Social Psychology
in Athletics

Social Psychology in Athletics

Bryant J. Cratty

University of California
Los Angeles

Prentice-Hall Inc., *Englewood Cliffs, N.J.* 07632

Library of Congress Cataloging in Publication Data

CRATTY, BRYANT J.
  Social psychology in athletics.

  Includes bibliographies and index.
  1. Sports—Psychological aspects.   2. Social
psychology.   3. Social interaction.   4. Competition
(Psychology)   I. Title.
GV706.4.C72   796'.01   80-22320
ISBN 0-13-817650-7

Printed in the United States of America

10 9 8 7 6 5 4 3 2 1

Editorial/production supervision and interior design by Marybeth Brande
Cover design by Miriam Recio
Manufacturing buyer: Harry P. Baisley

PRENTICE-HALL INTERNATIONAL, INC., *London*
PRENTICE-HALL OF AUSTRALIA PTY. LIMITED, *Sydney*
PRENTICE-HALL OF CANADA, LTD., *Toronto*
PRENTICE-HALL OF INDIA PRIVATE LIMITED, *New Delhi*
PRENTICE-HALL OF JAPAN, INC., *Tokyo*
PRENTICE-HALL OF SOUTHEAST ASIA PTE. LTD., *Singapore*
WHITEHALL BOOKS LIMITED, WELLINGTON, *New Zealand*

This book is dedicated to a girl who
runs fast and far, and yet who pauses
to see a butterfly, and to watch a squirrel,
and whose brown eyes follow the
sun into the Pacific at dusk.

Contents

Introduction

The earliest writings about athletics and sport contain reference to the social and psychologic dimensions of participation. Most scholars agree that the first experiment in social psychology, published before the turn of the century, was one that dealt with how an audience modified vigorous physical performance.

Despite this early interest in the psychosocial parameters of sport, not until the past two decades have reviews been written summarizing the thought and research data pertaining to the subject. The effects of the applause of fans upon performance, the nature of team interactions, the nature of leadership on the team, as well as other important subjects, while often the concern of the coach, have been accorded less attention by researchers and by those who summarize the scientific literature in book form.

In contrast, the history of sport psychology is relatively vigorous. By the early 1920s, in the United States as well as in Eastern and Western Europe, a number of books and studies had begun to appear dealing with various topics related to the psychology of sport. In the 1930s, few references directed toward physical educators failed to include a chapter dealing with the way athletic participation and physical activity could be a psychologically, intellectually, and socially uplifting experience.

Not until the late 1950s, however, did reasonably well-designed studies begin to appear in research journals, published in English, which dealt with the social-psychologic consequences of sporting endeavor. Even at present, a large amount of the work emanates from the laboratories of a relatively few individuals.

During the past two decades, small rays of light have been cast in this relatively gray area of knowledge. In 1964, an international committee for the study of sociology of sport convened for the first time, a meeting followed by more in Cologne, Vienna, and Moscow. In a number of languages, including English, German, and Russian, texts began to appear with increased frequency during the 1960s. These books dealt not only with motor learning and the psychology of sport, but also with sport and society. Books of readings took their places on bookshelves beside texts authored by Harry Edwards and collections of conference summaries edited by Gerald Kenyon, Gunther Luschen, John Loy, and others. A text by this writer, *Social Dimensions of Physical Activity,* was published in 1967, summarizing some of the then sparse literature.

In 1968, in an opening address of a section on "Actions and Interactions of Sport, Spectator, and Athlete" at the 2nd Annual International Congress of Sport Psychology in Washington, D.C., John Loy put forth a plea for a social psychology. Unfortunately, however, since that time too few scholars have answered his eloquent challenge. Largely absent in the literature are attempts to pull together material that reflects social-psychologic dimensions of sport. Books covering such topics as the audience effect or focusing on the sports team as a group organism are largely absent. It is the purpose of this text to deal with these and similar topics.

Social psychology has been defined as the attempt to understand how people affect each other. It is the study of conditions among people, as well as within them, that influence the totality of their relationships, their ability to work together toward some common goal, and their possible pleasure and displeasure with one another. Thus, such topics as group cohesion, attitude formation, dissension, aggression, group motivation, and interpersonal communication are respectable subtopics in social psychology.

Social psychology focuses not only on variables within and between individuals, but also on the totality or the "essence" produced by their association. At times, this essence, or basic ingredient, is different from whatever each individual brings to the group situation. That is, the sum of the parts in social psychology may be different from the nature of the individuals making up the whole of the group or of the team.

It is not difficult to justify the study of some of the above topics within the emotionally laden and socially rich environment provided by competitive athletics. The sports team can be likened to a work group under stress, but a work group in which the outcomes are noted and observed by a large number of people. It is thus the purpose of this book to examine current psychosocial theories and research as they pertain to the dynamic and often dramatic human events occurring in athletics. Further, the book is meant to meet the needs of university and college students wishing to learn more about the intricate social-psychologic machinations within and surrounding the athletic team. Coaches may also benefit from a review of the content, and for their benefit an "Implications for Coaches" section is contained in most chapters. The text is meant to be a stimulus to scholars interested in further research in what is still a rather barren field of endeavor. Finally, the content may aid athletes to better understand themselves and how they interact with other members of the team, the fans, and their coaches. Most fine athletes are students not only of their sport but also of themselves. Thus, the interested athlete may find out more about how he changes, and in turn is changed by, those around him or her.

In an attempt to meet the needs of the audiences mentioned above, the author tried to walk a delicate tightrope between theory and practice. It was believed that many readers not only know *what* might be done in various situations calling for group interaction in sport, but also may wish to learn *why* a certain psychosocial "event" might occur. It is for this reason that a chapter dealing only with theory was included (Chapter 2) and why most of the succeeding chapters contain various models attempting to explain the theoretical underpinnings of the topic and terms under discussion.

Thus, the chapters are meant to be read selectively. The reader who is more interested in applications may wish to forgo the material in Chapter 2 and instead deal primarily with sections containing applications. The university and college scholar, on the other hand, may wish to scrutinize the entire text and may benefit from the extensive bibliographies that accompany most chapters.

When attempting to summarize and to interpret available research, two types of studies have been examined: (1) Studies that illuminate general psychosocial principles of group interactions and (2) investigations that have focused specifically on sport as an environment worthy of study in and of itself.

The text was written not only because summaries of this type are largely absent, but also for the positive outcomes that may be derived from helping athletes and coaches as well as sports fans to become more sensitive to their own situations. Not only might such information, when applied, elicit much-needed positive changes in the conduct of coaches and athletes under pressure, but also some of the contents may encourage young researchers to search for the answers to important questions that now go begging.

Sport participation and viewing are seldom neutral experiences for those involved. Careful consideration of some of the discussions that follow may influence individuals who interact within sports situations, so that negative outcomes are minimized, while the opportunities for achieving positive social outcomes are maximized.

2

Theories and Models

This book focuses primarily on applications rather than theory. However, it is believed helpful to take at least a brief look at various ways social psychologists have studied group interaction and social influences. Experimenters on this topic have based their research on six primary types of theory, models that will be reviewed in the following pages.

One might ask, what is the worth of theorizing? Why can't we just get to the facts? Indeed it might be more helpful for some if we dealt only with the here, the now, the applied, and the "facts" as seen by the author. At the same time, it is obvious upon reviewing the literature, that there are some cleavages between various schools of social psychology. Not all experimenters base their efforts on the same basic assumptions, nor do all of them derive the same interpretations from apparently similar data.

Additionally, a reader or a student who not only looks at the here, the now, and the applied, but who also considers the why's (the underlying assumptions and theoretical bases), is likely to become able to (1) place apparently unrelated facts into manageable categories, (2) draw inferences from information with more facility and perceive new relationships, (3) better assess new situations and people, and (4) become more flexible when looking at personal reality and deciding on appropriate behaviors when working with others. Additionally, an individual well-grounded theoretically is able to anticipate problems when working with groups, rather than simply to react to unfortunate situations after they arise.

Six basic theoretical orientations will be briefly reviewed.

1. Social reinforcement theory, in which social behavior is conceived of as emanating from situations and encounters that are either rewarded or punished as the child matures into adulthood. ᶴᵘᵍᶦ ᵒᵘᶦᶳᶜ

2. Field theory, in which constructs from the biologic and physical sciences have been borrowed in order to explain complex psychosocial behaviors and interactions.

2. Cognitive theory, in which individuals are assumed to be directed not only by the appearance of social events and their own feelings, but also by their *thoughts and interpretations* of these events and feelings.

4. Psychoanalytically based theory, in which early psychosexual development is believed to be an important derivative of later social and psychological adjustments and behaviors.

5. Role theory, a collection of concepts brought together from sociology and psychology, predicated on the assumption that man either conforms or fails to conform to various "role sets" delineated by the societal context in which the individual finds himself or herself.

6. Gestalt theory, an antecedent of field theory and cognitive theory, the breaking away by the early German psychologists from the more mechanistic approaches to the study of human behavior is a landmark in the history of experimental psychology. Their contribution is also reflected in their emphasis on human powers to organize and interpret experience, experience that, holistically, they believed to be different from the mere reception of stimuli by the sensory end organs.

A number of basic issues differentiate between various approaches to the study of social psychology. Among these questions is whether or not man is simply a higher-level animal (whose interactions can at least be partly inferred by observing and assessing animal behavior) or an independent entity governed by emotions, social feelings, and interactions unique to his species. Further questions dealt with in various ways by theoreticians in social psychology include whether or not most social behavior is unconsciously motivated or consciously intended; whether social interactions are molded by selfish egocentric interests or by concern for one's fellow man; the degree to which adult social behaviors are the result of early childhood experiences; and of course, the nature-nurture question wrestled with for years by behavioral scientists reflected in the query as to whether social behaviors are learned or innate. A final question is whether man is a reflective thinking being, able to engage in self-determining behaviors reflecting his social competencies and ideals, or whether he somehow acts in a reflex-like manner when confronted with social stimuli, situations, and conditions.

Additionally, there are historical threads that connect certain contemporary attempts to formulate social psychologic theory. For example, social reinforcement theory stems from the theorizing of the early behaviorists who attempted to explain learning by strengthening stimulus-response connections; while many ideas within contemporary cognitive theory and field theory have their beginnings in the Gestalt school of thought. Psychoanalytic theory, while initially devised to aid in the rehabilitation of the disturbed through the examination of various unconscious psychosexual determinants of individual motivation and behavior, is currently represented by clinical practices engaged in as people are brought together in groups in efforts to understand various dimensions of their personalities.

PSYCHOANALYTIC THEORY

Introduction

Interpretation and analysis of the multifaceted writings of Freud is made difficult for several reasons: (1) The materials are extremely voluminous and (2) Freud's positions regarding psychologic and psychosocial mechanisms might best be described as a series of dynamic processes or evolutions, rather than as a static, well-formed system. Freud is seen, by those carefully inspecting his work, to have rather frequently modified his outlook on the importance of a number of factors integral to personality development and disintegration.

Nevertheless, his positions on social forces as they affect the formation of individual behaviors have been scrutinized by several contemporary scholars, who have summarized his positions regarding the role of the social-psychologic environment in the formation of the individual's psyche. Prominent among these scholars has been Bion, who published a series of papers in 1959, and other writers including Bennis, Shepard, Schultz, and Sullivan. More recently, at least two sport psychologists, Drs. Bruce Ogilvie and Tom Tutko, have also been influenced by Freudian concepts, reflected in their analysis of "problem athletes" published in 1966.

Overview of Freudian Theory

A comprehensive review of Freudian constructs and concepts is well beyond the scope of this book. The enterprising reader is encouraged to review Rapaport's, Blum's, and Lindzeys's summaries of Freud's theory of personality. At the same time, the uninitiated reader should not be expected to readily comprehend the discussion that follows without at least some superficial orientation to the ideas and basic concepts espoused by the first psychoanalyst.

Essentially, the "psychic apparatus" was viewed by Freud as consisting of three primary compartments. First, the *libido*, a store of vital energy, mental in nature, which was conceived of as derived from one source, sexual energy.

Second, the mental life of the individual is divided into three components (1) the conscious, consisting of events and content of which the individual is aware; (2) the preconscious, the part of the mind that can be readily recalled to the conscious, a component of the mind which plays a relatively minor part in Freudian theory, and (3) the all-important *unconscious*. This third portion of the mind plays a major role in Freudian theorizing and is considered a primary aspect of mental functioning. It is this emphasis by Freud that has made it difficult for many of Freud's contemporaries, as well as those who followed, to objectify and verify through experimentation some of the major parts of psychoanalytic theory. Freud, however, postulated that various factors and behaviors substantiate the existence of the unconscious, including evidence from demonstrations of posthypnotic suggestion, the analysis of the meaning of dreams, memory and speech "slips," as well as the supposition that prolonged psychoanalysis purportedly reveals behavioral symptoms not immediately apparent in the personality of the patient.

Another component of the psychic apparatus advanced by Freud is the personality containing three major subsystems: the *id*, the *ego*, and the *superego*. The id is an unconscious repository of psychic energy, primarily derived from basic biological needs functioning since birth. Freud described the id as a "seething cauldron" of basic instincts, a somewhat hidden recess of man's animal-like being.

The ego, Freud suggests, is a mechanism that evolves rather early from the more primitive id; while the ego derives energy from the id, in the course of development, the ego becomes functionally differentiated, operating more within the world of time, space, and the real experiences of life. Freud's writings suggest that the ego is responsible for the perception of objects in the real world, particularly those that result in need gratification and tension reduction. Moreover, the ego is based upon logical inferences, conceptual behavior, and engages in what is termed "reality testing." The latter process consists of processing and evaluating information about the importance of and relationships between specific actions and behaviors on the part of the individual. Thus, while the ego derives energy from the id, it serves to control more basic impulses and consists of a hinge between reality and more primordial and base instincts contained in the id.

The third component of the personality, the superego, is a theoretical construct with relevance to students of social-psychologic behavior. The superego consists of the "social governor," or at least it is a reflector of behavior. It is composed of cultural values and societal expectations that have been perceived and adopted by the individual. The superego is a mechanism whereby the individual seems to be making moral demands on himself, demands formulated in childhood as the infant becomes aware of restrictions, controls, and reprisals emanating from parents and others close to him.

Thus, as a kind of mediator between the more basic and primitive id and the more civilized superego, the *ego* must often undergo strains and modifications. Various defenses emanating from the ego may serve to distort reality so that conflicting forces within the individual can somehow "live together." Mechanisms whereby the ego reconciles "wilder instincts" with the more sedate cultural values surrounding the individual are termed *ego defenses,* and comprise a list memorized by most first-year students of clinical psychology. They include:

1. Projection. The tendency to transfer one's personally unacceptable wishes or actions to another person or external object. Numerous examples from athletics could be cited, including the player who so dislikes himself that he perceives others (coach, fans, and/or teammates) as disliking or even hating him.

2. Reaction formation. The repression of an unacceptable feeling or condition by reversing it to a directly opposite emotion or condition. An example would be to deny one's real feelings about a coach, and instead reverse the less personally acceptable dislike, or hate, into liking, or even love.

3. Denial. Under extreme threat, an individual may, particularly if immature or emotionally disturbed, deny the existence of an object, situation, person, or threat. With maturity, or the assumption of better mental health, more accurate perceptions of reality are formed, and thus it is increasingly difficult for the individual to engage in denial. At the same time, mild forms of this kind of defense of the ego can sometimes be seen as young athletes, facing formidable opponents, reject the obvious threat to their self-esteem and deny the abilities of their future adversaries.

4. Sublimation. This mechanism, conceived of by Freud as a useful one for society, consists of behaviors that channel sexual energies into socially more beneficial forms. Behavior reflecting sublimation may consist of hard work, artistic-creative efforts, achieving vocational or professional excellence, or conceivably (although Freud did not dwell extensively on the subject) the seeking of perfection in competitive athletics.

In addition to emphasis on unconscious drives and motives, Freudian theory dwells extensively upon the importance of infant experiences and development, particularly psychosexual development, in the formation of the personality of the youth and adult. Freud lists four stages of psychosexual development from birth to maturity, including:

The oral stage, in which the infant derives pleasurable sensations from the region around the mouth while feeding. This stage lasts from birth through the first year or 18 months of life.

The anal stage, extending from around the first year of life until approximately 4 years of age, during which pleasure and problems revolve around the eliminative and retentive functions of the bowels and anal sphincter.

The phallic stage. This "plateau" in the child's development is characterized by the attempts of the child and youth to consolidate his personality by relating more and more to objects and events in the world outside his own body and family. During this stage, the child prepares for the upcoming and often stressful sexual events of adolescence.

The genital stage is a bridge between childhood and adulthood. Freud conceives of this adolescent period as a kind of explosion of psychologic and physiologic energies as the child awakens and manifests sexual and aggressive instincts that were last seen during the first three stages of development. Normally, the genital period ends as the adolescent changes into an adequate socialized adult, exhibiting the ability to sublimate the libido at times into appropriate channels, such as friendships, sports, and other creative and professional endeavors.

A thorough exposition of these five stages would include the way delayed or atypical psychologic development mainfests itself in behavior, indicating that the chronological age and psychosexual stage of the individual are not compatible and congruent. The adult who cannot easily form friendships with the opposite sex, the child who evidences thumb sucking behavior into middle childhood, the athlete who throws temper tantrums, or the child who remains overly preoccupied with processes of elimination are but four examples of this kind of mismatch. These discrepancies are thus of concern to psychoanalytically oriented clinicians who accept the major ideas within Freudian theory.

Freud wrote at least four works that deal with the behavior of individuals in groups.[1] Summarized, the major premises from these essays include the observations that

[1] *Group Psychology and the Analysis of the Ego,* 1922; *Civilization and its Discontents,* 1930; *Totem and Taboo,* 1913; and *The Future of an Illusion,* 1928.

1. An adequate functioning society is possible because of a balance being formed between constructive and restrictive demands of the culture and the often destructive nature of man's instinctual impulses and ego.

2. Initial processes of socialization emanate from the family. The processes of socialization thus involve the child's acceptance or rejection of strategies, customs, and constructions, which in turn form the child's superego.

3. Freud believed that as the result of (1) above, man and society were in a constant state of struggle, on the one hand societal constraints repressing basic urges, while on the other hand, if societal limitations break down, man's basic destructive and aggressive nature is likely to emerge. Thus, he believed that a viable civilization is possible only when societal forces exert external control over man's instinctual shortcomings.

4. Freud hypothesized that all social units into which adolescents and adults gravitate are in the main governed by behaviors acquired within the family. Freud viewed all group relationships and ties as being based upon processes of identification with a leader (father) figure. Ogilvie and Tutko (1966) reflect this Freudian principle as they explain at several points in the text that psychologic blocks between coach and athlete may result from unconscious efforts on the part of the athlete not to best the coach (father figure). To use their words: "To compete with and beat the father figure would subconsciously at least be tantamount to destroying daddy, which again would produce considerably mixed feelings of guilt and fear." (page 40)

They also explain that the athlete who is constantly trying to "con" the coach may in reality reflect fear of besting the coach (father figure) in direct ways. In turn, this results in the athlete employing more subtle means (conning) to resist the authority and constraints of the coach. These authors also claim that the depression-prone athlete may be a reflection of early and traumatic experiences (spankings) at the hands of parental authority figures—figures whom he associates with the coach, and who in the past, and perhaps in the present, stand ready to make him feel "no good" and unworthy despite his best efforts to please them.

A Freudian Look at Groups and Group Process

Bion (1959) published the results of a series of papers whose viewpoints reflect group dynamics within a Freudian framework. Although his observations are primarily obtained from his work with therapy groups, the concepts are broad enough to apply to any kind of "work group," including an athletic team.

Bion holds that the basic assumptions of groups emerge as the members begin to evolve reasons for the group's existence, at both the conscious and unconscious levels. Three basic qualities, Bion feels, are characteristic of all work groups:

1. Dependency assumption. The group has met in order to be nurtured and supported by a leader, upon whom the remainder of the group is dependent. Some of the statements by Ogilvie and Tutko also reflect this assumption, as do components of Freudian theory that dwell on parent-child relationships. Bion holds that while many groups are initially given an appointed leader (coach, father), with further interactions, a "natural" leader will often emerge; an individual even more able to assume a nurturing role in the eyes of group members than was the original authority figure.

2. Pairing assumption. Lines of communication and rapport established between two or more group members, regardless of their sex, imply some kind of sexual purpose. In line with the emphasis within Freudian theory upon sexual behavior and drive, Bion asserts that the group leader may aid in this pairing tendency and also is seen by others as one who may bring about further interactions that are unconsciously sexual in nature.

3. The fight-flight assumption. All groups have assembled for the purpose of either fighting or fleeing from something. The first of these basic tendencies, of course, is often exploited by the coach as he exhorts the team to "fight" the other team (enemy?) and engages in similar locker room speeches. However, if Bion's second premise is correct, the tendency to flee from potentially stressful situations is also present to various degrees in groups, a tendency most leaders of work groups, whether industrial, recreational, or athletic, usually wish to diminish.

In order to maintain group equilibrium and freedom from tension, Bion continues, the leader is effective to the degree to which he or she is perceived able to aid the group in either their fighting or fleeing tendencies. Bion further suggests that it may be the role of the leader to promise the possibilities of both fleeing and fighting at the same time. For example, the leader may permit individuals to merge into the group and thus avoid or flee personal responsibility and involvement, while permitting the group to prevail against imminent threats and stresses. Bion also postulates the existence of other characteristics of groups, including what he terms the "group mentality," with the word *mentality* used in the broadest sense. Thus, he suggests that group mentality involves the unanimous will of the group, contributed to by individuals in ways of which they may be unaware, and influencing members negatively when they feel they are at variance with group principles, norms, and objectives.

Bion, however, like other writers cited in this section, uses Freudian concepts to develop ancillary conceptual models and systems, rather than as a basis for empirical experimental work. As has been noted by more than one reviewer, Freud did not evolve principles and concepts that are highly amenable to experimental verification.

Implications

Freudian theory has also been taken to task for other reasons. Shaw and Costanzo, for example, state that Freud did not seem to provide structures that link his various ideas. Thus, the system seems at times to be a series of disjointed ideas lacking unifying threads.

Freud engaged in a great deal of self-examination in his writings, and while self-criticism is usually deemed to be a laudable undertaking, the writings that emerged are often so variable in their positions on a given question that interpreting them has been difficult.

Freud's assumption that sex and the death wish play overriding roles in the formation of the human personality not only led to resistance by scholars during Victorian times, but has promoted controversy and skepticism today. For this reason, various neo-Freudian splinter groups have formed during the intervening years, which accept only a part of Freud's ideas. Some scholars, for example, while accepting many of Freud's major ideas, disagree with him concerning the nature and importance of sexual drives and other postulates Freud viewed as basic.

To summarize some of his main ideas, however, the following statements seem valid.

1. Freud believed that all human behavior is formed by both genetic and historical antecedents, themes that have been adopted by numerous other scholars, notably learning theorists.

2. Freud's emphasis on the unconscious has stimulated a great deal of clinical thought and promoted efforts to evaluate the more subtle aspects of the human personality through projective tests of numerous kinds.

3. He believed that behavior was caused by a collection of structures and forces within the individual's total personality system. This premise has stimulated numerous others who followed him and has served to provide more expansive and comprehensive theoretical frameworks in recent decades.

4. Freud's insistence upon the effects of drive, even though largely limited to the sexual urges, has encouraged more recent attempts by theorists to consider an expanded list of human motives and drives when attempting to formulate theories of motivation.

5. Freud held the belief that behavior is regulated by a "flow of psychic energy." This concept has at times misled theorizers into believing that physical activity itself acts as a therapy and a sublimator both of the sex drive and of tendencies toward aggression. Some of the experimental evidence, as reviewed in the following chapters, questions this assumption.

6. Freud's suggestion that behavior is largely adaptive has stimulated some to examine the nature of stress and its reduction by various kinds of compensatory behaviors. This kind of assumption is reviewed in Chapter 9.

Overall, it is believed that the first psychoanalyst is best conceived of as a highly original thinker, a stimulator of ideas from which both his critics and his supporters have received a great deal of nurture.

Many current experimental methodologies, primarily those employed by learning theorists, bring into question many concepts basic to Freudian theory. However, his main contributions have been to encourage others to probe more deeply into the complexities of the mind and into the dynamics of group interaction.

THE REINFORCEMENT THEORISTS

Numerous observations regarding the effects of reward and punishment on behavior are contained in historical, philosophical, and religious documents dating back several centuries. At the turn of this century, scientific as well as philosophical forces, together with the emergence of creative theoreticians on both sides of the Atlantic, coalesced to produce the beginnings of one of the most productive research thrusts in the history of psychology.

Edward L. Thorndike in America in 1898, as well as Ivan Pavlov in Russia in 1902, made independent but similar discoveries concerning the results of rewards on animal as well as human behavior. Thorndike proposed that the strengthening of the bonds between sensory input and action occurred as practice was welded to positive consequences, while a weakening of these stimulus-response connections came about because of disuse and/or adverse results. This "law of effect" was simultaneously discovered by Pavlov in his experiments with salivation responses in dogs and labeled a "law of reinforcement." Although discovering similar principles, Thorndike sought answers to problems in education. Pavlov, on the other hand, initially sought to throw light upon the antecedents of salivation in the dog, and discovered that a bell rung simultaneously with the sight of food would later independently elicit the salivary response in the animals he studied.

Pavlov suggested as the result of his observations that this anticipatory response was a type of "psychic reflex."[2] His research on this and associated problems earned him the Nobel Prize in 1904. Some, hearing Pavlov's name associate him only with a mechanistic look at learning

[2]In his 1910 book *The Work of the Digestive Glands,* Pavlov substituted the term *conditioned reflex* for *psychic reflex.*

and physiologic reactions. However, during his last years his writings reflected expansive concepts relating to "higher mental processes" and the way the social context influences human learning and behavior.

During the decades following this early work, several prominent theorizers have expanded and refined the basic principles first illuminated by Pavlov and Thorndike. More recently, a number of social psychologists have carried out rather formidable research programs based on the laws of reinforcement and association.

Basic Concepts

Deutsch and Krauss (1965) have suggested that reinforcement theory is undergirded by three major principles: (1) Methodologically, the system takes the point of view of behaviorism, that is, that behavior in and of itself is worthy of study independent of neurological and/or physiological underpinnings. (2) The "structural principles" upon which the orientation rests are associational in nature. (3) The motivational principle best illustrating the concept of reinforcement inherent in the theory is *hedonism.* This latter assumption suggests that man is a constant seeker of pleasure and avoider of the unpleasant. Thus, all human motives can be understood with reference to whether the individual is moving toward pleasurable outcomes and consequences and/or avoiding unpleasant ones.

Methodologically, two main types of learning experiments underlie the initial work within this theoretical orientation: (1) classical conditioning, the result of Pavlov's efforts and (2) instrumental conditioning, derived initially from the work of Thorndike.

The well-known experimental arrangements by Pavlov presented meat powder, an unconditioned stimulus (UCS), to the dog, eliciting an automatic flow of saliva (the unconditioned reflex, or response). A neutral stimulus (sound of a bell) was presented just before the food was given to the animal and later elicited saliva without the presence of meat powder (UCS). The new response to the bell is called a conditioned reflex, or "conditioned response," and the sound of the bell is termed a "conditioned stimulus." The process is termed "classical conditioning."

Operant or instrumental conditioning involves procedures whereby the presentation, or omission of reward or punishment, occurs *after* an animal has made some specific response. The response to be conditioned must occur before it can be rewarded. Thus, the movement response must be in the animal's memory storage before the experiment, and must be elicited during the course of the experiment. In

instrumental or operational conditioning, responses are usually speci-
fied in terms of their consequences. Thus, no matter how an animal may
press a bar to obtain food, for example, the behavior will be rewarded
independent of the specific movement the animal may accidentally or
purposefully select.

There are a number of basic concepts within reinforcement theory,
independent of the experimental arrangements. These ideas include
the following:

Stimulus. An external or internal "event" that tends to alter the
behavior of the organism has three functions according to reinforcement theorists: (1) the triggering of built-in responses, as the stimulus
represents an alteration of what the organism feels or perceives; (2)
discrimination, or providing a set or predisposition to respond to a
second stimulus event; and (3) reinforcement, as a stimulus is elicited
as the result of a previous action on the part of the organism, thus
providing a reward. Some "mediational" theorists would broaden the
definition of a stimulus and suggest that it may also be conceptual in
nature, rather than only an external or internal alteration in the organism.

Response. For some reinforcement theorists, notably Skinner, the
response cannot be logically separated from the stimulus, and is defined
as an alteration of behavior occurring as the result of the presence of
a stimulus.

Response strength. The strength of the tendency of a response to
occur is measured in several different ways and is used as a measure of
the degree of learning that takes place. These measures include the
probability of its occurrence (in what percent of trials it is likely to
occur), the speed or rate at which a response occurs, and latency, or the
time it takes the response to occur after a cue or stimulus is presented.

Drive. Hull and other reinforcement theorists believe that drive
represents a basic force(s) that activates behavior. Drive level in turn
may be manipulated by alterations in the exernal environment. The
strength of drive is believed to be based on the time and/or the amount
of the deprivation of various needs, deprivations which in turn may be
measured by observing the speed, frequency, and/or the strength(s) of
the response(s) evidenced by the organism.

Thus, most behavior acts to reduce "drive states." The term *need* is
usually employed by reinforcement theorists to represent the results of
deprivation of physiologic necessities. Drive, on the other hand, is a
more comprehensive term, referring to the state of the organism and

related to psychologic as well as social wants and desires. Reflecting this more expansive use of the term are the writings of Dollard and Miller, who separate drives into two major categories: (1) primary, innate drives, which include hunger, pain, thirst, and sex and (2) secondary drives, including socially learned rewards not directly dependent on biological needs, and other rewards including verbal and monetary reinforcements as well as specific food preferences and the like.

Generalization.   The principle of stimulus generalization, first seen in the writings of Pavlov, refers to the tendency of an organism to respond in a similar way to a stimulus different from that to which the response was originally paired. Using this concept, the reinforcement theorists explain transfer of training. Transfer from task to task, it is assumed, will occur to the degree to which the stimuli are similar in two tasks. Transfer due to general instructional and/or learning set is also explained using the concept of stimulus generalization. In sport, for example, stimulus generalization is reflected in the athlete's ability to exhibit more than one response in stimulus situations dissimilar to those for which he was originally trained.

Discrimination.   The concepts of discrimination and generalization have been described as a "natural pair" by some observers. Just as organisms may conserve energy and become more efficient by generalizing from stimulus to stimulus, individuals also become more efficient as they become able to make precise distinctions between stimulus and response conditions.

Reinforcement.   Definitions of the term *reinforcement* differ markedly, even among reinforcement theorists. Some scholars, for example, often include only rewards involving the satisfying of basic physiologic needs. Others have expanded the list of reinforcers to include social approval and similar psychosocial constructs.

Most experiments suggest that the effectiveness of reinforcers depends not only upon the nature of the reinforcer and past experience, but also upon the time schedule during which the reward is "delivered" to the subject, whether human or animal. These schedules include (1) fixed interval, a reward presented at some fixed period of time after a previous reinforcement; (2) variable interval, at a variable period of time after previous reinforcement; (3) fixed ratio, reinforcement is provided after a given number of trials, independent of the time between the trials; and (4) variable ratio, refering to reinforcers presented at an average number of correct responses, i.e., if the average was to be 10, reinforcement may occur at one point after 5, then after 15, then after 10 correct responses, and so on.

Extinction.   The decreasing tendency to respond under conditions of nonreinforcement. The extent of the tendency to stop responding depends on several conditions, including the following: (1) the amount of prior reinforcement, (2) the strength of drive under extinction, (3) the amount of work or effort involved in responding, and (4) the schedule governing the administration of rewards during the learning period.

The resistance of humans to extinction of various social responses is important to consider for those who attempt to understand their social behavior. Some individuals, for example, are "turned-off" by someone else after a single social rebuff, while others may continue to relate to the offending party despite the lack of social rewards.

Overview and Critique

Reinforcement theorists are often criticized by others as being rather mechanistic and inhuman in their approach to learning. Others feel that intellectual and physiologic-neurologic underpinnings of behavior are often ignored by reinforcement theorists. Critics view as shallow the viewpoint that the behavioral scientist should be concerned only with rewards and outcomes, and not with the moral implications of behavior as well as with the more subtle intellectual and neurologic processes involved.

For the past 40 years, however, reinforcement theory in various forms has provided a disciplined and empirical approach to psychologic measurement and theory in many countries. Reinforcement theorists are forced to analyze behavior in minute detail. A carefully planned reinforcement schedule usually *does work;* behavior does change, and often in dramatic and useful ways. Moreover, it cannot be denied that humans are constantly in situations containing rewards and punishments coming from others. In turn, the human also emits rewarding and nonrewarding behaviors. Thus, to assert that reinforcement theory is not important is short-sighted. People constantly modify the behavior of those with whom they interact, whether or not either individual is consciously aware of the fact or not.

Several sport psychologists, including Rushall (1972) and others, have suggested plans for evaluating the kinds of reinforcing behaviors emanating from coaches during their contacts with athletes. They have suggested the coach may be made to see how he is changing the behaviors of his charges, for better or worse. With various behaviors, he or she may be exhibiting ways that are rather elusive, subtle, and of which he may be unaware. Dickinson's (1977) text is another good contribution of a S-R learning theorist to the athlete, and to sport.

Those who hold to the principles of behavioral modification, however, may arrange conditions that are not likely to elicit the changes they hope for. For example, the reinforcer (or the one who extends rewards) must be perceived by the person to be rewarded as desirable before positive change will take place. At times only the rewarder may believe the rewards are positive, while the one to be rewarded may view the same conditions, objects, or events as of no value or even of negative worth. An example would be coaching behavior which is brusque, strict, etc., and which *the coach* may feel indicates to the athlete that he "really cares." The athlete, on the other hand, may detest this type of behavior coming from an authority figure. The ever-smiling coach or teacher, similarly, may not realize that the reward he emits (a smile) is so easily and constantly exhibited as to lose its reinforcing properties because of its very frequency.

Theories of reinforcement may also tend to break down when applied in the real world in situations in which both rewarder and those to be rewarded fail to agree on what real improvement consists of. In several experiments within the past 5 years, more improvement was noted in the performance of physical skills (bowling was used in one study) when the participants were permitted to reward *themselves* when they perceived improvement, than occurred when a *nonparticipating observer* controlled the reinforcers in the situation.[3]

Reinforcement Theory in Social Psychology

Some reinforcement theorists have alluded to the presence and importance of social rewards in the learning process. If one also assumes that at least some social responses are learned, it is but a short step to the assumption that the application of concepts important to reinforcement theory will explain how social behaviors become modified and shaped. The models of social behaviors that are derived from reinforcement theory range from those explaining how two people influence each other in face-to-face confrontation to the ways in which the culture modifies the behavior of individuals and groups. Social theories with bases in reinforcement theory tend to be undergirded by a good deal of viable experimental evidence, rendering them helpful in the explanation of human social behaviors ranging from the formation of friendships, to the imitation of others, to the instigation of interpersonal aggression.

[3]Outside the sports context, one also sometimes sees retarded children who are intellectually incapable of associating a given reward with a given type of behavior that is purportedly being reinforced.

In the paragraphs that follow, the extensive research produced by social psychologists within a reinforcement framework cannot be reviewed. The reader may refer to the summaries by Shaw and Costanzo (1970), Deutsch (1965), and Krauss for a more thorough perusal of the various models. Additionally, discussions in the remainder of the book covering numerous facets of social behaviors within the sports team context are permeated by data emanating from social psychologists influenced by the theorizing of Skinner, Pavlov, Thorndike, Hull, Miller, and others.

Miller and Dollard (1939), dealing with the way social imitation occurs, represent one approach by reinforcement theorists to explain the modification of social responses. They suggest that three conditions must exist in order for imitation to occur. The first is spatial association in time, that is, the people must take the same bus, wait in the same line, etc. Second, one of the two parties must be perceived as more powerful, capable, smart, or effective than the other. Within this second condition, there must be a series of rewards and/or punishments, which may occur when the imitative behaviors begin to take place. Finally, they postulate the existence of a complex imitative behavior, which they term "copying." In this context, the imitator begins responding not only in direct ways to the model he is imitating, but also to his own responses in the chain of behavioral sequences.

Extension of Miller and Dollard's basic model has resulted in a considerable number of data-based assumptions by Bandura and his associates (1959) as they studied the formation of aggressive behaviors. They advance the hypothesis that before imitating another person, the imitator engages in various kinds of mediating (thinking) behaviors. These thoughts involve attaching verbal labels to what is seen, evaluating the model to be imitated, and weighing the possible consequences for imitating the model. Some of Bandura's work will be reviewed in the chapter on aggression.

Homans, as well as Thibault and Kelley, has formulated principles that purportedly govern the quality and quantity of human interaction by relating to concepts found within reinforcement theory. It is suggested, for example, that whether or not two individuals begin or continue to associate is dependent on perceived outcomes of their confrontation. If their pairing is perceived to yield maximum positive outcomes for both, their interactions will continue. However, if one member receives considerably fewer or more rewards than the other, the pairing is likely to be altered or even terminated.

Thibault and Kelley have formulated a list of conditions important to consider when evaluating the quality of the interactions of a dyad (two-person group). This list includes the following:

1. Abilities. The person another usually enjoys associating with is generally perceived as possessing abilities not in the repertoire of the one
   desiring the association.
2. Similarity. Individuals with similar attitudes and orientations are more
   prone to select each other as friends, mates, or partners than are those
   with dissimilar interests, orientation, and values.
3. Proximity. There is considerable evidence that mere physical proximity is a positive impetus to social association, as at least one obstacle to
   the relationship has been minimized, i.e., getting to the other party.
4. Complementarity. Thibault and Kelley suggest that associations are
   formed and maintained when one member is able to reward the other
   with relatively little effort. Thus, when the rewards are high and the
   costs of giving rewards are low, associations are likely to be seen as
   pleasurable and worth maintaining.

In addition to these conditions, which are generally somewhat external to the actual interactions of two people, there are a number of
conditions that arise *within* as an immediate result of the socializing
process, according to Thibault and Kelley. These conditions include
whether or not behaviors emitted interfere with or facilitate sequences
of behavior coming from the other member of the pair, and the manner
in which compatible behaviors are somehow synchronized in subtle
ways.

Thibault and Kelley have devoted a considerable amount of thought
and research to discovering how power and power figures emerge in
group situations. They define power as the ability to affect the quality
of outcomes evidenced by the other person in the situation. Some of
these principles will be explored later in the chapters dealing with
athlete-coach interactions and interactions involving the team leaders
vs. other athletes on the team.

FIELD THEORY

Field theory in social psychology stems from the writings of Kurt Lewin
(1951), who in turn was influenced by, and a pupil of, the early Gestalt
psychologists in Germany during the first decades of this century. Lewin, student of Kohler and Koffka, proceeded to outline the manner in
which the social context, termed "life space," interacts with the personality of the individual. The classic Gestalt theory was focused primarily
on the nature of perceptual processes. Lewin's theorizing utilizes a
rather dynamic and fluid approach to social psychological analysis. Gestalt theory and Lewinian field are thus similar in the holistic manner

in which they approach psychosocial behavior; however, they depart from each other in the types of phenomena each deals with.

Lewin employed diagrammatic techniques and used terms borrowed from mathematics and physics to describe individual and group behavior as they are affected by the total psychologic and physical environment in which groups and people reside. Critical to field theory is the concept of life space, defined as "the psychological environment as it exists for the person at a given moment in time." Thus, Lewin was not preoccupied with the way past experiences influence current behaviors. The individual's life space, Lewin conjectures, contains several dimensions. For example, it is suggested that an individual's life space is separated into regions, which become increasingly differentiated and numerous as the person matures. It is also hypothesized that a more intelligent person has a more differentiated pattern of regions than does the less intelligent individual.[4]

The fluidity of the individual's life space refers to the ease with which an individual can move from one region to another, via actual locomotion or psychologic movement, as well as to the rigidity of the regions, reflected in the lack of boundary permeability. One's life space, Lewin suggests, may be divided into two additional dimensions, "reality" and "irreality." The former refers to the more objective aspects of life, while the latter are experiences composed of fantasy and imagery. These concepts are diagrammed in Figure 2–1.

Behavior thus refers to the "locomotion" of the individual from one region to another in his life space, movement that is either psychologic (change of thought patterns) or actual (walking from home to office). Locomotion is believed to be dependent on the individual's need system and the tensions the system generates.

The concepts of "force" and "force fields" are also critical to Lewinian field theory and refer to forces that cause change. If more than one force (psychologic, intellectual, emotional, and/or social tensions) impinge on the individual at a given time, behavior (locomotion) will occur to the degree in which the forces may be imbalanced, i.e., one is *pulled* toward one or the other. In turn, behavior of various kinds can be explained as an attempt by the individual to somehow bring his force field and the accompanying tensions into some kind of equilibrium. These forces are composed of those that *drive, repel,* and *restrain,* as well as forces corresponding to individual needs.

[4]In a theory of human abilities previously postulated by this writer, this same differentiated effect was seen as a function of age and intelligence when factoral studies of human abilities are surveyed. (See *Human Behavior: Exploring Educational Processes* and *Remedial Motor Activity.*)

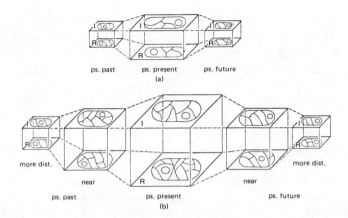

ps. past   ps. present   ps. future

(a)

more dist.   more dist.

near   near

ps. past   ps. present   ps. future

(b)

FIGURE 2-1. The life space at two developmental stages. The upper drawing represents the life space of a younger child. The lower diagram represents the higher degree of differentiation of the life space of the older child in regard to the present situation, the reality-irreality dimension, and the time perspective. (C = child; R = level of reality; I = level of irreality; Ps past = psychological past: Ps present = psychological present; Ps future = psychological future.) Reprinted with permission from K. Lewin, *Field Theory in Social Science* (New York: Harper and Row, 1951).

The presence of these forces, therefore, set up what Lewin terms *tension systems,* composed of two or more positive forces directed toward the same region of life space, or both a positive and negative force within the same goal region. Tension reduction, Lewin assumes, occurs when one force (e.g., need to complete a task) is reduced by behavior (e.g., completing the task). Moreover, tensions may be reduced in other ways, by substituting one behavior for another and by the satiation of needs. On the other hand, a conflict situation occurs when forces of equal strength impinge upon the individual at the same time, impelling action in opposite directions, or when the individual cannot easily substitute one activity for another that may be blocked in its execution. Through the use of such constructs Lewin, and others who follow his precepts, attempts to explain the instigation of interpersonal relationships, aggression, frustration, the influences of leadership on the behavior of subordinates, as well as parent-child interactions.

Critics of field theory point to the imprecision of some of Lewin's concepts, vagueness that has sometimes limited experimental verification. It has also been suggested that the theory deals not enough with overt motor behavior, but dwells primarily on the emotional, intellectual, and more deep-seated aspects of the personality.

Several scholars following Lewinian precepts have extended their views into various social phenomena. Heider (1958), for example, has expounded at length upon the nature of interpersonal perceptions. Cartwright (1959) has studied social power, drawing upon field theory for many of his terms and ideas. French has advanced a theory of social power and influence, which is amenable to the analysis of larger social groups.

Important to the central theme of this book is a theory of cooperation and competition outlined by Deutsch in 1949. Deutsch examined differences in interpersonal perceptions, and in self-perceptions on the part of the individual in cooperating *vs.* those in competing groups. In most sport situations, members both cooperate and compete at the same time. Deutsch's research and ideas are drawn upon in chapters that follow.

ROLE THEORY

Most scholars suggest that "role theory" is primarily a repository of a language, a set of terms denoting concepts that are helpful in the explanation of psychologic-social phenomena, rather than an iron-bound cohesive theory. The concept of role is historically derived from the stage. The Greeks and Romans first used the term to denote the way an individual behaves within a dramatization. The words in the writings of those who align themselves with various aspects of role theory have found their way, to a remarkable degree, into the vernacular.[5]

From its beginnings in linguistic history, the term *role* has changed very little. Within the writings of the social psychologist, it denotes the functions and collective behavior an individual manifests within a given social context.

Important, however, are ideas the social psychologist has associated with the concept of role. For example, even the most casual observer of the passing scene is aware that most people are called upon to assume a variety of roles. Often, these roles must be played within a short period of time. A man may arise in the morning as a head of a family. Driving to work, he becomes an unnamed member of the traffic stream, and is reacted to in this manner when given a ticket by the police. At work, he may be a subordinate on an assembly line or a member of top management. Finally, his evening activities may place him within an

---

[5]A comprehensive classification of the terms and concepts within role theory was carried out in 1966 by Biddle and Thomas.

athletic team, or in a classroom teaching a night class in automotive engineering.

Within each of these contexts, he is expected by those he encounters to act in certain ways, or at least to exhibit an acceptable range of behaviors, which if exceeded may brand him as unstable, unusual, or strange. Some have suggested that each social context has a number of expected roles an individual must at least loosely adhere to, roles that he and others subjectively define in a variety of social microsystems.

In each of these roles, the person may usually deviate somewhat, but not too much, from the rules prescribed by the segment of society in which he finds himself. Although each of us is expected to act somewhat differently in different situations, there are some consistencies in the way we behave. These consistencies reflect what some term "personality traits."

Some roles may markedly diverge from others, while others may be somewhat similar. In diagrammatic form, the concept of roles surrounding a central set of consistent behaviors (personality) may be depicted in Figure 2–2. Note that some of the boundaries between roles may be rather distinct, while others are less so. Some of the roles we assume are highly similar because of the similarity of social contexts, while others are quite different.

An important dimension of the roles enacted, according to the theorists, are the status systems encountered. As all societies and subsocieties are characterized by status systems, often an individual may have to adjust to occupying different positions in more than one status system

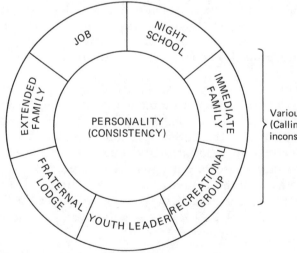

FIGURE 2-2.

at various times during the same day. Some of the status people enjoy has been allocated to them by higher authority and is termed "ascribed status," while a second type, status earned by the individual, is termed "achieved status."

There are two additional dimensions of status: (1) Vertical status reflects differences between levels of perceived competence and prestige, and (2) horizontal status implies different but equal positions in an organization among individuals who are on approximately the same level within the hierarchy. Thus, vertical status on a team would involve comparisons of locker room attendants vs. players vs. assistant coaches, and at the upper levels, head coaches. Horizontal status on a team reflects comparisons of different team members or of the assistant coaches as a group.

The concept of role conflict is important within role theory. Conflicts may arise when an individual has a limited amount of time and/or energy to give to two roles with which he or she must deal. The student-athlete who strives to earn both grades and a place on the team, as well as the husband-professional athlete who attempts to spend time with the family and to devote his emotions and energies to the athletic scene, are but two examples.

Role conflicts may be either mild or severe. They in general depend upon the personal resources within the individual, the number of roles they are expected to play, and the rigidity with which people in the various social contexts attempt to enforce stereotyped behaviors on the individual caught up in more than one social world.

Differences in position within the status hierarchy can cause emotional stress in the form of role conflicts. The highly paid professional athlete who receives the adoration of the fans in public, and who may at the same time remain under the jurisdiction of a coaching staff who "tucks" him into bed at 10:00 each evening, could have difficulties adjusting to status differences in the two situations. Thus, role conflicts may arise because of an incompatibility between the individual's personality and needs, and the rigidity and differences in the social roles into which they may be compressed as they travel from various parts of their social-psychologic environment.

Further reflection suggests that an individual is not always mindlessly thrown from role to role without his or her tacit participation and approval. Thus, the notion of "reference group," a concept first seen in the work of Hyman in 1942, is an important idea in the writings of the role theorists.

Basically it is assumed that the actions and behaviors of people within various social contexts are to some degree influenced by the group with which the individual *primarily* identifies. These groups and subgroups are of two types: (1) a group to which an individual is assigned by others (on the basis of education, age, sex, income, place of residence, etc.); this has been termed a "membership group"; (2) a group the individual uses as a basis of self-appraisal or comparison. Therefore, the group an individual seems to belong to (his membership group) may not be composed of the people with whom he or she actually identifies. Kelley has subdivided the latter type of reference group into two subgroups: (1) the "normative group," which consists of a source of values the individual has assimilated and (2) the "comparative reference group," which the person uses as a means of self-evaluation as well as for the evaluation of others with whom he comes in contact.

There has been a considerable amount of work carried out to determine what conditions and criteria influence the nature of the reference groups an individual both *perceives* himself a member of and *wishes* he was included in. Among the variables studied included the make-up of the membership, their number, the status and cohesiveness of the group, the demand by members for group conformity, and the clarity of the group's norms and standards. For the most part, stress is experienced by an individual whose actual social group (or membership group) is different from the idealized group to which the person may constantly be comparing his achievements, behaviors, and personal standards.

Of relevance to the central topic of this book is the work by Erving Goffman (1959). He developed a model for analyzing social interactions with reference to terms found in theatrical performances. This role theorist thus dealt with such terms as "actor," "performance," "part," and "routine."

Goffman, for example, focuses initially upon the manner in which the person erects a social façade. He compared this "front" with the one an actor maintains during his performance and suggests that people's *actual* personalities and temperaments may be in conflict with the social "wall" they throw up between themselves and others.

Goffman also discusses what he terms "the performance team," which he defines as a social group one of whose members may, at a given time, give away the show because of behavior(s) that are inappropriate to the role of the total group. As is true on athletic teams, Goffman points out that members of a performance team may differ in important ways from one another and yet maybe "thrown together" in order to perform a publicly viewed role in a given situation. Thus, each member becomes dependent on the good, or at least adequate, performance of the others. When analyzing such a group, Goffman suggests that four qualities are important: (1) The *technical* skills of the group, relating to operational efficiency; (2) the *political* nature of the group, reflected in group status, social power, and the ways in which rewards are distributed to maintain this power; (3) the *structural* qualities of the group, reflecting status divisions, and (4) *cultural standards* the group uses as comparative norms.

Overall the language, rather than the consistency and depth of role theory, seems to be the most important contribution of writers taking this approach to studying social interactions. For example, the concept of role, and the covert and overt ways in which people emit behaviors in various social contexts, has relevance for those studying the athletic team. The athlete is often caught up in powerful role conflicts, stresses that may impede his efficiency if not taken into account and understood by his teammates, as well as by those in authority.

The conflicts experienced by black athletes recruited from the ghetto of an eastern city to participate in a small conservative town may result in conflict situations that severely drain athletic as well as academic potential. The white athlete who is recruited to matriculate at a university whose academic standards are above his reach may similarly confront severe status, role, and other psychosocial stresses.

THE PERSONALITY OF THE GROUP

Raymond Cattell, a leading personality theorist, in 1948 proposed a set of postulates that relate to the study of athletic teams. Cattell suggested that a social group can be considered to have a unitary "personality," much as does an individual. He bolsters his argument by noting that (1) a group retains various characteristic behaviors despite changes in group membership, (2) groups are capable of responding as a unit to events, threats, and stresses directed toward one of their members, and (3) groups possess drives, evidence emotional states, and engage in collective deliberations much as do individuals.

Cattell used the word "synality" to denote the relationship and similarity of a social group to an individual's psychosocial functioning. He also suggested that group characteristics and tendencies can be made clear through the analysis of *structural characteristics,* reflected in the personal internal relationships among members; by measuring *population traits,* including intelligence, personality traits, and attitudes held by group members; and finally by evaluating what he termed "synality traits," or the effects the group has on another group, on the environment, and on individuals. Examples of synality traits include committee decisions, winning a game, aggression toward another group, digging a ditch together, and pulling together in a tug-of-war.

Cattell wrote that a group exists only insofar as it satisfies the psychologic needs of its members. Moreover, groups may get together to meet highly specific functions, rather than constituting all-pervasive forces in the lives of their members. The total psychologic energy available in a group Cattell dubbed "synergy." He subdivided this energy into two types: (1) maintenance synergy, the energy needed to hold the group together, and (2) effective synergy, the effort exerted to meet outside goals.

It is easy to draw examples of the latter two concepts from athletics. For example, if a team's internal conflicts require too much of the group's internal energy, or that of the coach, there may be too little effective synergy left to deal with opponents.

Cattell's observations and colorful terms have added a dimension to the study of group interaction. Groups do indeed at times seem to have a personality of their own and possess energies and emotions relatively independent of those apparently possessed by individual members. The concept of group synality is an important one, particularly when considering the often volatile, energetic, and dynamic forces impinging on and emanating from sports teams.

COGNITIVE THEORY

Cognitive psychology has enjoyed increasing popularity since the middle 1950s. Although having historical antecedents dating back to Kant in the 1700s, this trend of thought was often overpowered by associationism and reinforcement theory in America during the early part of the century. It has thus been only recently that psychologists and social psychologists began to explore ways in which cognitive processes interact with other aspects of behavior.

A cognitive psychologist assumes that the way an individual thinks about experience is an imperative intermediate function, occurring between the awareness of events and the behavior itself. Additionally, cognitive psychology within social psychology suggests that the ways people interpret a social experience is important to consider when assessing their subsequent behavior(s). There have been a number of theoreticians who have allied themselves with cognitive psychology. The work of only a few is represented in this brief review and in the remainder of the book.[6]

[6]Cognitive psychology as related to new concepts in human motivation is presented in Chapter 6.

Some of the initial concepts in this area were outlined by Festinger in the late 1950s. He suggested that when a problem is presented to an individual whose "pieces" do not seem to fit, "cognitive dissonance" is created. The person then attempts to reconcile the imbalance, to bring consistency to apparent ambiguity. This idea is a reflection of the gestaltic principle of perception, which suggests that people constantly search for a "good Gestalt," for a holistic and complete picture of a partially presented diagram.

Festinger also suggests that when a person is presented with a situation creating dissonance or confusion, he searches for consonance, for consistency. He looks for reasonableness, a reconciliation of what appeared ambiguous. His major premise has found its way into theoretical models for learning, motivation, and other components of the behavioral sciences. For example, some have suggested that the primary job of an educator is the production of confusion (creation of dissonance), which when intellectually placed in order by the learner provides the core of the educational process.

Within the literature in social psychology, Festinger's ideas have been applied in several contexts, for example, in searches for the ways people influence one another in group situations. Basically, it has been assumed that dissonance occurs when a group member's ideas, perceptions, attitudes, and/or opinions do not conform to the group's opinions. Further, this incongruency may be resolved in one of several ways: (1) changing one's *own* view, (2) seeking to change others in the group, and (3) finding others who support the same position, finding allies. These ways of exerting and reconciling interpersonal differences are often found on athletic teams.

According to Festinger, there are other circumstances that mold social influences, including the number of people holding the same or opposing opinions, the importance and attractiveness of those who agree or disagree with an individual, and the extent of disagreement in a group. The manner in which opinions and norms influence new team members' thoughts and actions is only one of the several ways in which Festinger's ideas may aid in the understanding of teams and team interactions.

Although they do not always check out when subjected to experimental scrutiny, the concepts advanced by cognitive theorists constitute a main thrust in contemporary psychology and social psychology. More about these contributions to the understanding of group communication, conflict, interpersonal attraction, and group stress and motivation is found in other chapters.

SUMMARY

Some of the major theoretical positions relating to social interaction in groups have been reviewed. The contents of the bibliography that follows should help the more enterprising student-reader to better understand the major positions discussed.

Several theoretical positions have not been discussed directly, for example, Gestalt theory, which formed the basis for some of the major concepts in cognitive and field theory. Fiedler's model for the study of leadership behavior will be covered in Chapter 10.

Despite their differences, the theories discussed contain several central ideas, similar concepts that are explained in different terminology by various writers. For example, the role theorist speaks of stresses that can occur when people must assume different behaviors in various components of their social milieu. The field theorist, in a similar way, discusses the "compartments of life space" through which the individual must travel, components with boundaries of varying degrees of permeability. Thus, both role theorists and field theorists are concerned with the diversity of social situations and behaviors with which people must deal.

To cite another example, aggression in children with aggressive fathers might be explained in several ways. The reinforcement theorist would postulate that the father is subtly rewarding his offspring for evidencing similar behavior. The role theorist would explain the influence of the aggressive father by a "role imitation" instruction, while the Freudian theorist would have still another and apparently logical explanation as to why a child born to a hostile parent evidences similarly brutal responses to people and situations.

Thus, a review of the theories should be accompanied by an attempt to stand back and look for what is *really* being said. Many of the concepts represent what may be described as common sense. Few of the data emanating from studies of social-psychological occurrences are at odds with what is already believed by lay observers of the human scene, according to some writers.

While this observation may be true in some cases, in others the expected "logical" results are not always confirmed when objective data are tabulated. Further, when social theory and subsequent findings do concur with what is commonly believed, this also is helpful. Such confirmation often leads to more precise attempts to obtain information in a more penetrating way than is possible by mere observation.

It is hoped that this overview of various theoretical orientations will help the reader place some of the information that follows into manageable categories. Sorting out what is being said and trying to see through jargon can aid in the formation of helpful insights into the nature of human interaction within the tense, physical, and emotionally laden contexts of competitive athletics.

QUESTIONS FOR DISCUSSION

1. Which of the theoretical positions discussed in the chapter is most acceptable to you? Why?
2. Can you take examples from sports interactions between coach and athlete that illustrate the manner in which reinforcement theory operates? Cite specific instances during practices or games in which a coach may be molding the behavior of an athlete by his rewards or punishments.
3. How many and what types of expected roles might a coach have to play on a given day? What conflicts might occur owing to the diversity of these roles? What about different roles an athlete may have to engage in during a given week?
4. In what ways do theories aid us to sort out data emanating from research studies?
5. What kinds of things may impinge upon an athlete's "life space" that will both aid and detract from his athletic performance.
6. What basic assumptions might a cognitive theorist make upon hearing a coach talk to an athlete? What basic assumptions might a reinforcement theorist make upon hearing the same conversation?
7. What is the meaning of, and implications for, the term *group synality* as used in the chapter?
8. Using the concepts of "modeling" and "social imitiation," describe how a young boy or girl, new to competitive sports, might be influenced by peers, coach, outstanding athletes in the sport, and/or parents.

BIBLIOGRAPHY

BANDURA A, WALTERS RW: *Adolescent Aggression*. New York: Ronald, 1959.

BENNIS WG, SCHEIN EG (eds): *Leadership and Motivation*. Cambridge: MIT Press, 1966.

BIDDLE BJ, THOMAS EJ (eds): *Role Theory, Concepts, and Research*. New York: Wiley and Sons, 1966.

BION WR: Experiences in groups, 1–7, *Human Relations*, vols. 1–4, 1948–1951.

BLUM GS: *Psychoanalytic Theories of Personality.* New York: McGraw-Hill, 1953.

BREDEMEIER HC, STEPHENSON RM: *The Analysis of Social Systems.* New York: Holt, Rinehart, 1962.

CARTWRIGHT D: A field theoretical conception of power. In Cartwright D (ed): *Studies in Social Power.* Ann Arbor, Michigan: Institute for Social Research, 1959, pp 183–200.

CATTELL R: *Personality, A Systematic, Theoretical and Faculty Study.* New York: McGraw-Hill, 1950.

CRATTY BJ: *Human Behavior.* Wolf City, Texas, Universities Press, 1972.

––––––. *Remedial Motor Activity for Children.* Philadelphia: Lea and Febiger, 1975.

DEUTSCH M, KRAUSS M: *Theories in Social Psychology.* New York: Basic Books, 1965.

DICKINSON J: *A Behavioral Analysis of Sport.* Princeton: New Jersey, Princeton Book Co., 1977.

DOLLARD J, MILLER NE, DOBB LW, MOWRER OH, SEARS RH: *Frustration and Aggression.* New Haven: Yale University Press, 1939.

––––––. MILLER NE: *Personality and Psychotherapy,* New York, McGraw-Hill, 1950.

FESTINGER L: *A Theory of Cognitive Dissonance.* Evanston, Illinois, Row Peterson, 1957, Stanford, California (reprinted by Stanford University Press, 1972).

––––––. *Conflict, Decision, and Dissonance.* Stanford, California: Stanford University Press, 1964.

FIEDLER FE: *A Theory of Leadership Effectiveness.* New York: McGraw-Hill, 1967.

FREUD S: *Totem and Taboo* (1913). In Brill AA (ed): *The Basic Writings of Sigmund Freud.* New York: Random House, 1938, pp 60–68.

––––––. *Group Psychology and the Analysis of the Ego* (1921). London: Hogarth Press, 1945.

––––––. *The Future of an Illusion* (1928). London: Hogarth Press, 1949.

––––––. *Civilization and its Discontents.* London: Hogarth Press, 1930.

GOFFMAN E: *The Presentation of Self in Everyday Life.* Garden City, New York: Doubleday, 1959.

HEIDER F: *The Psychology of Interpersonal Relations.* New York: Wiley, 1958.

LEWIN K: *Field Theory in Social Sciences.* New York: Harper and Row, 1951.

LINDZEY G (ed): *Handbook of Social Psychology,* 2 vols. Cambridge, Mass.: Addison Wesley, 1954.

OGILVIE B, TUTKO T: *Problem Athletes and How to Handle Them.* London: Pelham Books, 1966.

PAVLOV IP: *Conditioned Reflexes.* London: Oxford University Press, 1928.

RAPAPORT D: The structure of psychoanalytic theory, a systemizing attempt. In Koch S (ed): *Psychology: A Study of a Science,* Vol. 3. New York: McGraw-Hill, 1959, pp 55–183.

RUSHALL B, SIEDENTOP D: *The Development and Control of Behavior in Sport and Physical Education.* Philadelphia: Lea and Febiger, 1972.

SCHULTZ DP: *Panic Behavior: Discussion and Readings.* New York: Random House, 1964.

SHAW ME, COSTANZO PR: *Theories of Social Psychology.* New York: McGraw-Hill, 1970.

SHEPARD CR: *Small Groups, Some Sociological Perspectives.* New York: Harper and Row, 1964.

SKINNER BF: *The Behavior of Organisms, An Experimental Analysis.* New York: Appleton-Century-Crofts, 1938.

SULLIVAN HS: *The Interpersonal Theory of Psychiatry.* New York: Norton, 1953.

THIBAULT JW, KELLEY HH: *The Social Psychology of Groups.* New York: Wiley, 1959.

THORNDIKE EL: Animal intelligence, an experiental study of the associate processes in animals. *Psychological Monographs* 2:4 (Whole No. 8).

3

Early Social Experiences and Later Athletic Participation

The ways adolescents and young adults interact in competitive athletics are molded by a number of factors. Some of the more apparent forces are the size and constituency of the group and the variables acting on the group at a given time, including leadership and follower behaviors.

Among the less obvious variables, however, are those buried in the past of the youngsters. Whether one cleaves to the teachings of Freud, Pavlov, Skinner, or Bruner, it is difficult to deny the influence of early childhood experiences on at least some of the behaviors people exhibit later in life.

Shortly after birth, infants begin to react voluntarily to important others within their immediate life space. By the third or fourth month, they reserve smiles for familiar faces, while strangers are looked upon with some concern. Young children quickly learn how to elicit helpful responses from the powerful figures by whom they are surrounded. By the second month, cries of different kinds are emitted to denote various mood states and desires.

As children mature further, they find themselves in a family unit, a group containing reward patterns, status hierarchies, tensions, pleasures, and most important, people critical to both their physical and psychologic well-being. Both present and future behaviors are thus molded by the attractiveness, the trustworthiness, and the power of those with whom they come in contact during their early days, months, and years of life.

The literature suggests that the following behaviors and relationships are important to the later functioning of the child and youth on an athletic team.

1. The way early childhood experiences influence the child's feelings about power, authority, and status.
2. Ways parental behaviors mold the youth's needs for achievement and strivings for success.
3. Ways family habits and attitudes about physical activity may influence the offspring's feelings about participation in competitive sport.

A final section of this chapter deals with the way peer status and personal feelings of mastery can be gained through physical activity. The important topic of the psychologic influences of sports competition itself upon the youth is covered in indirect ways, both in this chapter and in those dealing with motivation, aggression, group cohesion, and leadership.

THE EARLY SOCIAL ENVIRONMENT AND FEELINGS ABOUT POWER, STATUS, AND INFLUENCE

Young children usually find themselves in an environment containing powerful figures who almost completely dominate their every move and thought. Their parents are able to control their movements from one place to another, as well as exert a number of subtle social and emotional constraints on their thoughts and actions. The degree to which the parents employ these sanctions, prohibitions, and rewards depends on a number of factors, one of which is the way *they* were raised as children. Additionally, the effectiveness of the parents' influence is dependent upon the child's perceptions of their power, as well as their consistency in its use.

A large number of studies have attempted to link parent-child interactions with contemporary as well as future social behaviors of children. Frequently, these data are argumentative, vague, or downright unbelievable. However, there *are* patterns emerging from some of the more carefully conducted research, which are beginning to sketch a picture of the behaviors reflecting family authority, and which may reflect the way the youth later reacts to power figures, equals, and subordinates on athletic teams.

Research, for example, indicates that about 95 percent of all children are punished physically at some time during their early lives. This punishment begins during the first year and tapers off somewhat at about the age of 10. Punishment, in direct physical ways, is more prevalent within lower socioeconomic groups than in middle or higher income groups in the United States. However, the distinctions between these groups and child-rearing practices are becoming less marked.

This may be occurring because of the diffusion of information concerning "acceptable" or "good" child-rearing practices seen in the popular media, including television, magazines, and books.

Parental authority manifests itself not only through the administration of spankings, but also by physical restrictions on a child's movements. For example, in a survey by Sears et al. (1957), one-half of the 400 mothers surveyed reported that they exercised considerable authority over the child's actions in the home, while 30 percent designated certain parts of the home in which the child could move without hindrance, leaving 70 percent which to some degree was "off limits" to unbridled actions on the part of their offspring.

In this same survey, Sears studied parental sanctions on mobility *outside* the home. Again, marked differences were noted. Eleven percent of the parents restricted their children's movements to the yard of their own home, 53 percent to "his side of the street," while 1 percent placed restrictions on more distant territory.

There are probably ethnic and/or socioeconomic differences in the freedom given children to explore their neighborhoods, but the number of valid studies exploring these differences is not great.[1]

The 1960s brought studies investigating some of the questions under consideration. For example, Martin Hoffman (1960) explored what he termed "power assertions" by parents and the amount of hostile and assertive behavior exhibited by their children. He focused on specific measures of what were termed "unqualified power assertion" reflected when the parent tried to establish authority over the child without any attempt to explain *why* that power was being exercised.

The study contained measures of the extent to which the child resisted assertive behavior by his playmates, comparisons of the frequency with which husband and wife exerted power over each other, as well as measures of the extent to which unqualified power was found in working-class as well as in middle-class families.

The "power-laden" behaviors of nursery school-age children were observed by Hoffman in play groups over a 2-month period. Recordings of what the child did and said were obtained, using a "shorthand" that included drawing stick figures to represent interpersonal reactions.

Among the findings were the suggestions that there were marked class differences in the incidence of power assertions exhibited by working-class fathers in contrast to middle-class fathers. Additionally, a good

[1]The reader interested in cultural, ethnic, and racial differences in early child-rearing practices, including handling techniques, should consult the article by Werner in *J Cross-Cultural Psychol* 3:2 (June 1972), 111–134. Racial differences in motor behavior are also covered in Cratty, *Perceptual and Motor Development in Infants and Children* (Englewood Cliffs, N.J.: Prentice-Hall, 1979), chap. 11.

amount of "displaced assertiveness," resistance to the power of others, and hostility was seen in children whose parents engaged in more than a usual amount of "unrestricted power assertiveness." Interesting data also emerged when the interactions of husbands and wives were recorded. For example, a wife whose husband scored high on power-assertive behaviors directed toward her was highly likely to engage in this same kind of behavior toward her child or children. Thus, unreasonable power directed toward her seemed to be displaced toward her offspring, rather than directed back toward its source, her husband.

Specifically, there were high and positive relationships, especially among child-mother groups in the working class, when power exerted by parents and power exercised by their children toward other children were contrasted (r's ranging from + .67 to + .76). The same relationships between father-child pairs were not so clear-cut, perhaps indicating the marked influence of prolonged daily exposure to the mother on a child's behaviors.

Hoffman (1960) concluded that the mother, because of her constant presence, is more likely to be an "agent" of power and discipline than is the father. However, the data also indicate that the powerful father exerts strong yet indirect influences on the child's assertiveness through behaviors initially directed toward his wife.

The data suggest that the ways a child may interact on teams later in life may have their antecedents in the assertiveness of family members to whom he or she has been exposed in childhood. Thus, the coach who finds a youth resistant to dogmatic suggestions and constraints might reflect upon the facts just presented. A youth on a team may need more than simple unrestricted power assertions. Because of his early experiences with authority in the family, he may react to highly authoritarian behavior with the same kind of hostile, resistive, and aggressive attitudes reported in Hoffman's study. Instead, it may be more productive with some youth to take a less assertive approach, one in which coaching "commands" are accompanied by reasons and rationale.

In a program of research, reported in several articles published in 1960, a broader look was taken at child-rearing practices and the subsequent behaviors of children than is seen in Hoffman's study. Harvey and his colleagues (1961) postulated that there are four "conceptual systems" under which children are reared. Analysis of these systems, they conjecture, may predict the type of behaviors children will evidence in various social situations. These four "systems" are described as follows:

1. In the first system, the most "concrete forms" of parental authority are exercised and experienced. The parent not only functions as a source of authority but also consistently reinforces absolutes. Parents working within this framework identify highly with institutional and religious

as well as national authority. In turn, they transmit this trust to their offspring. Social roles and status symbols are important to parents. According to Harvey, an aura that includes "absolutism" and "systems of closed thought" permeates this complex of child-rearing behaviors. This system he calls "absolute authority."

2. The second system, comprised of parents who present the child with a nonstable diversity of choices, is marked by capricious and arbitrary child-rearing practices. Much of the time more diversity, choices, and ambiguity are presented to the child than he or she can understand and assimilate. Reliable and stable guidelines for thought and behavior are largely absent. Harvey calls this system "capricious child-rearing."

3. In the third system, the child is surrounded by overindulgent parents. One or both parents serve as a buffer between the child and the demands made by the environment and by other authority figures and institutions. This child's opportunities to explore social alternatives and to manipulate the social context are restricted. This third system is called "overindulgence."

4. The fourth child-rearing system is marked by opportunities afforded the child to explore the environment, with nonpunitive acceptance given to what may be unorthodox solutions to problems. The child is thus given freedom to explore both the social and physical world. This fourth system is labeled "exploration permitted."

Harvey and his colleagues conducted a series of studies in attempts to determine the type of person "being turned out" after being exposed to the various systems described. Their overall conclusions are worth considering, particularly when viewing coach-athlete interactions on sports teams and trying to understand the relationships between athletes on teams.

Table 3-1 shows several types of social-emotional behaviors that might be exhibited by athletes who are products of the four systems of child-rearing. There are, however, obvious drawbacks to the whole-hearted acceptance of Harvey's model, which contains rather categorical and somewhat rigid sets of concepts. For example, it is probable that many children are raised within a combination of child-rearing styles. It is not uncommon to find that mothers and fathers do not agree on how to raise their children.

However, a consideration of these categories, together with forming hypotheses about behavior evidenced by children who have been exposed to each, can afford coaches some insight into the often obtuse attitudes and acts exhibited by younger team members. Further, coaches may try to examine how they themselves were reared and then compare the type of coaching behavior they employ to the type of behavior seen in children they are coaching, who may have been exposed to different child-rearing styles.

For example, the authoritarian coach, perhaps reared in an absolutist atmosphere, may have great difficulty relating well to an athlete who has been raised in the exploration style. The coach who has been raised in a capricious manner may have difficulty relating to a youth who is highly rebellious and distrustful of authority. Perhaps the most congenial pairings of coach and athlete are those in which both have come from authoritarian backgrounds. Authoritarian parents tend not only to produce authoritarian youth, but authoritarian children in turn are likely to accept authority with little question. When both coach and athlete have been reared in ways likely to produce flexible and exploratory behaviors, a compatible "wedding" between coach and athlete is also likely.

Within Harvey's classification system, there are at least twelve combinations of child-rearing configurations, reflected in their pairing of behaviors of coach and athlete. Given a 5- to 40-member team, a large number of combinations is possible.

The interactions between authoritarianism in the coach and behaviors of athletes, reflecting the various child-rearing systems discussed, should be explored further. The studies by Hendry and others (1972) point out that for the most part coaches tend to lie at the strong end of the authoritarian-permissive continuum, found on several instruments purporting to measure personality. However, as will be seen in the chapter dealing with leadership, many effective coaches are now being found to possess qualities that reflect a more humanistic approach to working with others than the coaching stereotype has traditionally reflected.

Finally, the "conclusions" appearing in the chart are highly speculative. Indeed, the need for research on this type of relationship is obvious, since the available material is minimal.

PARENT ATTITUDES AND CHILDREN'S SPORTS PARTICIPATION AND ATHLETIC ABILITY

In addition to providing models of authoritarianism and permissiveness, and engaging in subtle "child-molding" behaviors, parents influence their children's feelings about competitive athletics in a number of concrete ways. The parents may or may not provide recreational opportunities for the family. They may take the child to the park and play with him or her at an early age, or they may not. Equipment and facilities may or may not be provided for recreational activities. While participating in sports activities in view of their children, the parent

TABLE 3–1. Childrearing systems and athletic behavior.

System	General behavior	Hypothesized behavior on a sports team
#1 Absolute authority	High score on authoritarianism, scales himself (or herself), accepts authority without question, rigid in belief system, and conforms to positive ideas about God and similar absolute authorities. Avoids conflict by avoiding nonauthorities, i.e. nonmajority opinion.	Happiest with an authoritarian coach, and such a coach would be happiest with them. Works hard, accepts strategies without reason; resents "trouble makers" on team, not influenced by agitators on team; believes in the good of athletics without question; would place morality, patriotism, and athletics as co-joined values.
#2 Capriciousness	Low on authoritarianism themselves, mistrustful of authority, as authority figures have not proved reliable in their past; rebellious attitude toward unexplained demands, lack stable guidelines to their behavior, seem to be in a psychologic vacuum, which may be filled with ideas from perceived power figures at either end of a conservative-liberal continuum. Avoid dependence on tradition, God, and most of the reference points that serve #1.	May be difficult to coach, particularly if coach is high in authoritarianism; need stable reinforcement system, need a system and authority figures which are dependable and trustworthy, may be easily led by dissident members of team, or by more stable ones, and/or may change in their alligince to team, goals of the team, and/or to the coach as the season progresses. Will be motivated little by appealing to loyalty to their school, team, or coach.

#3 Overindulgence	Overindulged children are likely to be socially manipulative of authority figures, as they have been able to coerce their parents. They harbor feelings of power and omnipotence over situations, as they have been led to believe that about themselves via parental indulgence. They seek a large number of friends to avoid being thrust on their own resources due to early overprotection. They acquiesce to authority.	Likely, at times to exhibit paradoxical behaviors. They are at once friendly to teammates and ingratiating to the coach, but may not do well under stress of competitions, particularly if they fail; however, they may be overly expansive of their roles in winning. Conceivably they do better in team than individual sports, as the overindulgence they have experienced does not prepare them for independent action, unsupported by others. They need constant approval from coach (father) figures.
#4 Exploration	The youngster is generally able to function well in abstract, ambiguous, or confusing situations. He is not unsettled by inconsistent authority, and will weight authority, while depending on his own insights and explorations at the same time. He is capable of examining alternatives without undue stress, is flexible intellectually, and is more open and sensitive to minimal cues in his environment.	This may be a youngster who appears to be relatively compliant on a team, but who at the same time depends on his own resources for guidance. He will not become easily rattled if a change in game strategy is suddenly required, nor will he have difficulty accommodating to new teammates, coaches, etc. He scores low on a scale of authoritarianism. He may be difficult for an authoritarian coach to understand, but not as difficult as #2 to deal with. Suggestions from this type of athlete may be useful to the team; while he or she will likely be extremely sensitive to the subtle social nuances of what is occurring in the team situation.

may exercise varying degrees of control and constraint upon the vigor of the behavior expressed both by them and by their offspring. The parent may take an active or passive part in family recreational activities in which sport plays a part.

In these and other ways, the parent transmits attitudes and values about physical activity in general and about participation in specific sports. Emphasizing the important ways in which families influence their children in sport is the study by Balazo (1975), in which the backgrounds of 24 female Olympic athletes were surveyed. In this retrospective study, the author concluded that both parents had been highly supportive of their daughters' efforts at early ages.

Thus, it is not surprising that the few research studies that have been carried out point to (1) the positive correlation between parental attitudes about physical activity and their children's participation in sport and (2) the relationships between parental attitudes and abilities and their children's actual performance capacities. These studies also contain data indicating the different ways families of boys and girls who want to participate in sport interact with their children, in contrast to relationships in families whose children do not choose to compete in athletics.

Snyder and Spreitzer (1973) indicated that family practices revolving around sport were predictive of the participation of both boys and girls in competitive athletics. The studies by Orlick (1972, 1978), which will be discussed, reflect similar relationships. Data from work by Scott (1952), McGee (1956), and Skubik (1956) indicate that parent attitudes toward physical education influence the attitudes and behaviors of their children, both in physical education classes and in competitive youth sport programs.

The husband and wife may hold generally similar attitudes about the value of sports participation. Data from a study by Zeller (1968) document this by revealing a high and positive correlation between the attitudes of husbands and wives toward physical activity and sport. Thus, most of the time, the child may be influenced by both mother and father when deciding whether or not to engage in competitive sport.

Attempting to draw positive conclusions about the influences of *any* parental behaviors and attitudes upon these same acts and attitudes in their offspring is a tenuous undertaking. Forming these generalizations about sport participation is fraught with peril, for in addition to transmitting their *attitudes* about things, objectives, activities, people, and situations to their children, parents also transmit *inherited characteristics.*

For example, several studies have found that there are relatively stable and positive correlations between father and son performances in such basic activities as sprinting and broadjumping, while studies from Bulgaria in the 1970s uncovered rather high father-son relationships between the *tempo* of running behavior while sprinting.

Thus, sorting the influences of inherited traits and attitudes, and the intergeneration transmission of both, is rather complicated. Figure 3-1 attempts to depict some of the possible interactions among parent-child performance, attitudes, and abilities in sport.

Some of the studies contain evidence that generally confirms "common sense." For example, in a study by Lawrence Rarick (1949), marked differences in parental behaviors were noted when the backgrounds of ten third-grade boys and girls who scored high on seven

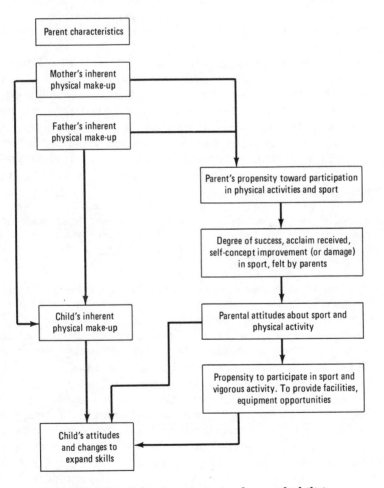

FIGURE 3-1.   Inheritance, attitudes, and abilities.

physical performance tests were contrasted to parent-child interactions among ten boys and girls who scored low on the same tests. These 20 extreme cases were culled from a total of 172 children who were administered the test battery in an elementary school.

In addition to the expected strength and size differences between the two groups, prolonged interviews with parents revealed the following: (1) Eight of the ten children scoring high reported frequent parent-child play interactions, while none of the low-scoring children reported this support from their parents. (2) Parents of the 10 highest-scoring children reported that provisions were made for a play area in their own yard, while none of the poorer performing children said that they had been provided this recreational space at their homes. (3) One-half of the better children frequented playgrounds, while one half of the 10 children who performed poorly said that they visited their local recreational area.

Also of note were the statements by parents that all the children who performed well participated in active play after school, while none of the less able children did so. During the period of early childhood, not only did more of the superior group evidence precocious motor development (early walking, etc), but they also indicated preferences for physical activities involving the larger muscle groups. Among the poorer performing children, most preferred to engage in passive activities requiring manual dexterities during their early childhood years.

Rarick concluded that:

> Parental interest as indicated not only by the provision for adequate play facilities, but also by active parent-participation in the child's activities is an important factor in helping children gain a high level of motor development.

More recent evidence has been obtained in a series of studies by Terrence Orlick (1972), from Ottawa, Canada. A survey interview was made of boys in the eighth grade, just before they became eligible to sign up to participate in youth ice hockey. There were marked differences in the responses obtained from parents whose boys chose to participate and the parents of those boys who did not.

The parents of the participants evidenced an interest in sports in a number of ways, ranging from watching televised sporting events to providing sports equipment for their boys. The parents of the boys who did not wish to participate seemed to find nonathletic ways to relate to their sons. The mothers of the boys electing to compete said that they actively encouraged vigorous play, as opposed to quiet play encouraged by mothers of the nonparticipants in the rugged and fast sport. Overall, upon inspecting parent behaviors, there was a high degree of predictability, of whether or not a boy chose to enter the competitive situation.

Although the Orlick study was limited to boys, a more recent investigation by Snyder and Spreitzer (1973) revealed that family behavior relative to sport was predictive of the participation of both boys and girls.

In the late 1950s, I encountered an interesting situation when testing freshmen in a swimming assessment at UCLA. Failure in the test necessitated participation in a beginning course during their first year at the university.

Just prior to the test, the students were given a questionnaire on which, among other things, they were asked to indicate whether or not their mothers and fathers could swim. After a few administrations of this test, our responses became almost reflex-like. We reached for the pole to "fish out" students who indicated that they had nonswimming mothers!

Whether nonswimming mothers failed to provide opportunities for the youths to learn to swim and/or whether maternal fears were somehow transmitted to the children was difficult to ascertain. However, the degree of predictability of test failure based on that one question was remarkable.

In her study of parent attitudes and the motor performance of their children, Zeller (1968) obtained data that tended to confirm much of what is assumed about the molding of youthful attitudes and performance by parental attitudes. She surveyed the attitudes about physical activity of 111 parents and contrasted their reports to the physical performance of their children.

She found that parent attitudes toward physical education and parent participation in physical activity were correlated, as were the attitudes of wives and husbands. Most important were the moderate positive correlations between the attitudes of parents and the actual performance scores of their offspring.

Schnabl-Dickey (1977) also found relationships between certain parental behaviors and the physical performance of their preschool children. Both throwing skills and jumping abilities seemed to be reflected in the manner in which parents had reared their children.

The handful of studies reviewed indicate that there are positive effects upon children's sports performance emanating from parents; studies illuminating the converse relationship seem absent. There is only inferential evidence that a *too* enthusiastic parent may blunt a child's performance. Stevenson, Klein, and Knights (1948) found, for example, that the influence of parents as rewarding or punishing agents seems to diminish as exposure to parental demands increases.

There may be a curvilinear rather than a simple linear relationship between children's sports performance and the enthusiasm exhibited by parents about sport. That is, parental attitudes toward sports participation by their children may have a positive effect until a point is reached when parent pressure tends to reduce the performance potential of the child. As parent opinion and parent-child tensions become extreme, the children may become reluctant to incur parent displeasure by exposing themselves to the stress of competitive sport.

Readers who have had even minimal exposure to the youth sport movement are aware of the too-interested-parent syndrome and the often deleterious effects upon young people's physical and mental health. I have become aware of the same eager parent syndrome manifested at the university level. Even at major universities, some parents come to practices daily and at times become so vocal that their attendance has to be terminated.

BIRTH ORDER, FAMILY COMPOSITION, AND SPORTS PARTICIPATION

Several scholars have explored the role of birth order as potentially influential on a number of psychologic and social attributes and behaviors. From a psychoanalytic standpoint, Toman's *Family Constellation* (1961) poses interesting hypotheses about the way "power positions" and "subordinate roles" within the family, experienced early in life, influence relationships in adulthood. Toman makes a strong case, using divorce statistics, for the fact that a marriage will be more successful when the partners come from opposite ends of the sibling power continuum. That is, the most successful pairing of males will come about when a first-born male marries a last-born wife or when the first-born female weds a last-born male. In both cases, the partners have been accustomed to opposite roles as children, and thus are likely to be compatible, one leading, the other following. Although admitting his formulas relating birth order to later success and failure are not absolute, Toman states that since most of us have spent a good number of our formative years in these family relationships, family make-up should at least be considered when evaluating how people deal with adult relationships.

There is some literature exploring the hypothesis that first-borns, raised more protectively, are less risk-taking as adults. Schacter, in *The Psychology of Affiliation* (1959), reported that first-borns are more averse to physical pain than children born later in the family. In data by Torrance (1954), it was seen that first-born fighter pilots in combat were less effective than those born later.

Recent studies of birth order continue to discover differences. Rothbart (1971), for example, found that mother-child interactions were different. First-borns received more technical help from mothers and evidenced more pressure for achievement than those born later. Miller and Maruyama (1976) found that first-borns were not as social as were those born later. The second- and third-born children evidenced better skills and were better liked than their older brothers and sisters. This study surveyed 1700 grade-school children.

Reflecting on this and other similar information, several researchers concluded that first-borns might be expected to evidence different patterns of sports participation than those born later.

The data from more than one study support this contention. For example, Helmreich and Collins (1969) found that first-borns responded with more fear to the prospect of physical harm than later-borns. While in a more definitive study by Nisbell (1969), it was found that first-borns were less likely to play dangerous sports, and were underrepresented in contact sports including football, rugby, and even soccer. More recent work by Casher (1977) indicates that third-borns are the most adventurous of all with regard to vigorous sports in which injury is a potential hazard.

In most studies, however, first-borns are seen to be as likely participants in sports in general as are later-borns. The differences seem to lie in just what sport is chosen. The first-born, perhaps overprotected, fearing failure because of achievement related child-rearing behaviors, is less likely to risk either failure or injury in sports.

FORMATION OF ACHIEVEMENT NEEDS

The word achievement is often heard in locker room talks, during preseason exhortations, and at the team banquet at the end of the season. Many believe that in the competitive societies of the 1970s, achievement is good, and that people who evidence high needs for achievement are worthwhile individuals. Most also hold to the proposition that one needs to have high goals and aspirations in order to succeed in athletics.

Children and youth in modern society hear these admonitions to "make good" loudly and clearly. Paul Weiss (1969) in his philosophical analysis of sport suggests that one of the main motives of youthful sports participants is to gain measures of success, to exhibit excellence by extending their young physiques in games and sport. Whereas excellence in science and literature may be more difficult to attain until later in life, the young have at their disposal a valuable tool, their bodies.

The concept of achievement became an important one to various psychologists interested in the evaluation and development of the personality, particularly during the 1940s. During this decade, personal attributes purportedly important to military performance came under the scrutiny of members of the psychological community, including Henry Murray (1943). Their theories and tests began to reflect their interest in what was termed "need systems," a concept that evolved from the earlier and less precise notion of "drive," which was much used in the literature during the first decades of the century.

Of much interest to Murray, McClelland, and others was the finding that people, to varying degrees, either sought excellence or were not overly concerned with achievement. Atkinson (1964), one of the more vigorous workers in this area, defined need for achievement as a "capacity to experience pride in accomplishment."

From the interest and work on the topic of achievement has come the Thematic Apperception Test, designed to evaluate this sometimes elusive quality. The testing protocol involves presenting a series of pictures, each for a brief period (20 seconds). Afterward, the subjects are required to write a story about what they saw. The pictures depict interactions between people, usually in a factory or office situation. While the responses of those being tested are guided by such questions as "What is happening?" "Who are these people?" "What has led to the situation?" "What has happened in the past?" "What will happen in the future?" "What is being thought, by whom?" "What is wanted?" and "What will be done?"

Responses are scored according to criteria that include whether or not the individual emits responses containing "achievement imagery" and responses with references to standards of excellence; criteria also include whether or not their story evidences a need (they need to do a good job), positive affect (they feel better that the job is done), positive goal anticipation (they believe they will turn out the product), or blocks to success (they did not know enough).

Further work on this topic by Atkinson and others resulted in the formulation of the concept of the need to avoid failure. This need, related to "failure anxiety," is often measured by the Mandler-Sarason Test Anxiety Questionnaire.[2]

The developmental antecedents of the fear of failure in young children may be different from conditions that produce the need for success. According to work by Teevan and McGhee (1972), children with high needs to avoid failure were those whose mothers expected inde-

[2]A review of the history of these concepts and measurement problems is found in B. Weiner, *Theories of Motivation,* (Chicago, Rand McNally, 1973), chap. 5.

pendence and achievement from their offspring earlier in life than was true of children who evidenced less fear of failure to achieve. In this same study, it was found that the reward systems used by mothers differed. In children whose needs to avoid failure were high, the mothers were generally neutral when the children experienced success and punished them when they failed. On the other hand, the mothers of children who evidenced low needs to avoid failure tended to reward their offspring following success experiences.

A large number of studies conducted in businesses, government, and educational institutions have produced data that have refined and elaborated on the concept of need achievement. One important direction of this research has been the attempt to ascertain what kinds of family behaviors and parent-child interactions produce children and youth possessing high achievement needs. The data from a study by Rosen and D'Andrade (1958) is often discussed in this context.

In their investigation, 20 boys evidencing high needs for achievement and 20 who scored low on needs for achievement were identified. Two social psychologists went into their homes and presented the boys and their attending parents five tasks. Four involved manual dexterity. To a large degree, however, the tasks required mental as well as physical processes. The parents were placed so that they could regulate the difficulty of the tasks given to their children. For example, they could decide at one point just how far back from a peg they should ask their boy to stand when trying to ring it with a quoit. In another task, the parents were in control of how many letters were given to the child at one time as he tried to form words in a kind of Scrabble game.

When analyzing the findings, the researchers noted several differences between parent-child interactions when contrasting the communications going to and being received from parents and offspring. For example, the boys who scored high in "achievement imagery" were confronted with high goal setting by their parents, who seemed more interested in presenting challenging situations than in the absolute scores they obtained. This same group of parents extended general rather than specific help, as their progeny also would either reject help, or accept only general comments. The "high achievement" boys rejected specific help in how to make their scores higher, rather than keeping the tasks challenging ones.

On the other hand, the parents of the boys low in achievement needs seemed more concerned about how their boys "looked" when performing. They concentrated on how high the scores were, rather than how the task was done or the challenge to their sons. These parents would, for example, place their sons close to the peg to throw quoits, so that high scores were achieved. However, the "high achievement boys" scored better on more of the tasks, despite these attempts by the others to inflate scores.

Information from studies by Winterbottom (1958), as well as research by others, point out that early independence training by parents produces children who are relatively difficult for others to influence and who evidence high needs for achievement. Also Sampson's work (1962, 1965) suggests that high needs for achievement are related to birth order, particularly among girls. That is, first-born females are slightly more resistant to social influences, and also evidence more need for achievement, than girls in other ordinal positions in the family. First-born males, on the other hand, seem less resistant to influence by others than later-born males. There is also some evidence that the greater dependency seen in some first-born males reduces their needs to achieve and heightens their need to affiliate.

From studies such as these, the child-rearing antecedents of children and youth with high achievement needs are beginning to emerge. As Rosen and D'Andrade stated, the parents of children who wish to do well in many tasks seem to be "pulling from ahead" rather than "pushing them from behind." In their work, it was found that the fathers would at times emit remarks that were particularly crushing to the egos of the boys as they performed. Data such as these suggest that individuals scoring high on achievement imagery on the Thematic Apperception Test and similar instruments usually evidence a cluster of characteristics when confronted with situations that call for achievement. These include the following:

1. Goal setting, self-estimation, and similar behaviors are different for those with high and low achievement needs. Individuals with high achievement needs tend to select and set intermediate attainable goals, rather than voice aspirations that are either unreasonably high or ridiculously low. Individuals whose achievement needs are low often set goals that are too easily met or are not possible of attainment. In either case, when the subsequent performance takes place, easy excuses are possible ("Of course, no one could do that well").

2. Most success and the strongest achievement orientation is seen in individuals who need to achieve success, in contrast to those who work hard because of fear of failure. However, the need to avoid failure is a stronger impetus to hard work than are motives of those scoring low on tests of achievement needs.

3. To some degree, programs that attempt to enhance achievement needs by schoolchildren and businessmen have been reasonably successful. Seminars dealing with goal setting, personal expectations and evaluation, and strategies for achieving success in direct ways can work positive changes in youthful sports competitors. These methods have been employed during recent years with youthful swimmers competing at top levels in the United States.

For the most part, however, studies of achievement needs have not been carried out within athletic settings. When motor tasks were used, it was because of the necessity to score performance precisely rather than because the researcher was interested in physical activity itself. Most of the work has concentrated on academic success in school, as well as on success in business or on the assembly line.

Perhaps the greatest weakness in the work on achievement needs is that the tests themselves employ pictures that bear little resemblance to situations found in the gymnasium or on the athletic field. Thus, responses inform the experimenters about the feelings experienced when viewing a commercial environment but little about achievement imagery in athletics. For example, children in the less privileged sections of large cities usually score low on the TAT and other tests of achievement needs, since pictures of factory and office settings mean little to them. However, these same youth inhabit the local playgrounds and strive to achieve success in pick-up games in all sports far into the night.

Thus, drawing valid conclusions from data emanating from hundreds of studies of achievement needs which are pertinent to athletic competition is a somewhat tenuous undertaking. However, some generalizations may be formulated.

For example, it is probable that as children are born and mature, a "diffusion effect" occurs relative to achievement needs. Initially, perhaps from about 2 to 4 years, children begin to formulate generalized notions of just how achievement oriented their families are. They then begin to make rather vague and generalized formulations of goals relative to what is expected, and what they expect of themselves.

With further exposure to their own relative success and failure, and to the family's reactions to their strivings, the children's feelings about achievement become more specific. They begin to select, to choose to value achievement in some tasks and not in others. Both Scanlan (1978) and Thomas (1978) have recently written about similar concepts as they have discussed the development of competition and achievement in children. For example, in this second period a child may begin to select fields of endeavor which to some degree have been suggested by family norms—the arts, the sciences, athletics, or perhaps literature.

During middle and late childhood, a third stage is reached. During this time, children's feelings about achievement begin to differentiate even more. Depending on various cultural sanctions, restrictions, and the availability of coaching and facilities, they will begin to decide what kinds of physical activities (if any) may be worthwhile and which ones are of less value to them. Thus, as feelings of competence and self-esteem become directed and polished, so do the choices of what to pursue and what to avoid.

It is obvious that the athletic coach and team members may enter a child's life during this last stage. The child's self-concept and achievement need pattern is either still in a state of flux or beginning to become solidified. Thus, the coach of younger boys and girls often has an easier time directing their energies than may a mentor working with older children or youth.

The young athlete with high achievement needs may evidence several kinds of behavior to which the coach should react in positive and supportive ways. He or she may, for example, not be overly social with others on the team, preferring instead to concentrate upon personal performance. High achievement athletes may need constant information about the relative success of their performance, more so than others on the team. Unique characteristics of their goal-setting behavior have already been alluded to. They are generally concerned about setting attainable goals rather than unrealistically high or low ones.

Finally, the coach should realize that even a relatively young man or woman has been exposed to years of achievement-related parental training, engendering attitudes that may be independent of objective performance capacities. When confronted with a young athlete of this type the coach may have to accommodate in several ways. For example, if the athlete's need to achieve is low despite outstanding athletic ability, the coach should try to retrain and promote achievement-related behaviors, instead of simply becoming angry or frustrated because the athlete does not seem to try hard enough.

Further illumination of the complex interactions of achievement motivation, parental training, and athletic success should come about when tests for achievement needs contain achievement imagery related to athletic participation. The instruments presently available are not compatible with the hypothesized, task-specific nature of achievement motivation reflected in the feelings of children past the age of 6 or 7.

GAINING STATUS VIA ATHLETIC PROWESS IN CHILDHOOD AND ADOLESCENCE

Children at play quickly establish a status hierarchy, similar to those seen in factories and government offices. The "pecking order" in numerous animal communities has also been studied with thoroughness and sophistication during the past decades.

In studies carried out in the 1930s and 1940s, it became apparent that a minimal or moderate amount of physical ability in young children was necessary for at least some status in play groups. This physical ability became increasingly important as the child progressed from the informal play groups in the second and third year to more structured teams in middle childhood.

If it is true, as Hardy suggested, that "social recognition during the elementary years is closely related to the individual's ability to distinguish himself from his associates," it is reasonable to believe that one of the more important and obvious ways a child can be different (and better) is by demonstrating skill in physical activity.

Parten (1933) and Hardy, in research carried out in the 1930s, found that children designated as "best liked" and "popular" by both teachers and other children were those whose physical achievements were superior in such tasks as running, throwing, balancing, and the like.

Lippitt and his colleagues (1952) documented the fact that children who achieved status and power in a summer camp situation were those who could best initiate and direct the physical activities of others. Thrasher (1926) in his classic studies of youth gangs, also documents the importance of physical toughness in this context. Coleman's work in the 1950s on the "adolescent society" also illuminates the manner in which high school athletics enhances the social acceptability not only of the athlete in direct ways, but also of those who are in any way associated with sport, including cheerleaders and the like.

In studies carried out in the late 1960s, I found that children designated as clumsy through physical ability testing evidenced lower self-concepts than did those who were not labeled in this manner. For example, on questions on a self-concept test (a portion of the Piers-Harris), the awkward children and "normals" evidenced significant differences. Of the boys with movement problems, 57 percent said that "their friends made fun of them," while of the boys free of coordination problems, only 34 percent answered in this manner. Boys with coordination problems tended more often to answer that they were not strong, that they preferred to watch rather than to play games, and that they were "sad most of the time."

Similar differences in responses to this same self-concept test were obtained from girls. Twice as many who had movement problems said that they had trouble making friends than did girls free of coordination problems.

Puffer (1905), studying leadership in adolescent games, found that skill at play was predictive of leadership roles assumed. Marks, studying the adolescent, also observed that boys who participated more in sports were most readily accepted than those not easily assimilated into games. The physically more adroit, Marks noted, were those who were also likely to carry out their impulses in direct action.

Thus, rather early physical skill has at least some influence on the achievement of social status in both children and youth. During adolescence, the influence of physical prowess probably has different effects, depending on the values with which the youth is surrounded. In certain families physical ability is a social imperative, while in others the prevalent value system is not as physically oriented.[3]

IMPLICATIONS FOR THE COACH

This chapter has numerous implications for the coach attempting to understand and to improve the athlete. To begin with, the coach should not make the assumption that he or she is the first important authority figure in the life of the youth on the team. Rather, the coach should attempt to ascertain in both direct and indirect ways: (1) what associations the athlete has had in the past with parental authority figures, (2) how the athlete feels about authority figures in general, as reflected by prior experiences in the family, and (3) how he can, if possible, continue in a positive way to act as a supportive authority figure.

This kind of information can be obtained directly through interviews, structured and unstructured, as well as by asking athletes to write (or tape) an autobiography, placing emphasis on how they interacted with family members during the formative years of their lives and athletic careers.

Indirectly, the coach may carefully observe contemporary interactions between an athlete and family members, particularly parents, to determine not only the past quantity and quality of their relationships, but the current manner in which the parent(s) deal with the athlete's performing efforts.

This kind of information may lead the coach to make decisions relative to the kind of behavior(s) appropriate when dealing with the athlete in contemporary situations. For example, if the athlete has had a strained relationship with the parents and suffered undue stresses relative to achievement of excellent performance, the coach may choose to take a gentler approach, more supportive than judgmental. On the other hand, if the athlete has apparently thrived on parental pressures

[3]I recently tried to improve the skills of a boy who declared that he did not think the program was really important, as he was going to be a movie producer when he grew up, like his father who was prominent in the "business."

that are rather direct in their emphasis upon athletic achievement, the coach may choose a similar way of dealing with the athlete.

Interviews and autobiographical data may also reveal that changes are occurring in the way the athlete perceives his or her performance. In the past, for example, the athlete may have initially believed himself a less valued member of a family, an individual whose value could only be enhanced by striving for athletic superiority. However, from a contemporary standpoint, the coach may ascertain that the athlete is no longer in great need of parental approval for good performance, and rather is looking for other reasons to strive and work hard on the practice field. In the latter case, the coach may aid the athlete to readjust values and motives, from those dependent on parental approval to those reflecting achievement of excellence for its own sake. Such a change aims to satisfy the athlete's sense of personal mastery, rather than to please others.

Further, the sensitive coach should attempt to ascertain what factors in the athlete's early family history may heighten probabilities that the performer may encounter emotional health problems when subjected to the strains and stresses of competition. Individuals who reveal that not only inordinate pressures have and are being placed upon them by family members, but that their personal sense of worth may be judged harshly if they do not do well, may be more likely to suffer performance decrements, at times resulting in psychic breakdown. On the other hand, athletes with a sense of self-esteem based on qualities in addition to physical excellence may suffer less and not overreact when either winning or losing.

Finally, the coach may, upon ascertaining the degree of independence training engaged in by power figures in the athlete's past (coaches and parents), make decisions about: (1) how many and what types of decisions the athlete may be comfortable in making about the present training program, (2) how the athlete can be encouraged to participate more democratically in problems that arise in training and competition, and (3) whether or not the athlete will profit from more or less control over his or her destiny as a performer, both at present and in the future.

SUMMARY

Much of the available literature contains data that are more inferential than substantive. Research pointing to cause-effect relationships between early developmental experiences within a social context, and later sports participation is difficult to locate. The difficulty of carrying out appropriate longitudinal studies precludes dogmatic statements relating child-rearing practices and early peer acceptance to later behaviors and tendencies to participate in athletics.

At the same time, factors of several types apparently exert at least moderate influences on whether or not the child becomes a sports participant. These include (1) the inherited physique characteristics acquired from parents, (2) the tendency to be active or inactive, (3) the little understood but probably inherited precision of movement capacities, and (4) parental attitudes and propensities for participation and success in vigorous play and competitive sport.

For the most part, if studies of the authoritarian personality of coaches are valid, the child entering sport, despite his *own* experiences within a family constellation, must somehow come to grips with an absolutist kind of social environment. The degree to which he or she can accomplish this is probably related to the child-rearing pattern he or she experienced. Youth who have been conditioned by their parents to accept authority without question are likely to be more comfortable in a socially rigid sports situation than those who have been subjected to more permissive child-rearing practices.

Other information in the chapter corroborates what would be considered common sense. A more active or less active adult tends to marry a similarly constituted mate. In turn they transmit their interest, or lack of interest, in physical activity to their offspring. They have also bestowed to varying degrees upon their offspring genetic influences that may or may not contribute to athletic participation.

The child may not only receive support from parents for success in physical activity, but also may be socially rewarded by peers for prowess displayed on the play field. These early status rewards may persist into adolescence and adulthood, and more than one athletic coach enters the occupation to perpetuate the reward system he or she has enjoyed as a youth by promoting vicarious success through directing the actions of the team.

To varying degrees, parents engage in what is termed "achievement training" with their offspring. This kind of child-rearing behavior, if directed toward achievement in physical activity, has obvious benefits to the coach who encounters the child in a competitive situation. On the other hand, the youth who possesses good or adequate physical qualities yet was exposed to family child-rearing patterns that did not emphasize achievement related behavior may cause a coach more than a little consternation. This youth may appear to be exerting less than optimum effort during practices and games. Further research exploring achievement needs with children could provide helpful guidelines as to how one can engage in achievement training in competitive sport.

QUESTIONS FOR DISCUSSION

1. What parental behaviors are likely to produce a child who is overly aggressive in sport? What kinds of parental child-rearing behaviors are less likely to produce an overly aggressive athlete in later life?
2. How are achievement needs subtly trained for by parents? Can you give a specific example of how this training might transpire, using an incident in your own life?
3. What are the likely effects of birth order on athletic competition later in life?
4. What role do parental attitudes play in the molding of children's tendencies to participate in competitive sport? Can you separate the effects of parental attitudes from the genetic characteristics they may also be transmitting to their offspring?
5. Using Harvey's classification system, predict how a youthful athlete may react to a specific situation in which he or she is confronted by a coach's admonitions.
6. What variables might mold both competitive behaviors in young children and their needs for power in play groups as well as in their initial confrontations with a sports team?
7. What problems arise when attempting to measure achievement needs, relative to sport, in young children and youth?
8. Why might an awkward child's self-concept *not* be enhanced through a program of skill development that actually improves performance level?
9. How might parents whose needs to have their children's performance in sports at too high a level inhibit the efforts of their children? Can you diagram this kind of relationship?

BIBLIOGRAPHY

ATKINSON JW: *An Introduction to Motivation.* Princeton, New Jersey: Van Nostrand, 1964.

BALAZO EK: Psycho-social study of outstanding female athletes. *Res Q* 46:3 (1975), 267–74.

CASHER BB: Enticing research directions: Fear of success, danger, and birth order. In Landers DM, Christina RW (eds): *Motor Behavior and Sport,* Vol. II. Champaign, Illinois: Human Kinetics Publisher, 1977.

COHEN DJ: Justin and his peers, An experimental analysis of a child's social world. *Child Development* XXXIII (1962), 697–717.

COLEMAN JS: *The Adolescent Society.* New York: Free Press of Glencoe, 1961.

CRATTY BJ: Athletic and physical experiences of fathers and sons who participated in physical fitness testing at Pomona College, California. *J Educ Res* (1959), 207–211.

———. *Children and Youth in Competitive Sport.* Freeport, New York: Educational Activities, 1974.

———. Comparison of fathers and sons in physical ability. *Res Q* XXXI (March 1960), 12–15.

———, Ikeda N, Martin MM, Jennett C, Morris M: *Movement Activities, Motor Ability and The Education of Children.* Springfield, Illinois: Thomas, 1970, chap. 1.

———. *Social Dimensions of Physical Activity.* Englewood Cliffs, New Jersey: Prentice-Hall, 1967, chaps. 5 and 8.

———. *Teaching Human Behavior Through Active Games.* Englewood Cliffs, New Jersey: Prentice-Hall, 1975.

GELFAND DM, HARTMANN DP: Some detrimental effects of competitive sports on children's behavior. In Magill RA, Ash MJ, Smoll F (eds): *Children in Sport, A Contemporary Anthology.* Champaign, Illinois: Human Kinetics Publisher, 1978.

HANDEL G (ed): *The Psychosocial Interior of the Family.* Chicago: Aldine, 1955.

HARVEY OJ, HUNT DE, SCHRODER HM: *Conceptual Systems and Personality Organization.* New York: Wiley, 1961.

———. Some cognitive determinants of influencibility. *Sociometry* XXVII (1964), 208–221.

HELMREICH L, COLLINS BE: Situational determinants of affiliative preference under stress. *J Pers Soc Psychol* VI (1969), 79–85.

HENDRY LB, WHITING HTA (eds): The coaching stereotype. In *Readings in Sports Psychology.* London: Henry Kimpton, 1972.

HOFFMAN ML: Power assertion by the parent and its impact on the child. *Childhood Dev* XXXI (1960), 129–143.

LIPPITT R, POLANSKY N, REDL F, ROSEN S: The dynamics of power. *Human Rel* V (1952), 37–64.

LITTLE SW, COHEN LD: Goal setting behavior of asthmatic children, and of their mothers for them. *J Pers* XVIV (1950), 377–389.

MAGILL RA, ASH MJ, SMOLL F: *Children in Sport: A Contemporary Anthology.* Champaign, Illinois: Human Kinetics Publisher, 1978.

MARTENS R: *Joy and Sadness in Children's Sports.* Champaign, Illinois: Human Kinetics Publisher, 1978.

McClelland DC, Winter DG: *Motivating Economic Achievement.* New York: Free Press, 1969.

McDougall W: *Outline of Psychology.* New York: Scribners, 1923.

McGee R: Comparison of attitudes toward intensive competition for high school girls. *Res Q* XXVII (1956), 60–67.

Mensh IH, Glidewell JC: Children's perceptions of relationships among their family and friends. *J Exp Educ* XXVII (September 1958).

Miller N, Maruyama G: Ordinal position and peer popularity. *J Pers Soc Psychol* 33:2 (1976), 123–131.

Murray HA: *Explorations in Personality.* New York: Oxford University Press, 1938.

———. *Thematic Apperception Test Manual.* Cambridge, Mass.: Harvard University Press, 1943.

Nisbell RE: Birth order and participation in dangerous sports. *J Pers Soc Psychol* VIII:IV (1969), 351–353.

Orlick TD: Family sports environment and early sports participation. Paper at the Fourth Canadian Psycho-motor Learning and Sports Psychology Symposium. Waterloo, Ontario: University of Waterloo, October 1972.

———, McNally J, O'Hara T: "Cooperative games: Systematic analysis and cooperative impact." In Smoll FL, Smith RE (eds): *Psychological Perspectives in Youth Sport.* Washington: Hemisphere, 1978.

Parten MB: Leadership among pre-school children. *J Abnorm Soc Psychol* XXVII (1933), 430–440.

Puffer JD: Boys: Gangs. *Pediatric Seminar* XII (1905), 175–212.

Rarick G, McKee R: A study of 20 third-grade children exhibiting extreme levels of achievement on tests of motor proficiency. *Res Q* XX (1949), 142–152.

Rosen BC, D'Andrade R: The psychosocial origins of achievement motivation. *Sociometry* XXII (1959), 185–218.

Rothbart MK: Birth order and mother-child interactions in achievement situations. *J Pers Soc Psychol* 17:2 (1971), 113–120.

Sampson EE: Birth order, need achievement, and conformity. *J Abnorm Soc Psychol* LXIV (1962), 155–159.

———, Maher BA: The study of ordinal position, antecedents, and outcomes. *Progress in Experimental Personality Research.* II. New York: Academic, 1965.

SCANLAN TK: Antecedents of competitiveness. In Magill RA, Ash MJ, Smoll EL: *Children in Sport: A Contemporary Anthology.* Champaign, Illinois: Human Kinetics Publisher, 1978.

———, PASSER MW: Anxiety-inducing factors in competitive youth sports. In Smoll EL, Smith RE (eds): *Psychological Perspectives in Youth Sport.* Washington: Hemisphere, 1978, chap. 5.

SCHACHTER S: *The Psychology of Affiliation.* Stanford, California: Stanford University Press, 1959.

SCHNABL-DICKEY EA: Relationships between parents' child-rearing attitudes, and the jumping and throwing performance of the preschool children. *Res Q* 48:2, 1977.

SCOTT P: Comparative study of attitudes toward athletic competition in the elementary schools. Unpublished Ph.D. dissertation, State University of Iowa, 1952.

SEARS PC: Levels of aspiration in academically successful and unsuccessful children. *J Abnorm Soc Psychol* XXXV (1940), 489–536.

SEARS R, MACCOBY EC, LEVIN H: *Patterns of Child Rearing.* Evanston, Illinois: Row and Peterson, 1957.

SEEFELDT VD, GILLIAM T, BLIEVERNICHT D, BRUCE R: Participatory patterns and characteristics of youth athletes. In Smoll FL, Smith RE (eds): *Psychological Perspectives in Youth Sport.* Washington, Hemisphere, 1978, chap. 2.

SKUBIK E: Studies of little and middle league baseball. *Res Q* XXVII (1956), 97–110.

SMOLL FL, SMITH RE: *Psychological Perspectives in Youth Sport.* Washington, Hemisphere, 1978.

SNYDER D, SPREITZER EA: Family influences and involvement in sport. *Res Q* 44:3 (October 1973), 249–255.

STEVENSON H, KLEIN R, KNIGHTS R: Parents and strangers as reinforcing agents for children's performance. *J Abnorm Soc Psychol* XXV (1948), 35–71.

TEEVAN R, McGHEE PE: Childhood development of fear of failure motivation. *J Pers Soc Psychol* III (1972), 348–358.

THOMAS JR: Attribution theory and motivation through reward: Practical implications for children's sports. In Magill RA, Ash MJ, Smoll FL: *Children in Sport: A Contemporary Anthology.* Champaign, Illinois, Human Kinetics Publishers, 1978.

THRASHER FN: The gang as a symptom of community disorganization. *J Appl Sociol* (January 1926), 3–21.

TOMAN W: *Family Constellation.* New York, Springer, 1961.

TORRANCE EB: A psychological study of American jet aces. Paper presented at the Meeting of the Western Psychological Association, Long Beach, California, 1954.

WEINER B: *Theories of Motivation, from Mechanism to Cognition.* Chicago, Rand, McNally, 1973.

WEISS P: *Sport, A Philosophical Inquiry.* Carbondale, Illinois, Southern Illinois Press, 1969.

WELLER L: *The relationship of birth order to anxiety. Sociometry* XXV (1962), 415–417.

WERNER EE: Infants around the world; cross-cultural studies of psychomotor development from birth to two years. *J Cross-Cultural Psychol* III:II (June 1972), 111–134.

WINTERBOTTOM MR: The relation of need achievement to early learning experiences in independence and mastery. In Atkinson JW (ed): *Motives in Fantasy, Action and Society.* Princeton, New Jersey, Van Nostrand, 1958.

ZELLER J: The relationship between parental attitude toward physical education and the physical performance of the child. Unpublished Master's thesis. UCLA, Department of Physical Education, 1968.

4

Competition and Cooperation

The term *competition* is used in sport by coaches, fans, and athletes alike. The word *competitor* is often substituted for the term *athlete* when speaking of members of sports teams. Within the vernacular, there is general agreement on the meaning of competition: it denotes the process of trying hard to win, to get something someone else wants.

It is difficult to discuss concepts related to the word *competition* without referring to cooperation. In many instances, both competition and cooperation occur almost simultaneously, as an athlete competes with others while cooperating with members of his or her own team to best their opponents.

Social psychologists during the past 20 years have become interested in both competitive and cooperative behaviors. At times, they have devised clever experiments with which to delve deeply into the factors influencing striving and collective behaviors that the words denote.

Among the questions and problems that have been explored, several are of potential interest to the coach and athlete. Some of these are:

1. What are the developmental antecedents of competitive behaviors seen in childhood?
2. When does one first see evidence of cooperative and competitive behaviors in children, and what forms do these efforts initially take?
3. When placed in situations in which motives to cooperate and compete may conflict, which types of behaviors emerge, or seem preferred?
4. What influences do friendship and previously pleasant and unpleasant associations have on competitive and cooperative behaviors within groups?

5. Are there personality traits predictive of the tendency to exhibit competitive or cooperative behaviors?
6. Are there sex and/or cultural differences in the tendencies to compete or cooperate?
7. Is the urge to compete general, or is an individual competitive in a given situation or for a given type of reward (social recognition, monetary considerations, etc.)?
8. What about the educability of cooperative and competitive behaviors? Can this type of education be engaged in sport? If so, how?

There is also a series of rather practical questions that are now being asked in the realm of sport, some of which reflect the preceding questions. For example, it is unclear whether or not an athletic team should be composed of all highly competitive types, or whether a balance of people evidencing both cooperative and competitive behavior is more desirable for good group performance. It is unclear at this point just how to predict at an early age what child will perform best in highly competitive sport later in life.

The optimum balance of cooperative and competitive tendencies within an individual engaged in sport is unclear at this time. It is not known just how competitive tendencies and the strength of cooperative behaviors are measured in athletes. It would also be desirable to know just how one might assign to either an individual or a team sport a person who evidences a preponderance of traits reflecting cooperative or competitive behaviors. The important interactions between aggression and competition have also not been fully explored.

The above questions form a basis for much of the discussion that follows. After reviewing the material in this chapter, the reader may begin to post tentative answers to some of the queries and in addition will become able to formulate even more penetrating questions.

Competition Defined

In efforts to bring more precision to the consideration of competition, social psychologists have suggested that the word may be considered within several classification systems. For example, theoreticians have usually started with attempts to define the word. In general, competition exists when two or more people struggle for some common goal or object. Further clarification of this concept of mutual struggle are the words "contritely interdependent." This means that if one individual achieves his or her goal, by definition the other(s) are prevented from reaching theirs.

In some competition, however, an individual may be able to reach a goal, while his or her opponents are still able to achieve at least some of their objectives. The losers in a game may, for example, enjoy the excitement of the physical workout. This second situation, whereby more than one individual may "win" something, is termed "promotively interdependent" by social psychologists.

Using other words, Luschen (1970) speaks of "zero-sum" competition. This denotes a struggle in which one individual wins totally and the other loses. In contrast, what is called "non-zero-sum competition" means that people may enjoy some degree of winning, or lose only partially. Whether one wins or loses in athletic competition, of course, hinges upon ideas of what success is all about. To some, success means conquering absolute standards or includes self-expansion through meeting the stresses of competition itself. This type of success may be independent of objective scores or marks achieved.

Still other definitions of competition appear in the literature, including that of Maller (1929) in his classic study of competition and cooperation among school children. He suggested that a cooperative situation is one that encourages an individual to strive with members of his group for a goal object, which is to be shared equally among all. Maller viewed a competitive situation, on the other hand, as one that stimulates the individual to strive against others for a goal object, which he hopes will become his sole possession.

A definition by Ross and Van den Haag (1957) also suggests that competition may be of several types. In what they term "indirect competition," an individual strives to better an impersonal mark, a record, or perhaps climb a mountain. "Direct competition," on the other hand, means actions involving another person(s) in a clearly personal contest.

Competition usually includes some kind of comparisons to various norms. Thus, Jones and Gerard (1967) stated that competition is either the attempt to compete with one's own personal assessments of what is good (comparative appraisal) or to depend on the evaluation of others (reflected appraisal).

In the world of sport, children, adolescents, and adults evidence individual differences relative to the type of appraisals they largely depend on. Some may be most influenced by the accolades and opinions of others, whereas others may "keep their own counsel" when evaluating their personal performance. It is probably true that during the initial stages of youthful sports competition children have to depend more on the opinions of others when evaluating their competitive worth. If these evaluations are generally positive, a child persists, and after a time gains the experience to evaluate his or her own quality of performance. Dependence on self-appraisal is seen more in mature athletes, who have extensive backgrounds in evaluating performance standards.

Most scholars agree that the culture molds competitive behaviors in both children and adults. Sutton-Smith and colleagues (1964) have suggested that certain primitive and modern cultural predispositions are likely to stimulate predictable kinds of competitive and cooperative behavior in children's games and in adult sport.

However, much of this theorizing remains highly speculative. It is unclear, for example, just how much the "total cultural pattern" in which the child or youth resides influences competitive sport behaviors, in contrast to the more immediate influences in performance situations. Peer pressures and presence, as well as parental and neighborhood standards, have great influence on how hard and for what a child or youth competes.

Orlick (1973) published an informative paper after visiting the People's Republic of China. Delving into relationships between culture and competition in sport he concluded that (1) within this large country great emphasis is placed upon friendship first and competition second, and (2) the involvement of the masses in sport is intended to improve people's health, and thus sport is practiced everywhere by everyone.

According to Orlick, Chairman Mao Tse-Tung taught that the improvement of the caliber of the people's sport performance is important so that they might have friendly competition with other nations, or as Mao states, "to increase friendship between China and the people of the world."

As a result, physical training teachers are encouraged to help the majority of the students to take an interest in active, vigorous sport. Thus, daily mass exercises are engaged in by factory workers, as well as by children in schools. Most people ride bicycles. The populace works together in the building of stadiums and other athletic facilities. If a factory needs a basketball court, the workers build it themselves, Orlick explains.

If Orlick's assessment of the competitive philosophy and sports climate of the People's Republic of China is correct, it marks a departure from the philosophies usually seen as athletes compete for some of the world's larger powers in international competitions. Most modern societies are reasonably competitive today, despite their unique political philosophies. The destinies of nations within the ever-shrinking world are so intertwined that attempting to ascertain reasons for athletes representing them to be competitive or noncompetitive seems pointless. Drawing inferences about how athletes from the so-called developing countries generate their competitive drive, by reference to studies carried out by anthropologists focusing on the nature of primitive cultures, also seems less than helpful. Athletes from these emerging nations in international competitions evidence the same fervor seen in competitors from the larger countries of the world.

Competitive vs. Cooperative Behaviors

A number of writers have contrasted competitive and cooperative behaviors using several kinds of reference systems. May and Dobb (1937), for example, contrasted the behaviors in the following manner. They suggested that both cooperative and competitive behaviors are similar, since both involve striving toward some "social end" by two or more people. In the case of competition, however, the end may be achieved by some but not all of those involved, whereas when cooperative behavior occurs, most or all of the individuals concerned are able to achieve the goal.

Further, they postulate that on the social level competition occurs when two or more are striving for the same goal or rewards that are scarce or difficult to attain, and the rules prevent achievement of these rewards in equal amounts by all concerned. The fact that the goals may be achieved unequally often acts as a stimulus to performance, particularly when the individuals have relatively few affiliative contacts with each other. Cooperative behavior occurs when individuals work toward goals that can be shared. Further, in cooperative situations, the rules require individuals to achieve the goal in relatively equal amounts, and they have the opportunity to enjoy many "psychologically affiliative" contacts with one another while striving for the end result.

Margaret Mead (1937) offers simpler definitions. She defines competition as "the act of seeing or endeavoring to gain what another is endeavoring to gain at the same time," and cooperation as "the act of working together to one end." But further, Dr. Mead suggests that there are different meanings to the terms "competition" and "rivalry." Rivalry, she writes, is behavior involving the "worsting" of another person. Competition is behavior oriented toward a goal, in which beating others, in a personal sense, may be a secondary consideration.

Deutsch (1950), in "A Theory of Cooperation and Competition," wrote about the logical psychologic implications of both competitive and cooperative behavior. Using terms taken from Lewinian field theory, Deutsch stated that the cooperative situation is marked by the fact that the "goal regions" for each of the individuals or subunits can be entered to some degree by anyone, only if everyone in the situation can enter the goal regions. Deutsch called this the seeking of "promotively interdependent goals."

In competitive social situations, if the goal regions are entered by one individual, it results in situations that prevent the others from reaching their respective goals. Deutsch describes this situation by the term *contritely interdependent goals*. Deutsch makes the important point that most "everyday situations involve few instances which may be labeled purely competitive or cooperative in nature." Most social interactions, he continues, "involve some kind of goal-centered behavior, involving complex sets of goals and subgoals, thus encouraging one to be both promotively as well as contritely interdependent at the same time." Deutsch uses the game of basketball to clarify his point, stating that while the team may be cooperatively interrelated and trying to win as a group, its members may be competing among themselves to become the "star" of the team.

During the early decades of this century, the concepts of competition and cooperation were discussed in terms of common sense. Later, however, more mature and sophisticated experimentation and theory building has resulted in refinement of the meanings of the two words.

For example, Thomas (1957), influenced by Deutsch's concepts, proposed that it is important to distinguish between interdependence with respect to the *goals* of a task and interdependence with regard to the *means* of reaching those goals. For example, if two coaches of the same team wished to use the same exercise apparatus at the same time to condition two athletes, it could be said that they were negatively interdependent with respect to the means (conditioning the players) but were working together toward bettering the total team performance. Thus, they were positively interdependent with respect to the goal, winning games.

Ravens and Eachus (1963) pointed out that some of the contradictory response reported in studies of cooperative and competitive behavior prior to that time could be explained with reference to the blurring of the meaning of the two terms. For example, competition would be expected to have negative effects on performance when there was high means interdependence coupled with goal interdependence. On the other hand, when the means remain relatively independent, an increased level of activity occurs in both cooperative and competitive situations.

Ravens further refines these ideas with the suggestion that means dependence may be of two types: (1) Behavior dependence, in which a person is dependent on the *performance* of another in order to reach some goal. An example of this in sport is when a forward in soccer-football depends on his teammates to receive a pass before scoring. (2) *Information dependence* occurs when knowledge from another is used by the performer to achieve some goal. The interaction and dependency between athlete and coach is an obvious example of information dependence in a competitive situation.

Development of Competitive Behavior
in Infants and Children

Competitive behavior in children may be seen at various levels of sophistication. For example, simple rivalry may be elicited in infants at rather young ages. Charlotte Buhler (1927) found that if an object is placed between two infants during the first two years of life, they will both try to grab it. However, it has been suggested that "real competitive behavior" in young children is marked by the ability to conceptualize about at least three things: (1) that some object, attention, or event is worth striving for, (2) that the "self" has an opportunity to acquire this object, and that (3) someone else is trying, at almost the same time, to achieve a similar goal.

Piaget places the onset of competitive behavior at about the time children begin to appreciate the rules that govern winning or losing, to perceive success and failure, and to compare their efforts to those of others. Thus, competitive behavior does not emerge until after the age of 4 or 5 years.

White (1960) discusses the evolution of competence, and children's perceptions of their abilities, within a Freudian framework. Initial feelings of autonomy are experienced during the anal stage, as chidren explore their environment. Self-esteem and assertiveness grow in the oral stage, during which there is an increased emphasis on motor accomplishments. During the phallic stage, children begin to imitate adult behaviors and power roles they perceive to be important. During these years, a child usually declares the intent to become a member of a powerful group, i.e., a policeman, cowboy, or some similar vigorous figure.

During later childhood, according to White, the peer group begins to assume major importance in the child's world. Their evaluations of his or her performance also elicit either seeking of competitive situations or a withdrawal from situations in which he is likely to be negatively judged. If the child has been judged primarily as a competent person and perceives himself as able, a competitive "mind set" is developed. He or she continues to seek evaluative situations involving competition, and an increased feeling of competency and autonomy develops in the child and youth.

Others have taken an operational, rather than a theoretical, approach to the study of competitive behavior in children. Greenberg, for

TABLE 4-1. Percentage of children exhibiting competition.

Age group	Present	Absent	Doubtful
2–3	0.0	89.5	10.5
3–4	42.6	55.6	1.8
4–5	69.2	23.1	7.7
5–6	74.4	15.8	8.8
6–7	86.5	5.4	8.1

SOURCE: Greenberg, P. T.: Competition in children: an experimental study, *Am J Psychol*, 44, 1932, 221–248.

example, using a block-stacking task, found that before the age of 3, competitive behavior was absent. By the fifth year, however, competitive behavior was recorded in about 70 percent of the children he surveyed. The experimental evidence, although scarce, generally substantiates the assumptions of Piaget, White, and others that competition in children is a learned social phenomenon rather than an innate characteristic, and does not appear even in rudimentary form until about 4 to 6 years of age.

Competitive behavior in children, according to Scanlan (1978), who has presented a rigorous model on the subject, emerges as the child is given positive social evaluations for efforts expended. With a continuance of these positive evaluations, the child will become an "evaluation seeker" rather than an "evaluation avoider," and evidence behaviors that most would term competitive. As increasing positive feedback from the environment is received for competitive efforts, the child's subjective perceptions of achievement-laden situations take on a positive tone, and more and more these situations are sought out by the successful child and youth. On the other hand, the child who receives a preponderance of negative social evaluations of performance in achievement-oriented situations withdraws from competition, writes Scanlan.

The Development of Cooperative Behavior in Children

Cooperative behavior appears in children at about the same time competitive behavior emerges. Between the ages of 3 and 5 years, Parten, Berne (1930), and Salusky (1930) recorded consistent instances of cooperative play in nursery school age children. By the age of 5 and 6, authorities suggest, children begin setting consistent standards for their own performance, select leaders, and begin to register sympathy for other children in their play groups.

Orlick has engaged in some of the more stimulating work with regard to cooperative behavior in children. In books as well as research articles, Orlick has attempted to describe how games can be made into cooperative rather than competitive experiences and tried to record changes in the cooperative behaviors of children as a result of the exposure to these games.[1]

The games he developed combined various combinations of cooperative means vs. independent means, as contrasted to both cooperative and independent goals or objectives. The cooperative behaviors in-

[1]The author of this text has also published a book describing how children may be taught about competitive and cooperative behaviors. See *Teaching Human Behaviors Through Active Games*, (Englewood Cliffs, N.J.: Prentice-Hall, Inc., 1975).

cluded both physical help given by children to one another and verbal cooperation of various kinds. In an introductory study published in 1978, Orlick was able to demonstrate that the incidence of cooperative behavior among kindergarten children increased as the result of exposure to a program of cooperative games. As improved methods of evaluation are developed, Orlick concludes, better understanding of the impact of such games will result.

Necessary Conditions for Competitive Behavior

Certain conditions are likely to optimize the occurrence of competitive behaviors: (1) One or more individuals should perceive a goal as worth striving for and rewarding if achieved. (2) Two or more people must believe that acquisition of the goal is desirable and that they are reasonably capable of acquiring it. (3) Interpersonal competition is likely to occur only when the potential opponents perceive their abilities are reasonably close in quality and quantity. Kohler (1927), for example, using a cooperative weight lifting task, has fixed the ratio of "closeness" at from 65:100 to 75:100. Perceptions of interpersonal differences greater than this will likely encourage some kind of teaching behavior; the more able will give the less able "lessons" in the task at hand, as winning would prove no challenge. Even the work of Buhler (1927), using infants, substantiates this concept of closeness as a requisite for competition. She found that infants differing by more than two and a half months would not compete for toys placed between them. Van Bracken also found that identical twins, whose abilities were equal, tended to compete more than did fraternal twins, whose skills were not alike.

Also, as has been pointed out, a level of maturity seems a requisite before competition occurs. Graves suggests that the effects of an audience are operative prior to the onset of "real rivalry," which occurs later in the child's life.

The Evaluation of Competitive and Cooperative Behaviors

Numerous types of games have been employed by social psychologists to assess the components of cooperative and competitive behavior during the past decades. Typical of the games involving manual dexterities was that employed in a study by Mintz (1951), who offered a small monetary reward to subjects who removed cones, attached to strings, from a narrow-necked bottle, as the water in the bottle gradually rose.

In the 1960s, subjects (unknown to each other) were placed in button-pressing situations that resulted in either rewards or punishments being meted out. The outcomes usually depended on whether buttons of a similar color were pressed simultaneously by two people out of sight of each other.

One of the most popular types of games used by social psychologists to study competitive and cooperative behavior is termed the "prisoner's dilemma" and is based on a not uncommon strategy used in real life when questioning two or more prisoners suspected of the same crime. The prisoners are usually separated, and each is told that the co-conspirator has confessed in order to obtain an advantage in the final proceedings. Each prisoner is thus urged separately to "make a deal" by confessing and obtain a lighter sentence by testifying against the other.

Thus, although the most advantageous thing to do is to protest innocence, each prisoner has to guess the behavior of the other, to make a decision whether to cooperate with the police or compete against the system, and to incur major or minor penalties involved with either decision. Thus, if each prisoner chooses to do what is best for *him*, without consideration of what the other will do, he will choose not to confess. But if he chooses not to confess and the other prisoner confesses, he will get the "book thrown at him."

During the past several years this type of game, with lighter penalties and rewards, has been used in a number of experiments by social psychologists. Amounts of money ranging from a few cents to several dollars have been used as incentives. A typical choice situation and subsequent rewards to be obtained appear in Figure 4–1.

The first figure appearing in each box refers to the winnings of the first person, the second figure to the winnings of the second. There are many possibilities of manipulating choices:

	If second person chooses A or B			
	A		B	
If first person chooses X or Y X	$3	$3	$0	$5
Y	$5	$0	$1	$1

FIGURE 4-1.

1. If the first person selects X and the second person selects A, it places them in the XA intersection, thus paying each one $3. However, if the

first person selects X and the second picks B, the payoff is nothing to
the first person and $5 to the second.

2. If the first person selects Y and the second A, the payoffs are $5 and
$0, respectively. In this case, the second person is letting the first win
grandly. If the choices are Y and B, the payoffs are $1 each.

Furthermore, the order in which the subjects select a course of
action can be varied in time: (1) the first person can select initially,
followed by the second, (2) both can select simultaneously, or (3) the
second person can be aware of the first person's choice, thus giving the
second person additional power. Some studies have afforded subjects
only one pair of selections, while others have involved as many as 300
selections; and at times the subjects were asked to contribute money for
disadvantageous choices.

Regardless of the variations, the essentials are similar from experiment to experiment. That is, the choice that apparently leads to the
most individual gain is in the long run not productive, and may be
self-defeating. Thus, both partners make assumptions based on various
amounts of data, feelings about the other person, and previous payoffs
resulting from their choices and the choices of their partners.

This is but one of a number of laboratory games contrived by social
psychologists to study competitive behavior. In the next chapter, a
number of tasks through which collective behavior has been studied are
enumerated. Included are those involving cooperative motor skills of
various kinds, in which two, three, or more persons can participate.

Competition, Cooperation, and Aggression

It has been suggested by those espousing the frustration-hypothesis
that *all* competitive behavior will inevitably lead to aggression on the
part of at least a portion of those involved. The reasoning is (1) in
competitive situations, not all can win; (2) the losers experience frustration at not meeting their expected goals; and (3) this frustration leads
to aggression.

During the 1950s and 1960s, a number of experiments in social and
sport situations were carried out. These often took place at summer
camps, using young boys as subjects. The findings were fascinating and
shed a great deal of light on possible interactions between competitive
and aggressive behaviors.

Three prominent studies of this kind were summarized by Carolyn
Sherif, in a paper delivered to the Scientific Congress prior to the 1972
Olympics in Munich. All three experiments had as their purpose the
study of conditions that accompany group formation, the ways in which

intergroup conflicts arise, and an examination of strategies that might possibly reduce intergroup conflict. All studies were conducted in isolated camps under the control of the researchers. The 20 to 24 boys in each study were apparently unaware that they were subjects in a field experiment.

The boys in each group were unacquainted with one another prior to the experiment and were purportedly in good mental and emotional health. It was not felt that there were significant ethnic or racial differences within the groups.

The experiments may be divided into three time phases: (1) a time during which the groups coalesced and formed communication patterns, hierarchical status feelings, and concepts about individual competencies, (2) an interval marked by intergroup conflicts, as the groups became competitive with each other, and (3) a period during which it was attempted to insert strategies intended to reduce or eliminate intergroup conflicts that had arisen.

During the initial phase of group formation, each group was unaware that others were using the facilities. It was a period marked by high activity and cooperative behaviors. Individual preferences were ascertained, and various group norms, roles, and relationships were worked out. During this period, for example, one group developed a "tough" self-image.

Sports and games were included in the groups' activities. At times, experiments were carried out using these games, which were unknown to the boys participating. For example, at one point the boys were encouraged to throw a ball at an unmarked target. It was found that the scores of the boys who had been given high group status were overestimated by the remainder of the group, while the scores of those with low status were underestimated.

The boys were free to choose their companions during this initial period. Reflecting other research findings obtained from athletic teams, it was discovered that although interindividual rivalry occurred, it did not impede intragroup cooperation. The boys' behavior, in general, reflected their social backgrounds. The 12-year-olds, the experimenters found, came to camp desiring sports competition, and possessed knowledge of game rules and accompanying skills.

During the second phase, in which competition between the groups was instituted, it was hypothesized that since only one group at a time could achieve important goals, intergroup conflicts would result. This hypothesis was substantiated, as initial conflicts ripened into outright hostility. Tournaments were terminated with hostile chants directed toward opposing teams. Verbal hostilities evolved into physical confrontations, after games or at night. Insults to person and property were planned and directed by one group against another. As two teams strained against each other in a tug-of-war, the experimenters noted, the "highest flames of hostility" were seen. Teams became closer socially as the stress of competing against opposition increased.

Momentary lapses toward group disintegration were prevented by leaders in the groups, as they directed verbal hostility against members of opposing groups. "Group bullies," previously disliked by their own members when isolated, became valued. Their hostilities were turned outward, against the opposing groups.

Indications that the games played did not have a cathartic effect upon interpersonal relationships was the continuation of verbal and physical hostilities when games were discontinued. When other circumstances brought the groups together, as when standing in a meal line, they continued to bicker and to fight.

It would at this point seem to some that the experimenters had a morbid desire to elicit hostility within the situations described. However, it was felt that they had to elicit a reasonably high level of intergroup aggression before instituting methods which would purportedly reduce aggression. They hypothesized that if an instinctual theory of aggression is tenable, it might be impossible to lessen intergroup conflict. They assumed that the groups would have to be disbanded to eliminate the unpleasant situations they had created.

On the other hand, if a simple frustration-aggression model was accepted, it might also be difficult to change the feelings group members had formed about their rivals and the situations. Despite these problems, the experimenters introduced several strategies in efforts to reduce intergroup hostility.

Initially, they tried to verbally persuade the boys to reduce the hostility they were directing toward one another. They were subjected to lectures, in which "love your neighbor" and similar platitudes were expanded on. While the messages were apparently accepted by the listeners, they applied them only to their *own* group and saw little application to situations in which the "hated others" took part.

A second strategy was then introduced, in which thirteen "contact situations" were arranged between groups. The boys were to be rewarded by associating in various ways, eating together and the like. This second strategy was also less than successful. In all cases, the contacts were employed as opportunities for renewed physical and verbal confrontations and exchanges between the groups. Following a number of these efforts, the experimenters finally threw in the towel and admitted the boys had defeated their second efforts at reconciliation.

A third method was then attempted. Situations were contrived that forced the groups to cooperate for what were termed "superordinate goals." These were fabricated so that each group could not achieve a highly desired outcome without the help of the other group. The situations included group efforts to discover a leak in the camp's water supply, as well as pulling together on a rope to free an entrapped truck carrying needed food to the boys during a hike.

This type of strategy seemed to succeed. Exposure to superordinate goals did observably reduce hostility and intergroup conflict. Although all members did not, at the same time, discard negative stereotypes about members of the other group, in time most seemed to do so.

The observations and findings from these studies hold important lessons for those interested in the social dynamics of sport, and particularly in the effects of sports competition. The data suggest that competition, in and of itself, does not reduce aggressive tendencies, and may even heighten them. The experimenters warn, however, that the findings are not taken from the real world of sport. For example, it could be construed that competition itself is not healthy; however, in the situations described, the teams were not only evenly matched but repeatedly competed *only* against each other. These two conditions are not always seen in regular arrangements for competing athletic teams. Volkamer has demonstrated that when teams of unequal competencies meet, intergroup conflict may result.

Data from these camp studies do suggest that inserting cooperative strategies and situations may help to regulate interteam hostilities. Frequently competing teams, while tending to exaggerate negative feelings about each other, may learn to reconcile their differences if the strategies outlined are employed. The authors further suggest that administrators of national level teams should keep superordinate goals in mind when arranging competitions. International good will might be introduced as a more laudable objective than simply winning a volleyball game.

Competition as Activation

Data from numerous studies of the effects of competition upon motor skill suggest that (1) if the performer perceives the performance context as competitive, he or she becomes activated; (2) when the individual prizes something that another (or others) may be simultaneously vying for, increases of muscular tension, blood pressure, and heart rates will be recorded. These and other measures indicate that the person is girding for a struggle or fight; (3) competitive situations result in physiologic and psychologic reactions similar to those seen in other stress situations. Thus, it is to be expected that skilled and simple muscular performance in competitive circumstances fluctuates in ways similar to those seen when an individual (or group) is placed under stress. The research indicates that competition is likely to enhance simple, direct, forceful muscular acts, or those requiring endurance. The data from Higgs' (1972) study of treadmill running under competitive and non-competitive conditions confirms this assumption.

People like competitive situations more than cooperative ones. Weight lifters hoist more in competition than in practice, balls are thrown farther (but perhaps not more accurately), and people run and swim farther and faster.

Recently acquired or complex skills, on the other hand, are likely to be disrupted under competitive conditions. Thus, the sensitive coach may have to prepare team members in different ways prior to contests. The immature performer on the gymnastic team may prove more able to perform strength moves on the rings, while the precision required on the side-horse may be "thrown off."

In track and field competition, similar differentiation of competitive effects may occur. The experienced sprinter may welcome competition and the surge of activation he or she experiences, and perform better. The less experienced sprinter, however, may fail to perform the intricate start with precision as the gun goes off. The hurdler just exposed to a modification in form will be thrown off under competitive circumstances. On the other hand, the hurdler or discus thrower who has kept his or her form constant will utilize the activation effects and perform better in competition. The inexperienced javelin thrower may toss the spear out of the stadium when competing in an international meet for the first time, while consistently fouling. The more experienced thrower, on the other hand, may also do well but stay within the prescribed boundaries.

Wankel (1972) and others have found that high-ability groups perform best under competitive circumstances, while low-ability groups perform poorly when subjected to the stress of the evaluation of others. In Wankel's study, noncompetitive groups performed best during the early stages of learning a balance task, whereas competitive groups performed best during the later stages. Thus, the hypothesis presented previously, using gymnastic teams and track and field experiences as examples, is confirmed upon inspection of laboratory data.

Competition interacts in interesting ways, both with the audience effect and with anxiety. Ryan and Lakie (1965), for example, found that (1) those with high anxiety and low need achievement performed best under noncompetitive situations, and (2) those with low anxiety and high achievement needs performed best in competition.

Data from studies by Vaught and Newman (1966), McGowen (1968), and Martens and Landers (1969) on anxiety and motor performance are somewhat conflicting. These conflicting findings could be the result of the numerous ways in which anxiety is measured and the variety of motor skills included in such experiments.

Hrycaiko (1978) found that child social facilitation positively influenced the performance of young boys in a hand-eye coordination task (rolling a ball up an incline with precision). Competition in the same experiment did not. However, the boys subjected to competition evidenced higher heart rates, indicating that perhaps their activation could not be channeled into improved performance of this precise task.

To accurately assess competitive effects on motor performance both in the laboratory and in the field, innumerable variables must be taken into account. These include optimum activation needed in the task, personality traits of the performers, previous exposure to competition, the presence of an audience, the stage of learning that is involved, the type of task required, and the presence of co-actors. Many of these variables are discussed in the chapters that follow.

IMPLICATIONS FOR THE COACH

The preceding discussion holds innumerable implications for the coach, only some of which were dealt with. A review of the data will, it is hoped, aid the coach to become sensitive to individual differences in a youth's precompetitive molding by parents, peers, and the subculture in which he or she resided. The coach should also be aware of the performance differences that are likely to occur as the less mature athlete enters the competitive arena for the initial attempts at success.

Further, the athletic mentor should be encouraged to come to grips with various amounts of rivalry and competition *within* the athletic team. If not overdone, interpersonal rivalry for team positions is a healthy sign of caring on the part of the athletes.

The coach might also become better able to deal with a youth whose apparent motives to compete are not congruent with his or her physical potential. Some children and youth, because of some of the child-rearing styles already discussed, may prove particularly frustrating to a coach whose own early needs to achieve within an athletic environment have been extremely high. A tolerant attitude toward the young athlete whose subjective expectations of winning are negative is a product of previous social evaluations that have also been negative. The coach should attempt to aid such young people to formulate more realistic and positive opinions of themselves and their performance potentials. A gradual remolding of values and attitudes about success is often more successful than simply demanding a competitive attitude on the part of an immature child or youth.

The different effects of activation on competition should also be recognized by the coach. Activation is elicited by exposing the athlete to an audience, by verbal exhortation, by mentally realigning the athlete's values about the forthcoming contest, and by exposure to the competitive situation. Thus, a thorough knowledge of the effects of competition (activation) on simple, complex, well-learned, and slightly learned skills will probably elicit fewer surprises when relatively inexperienced athletes are placed in competition for the first time.

The sensitive coach should also be aware that the presence of both cooperative and competitive behavior, in competition and during practices, may prove stressful and self-defeating for the athlete if carried to extremes. If during a practice workout for distance runners, to cite one example, two participants are found to be angrily competing during each of the intervals they are asked to run, it may be wise to separate them during practice sessions. If this is done, they are not overstressed, and they can harbor competitive urges and direct them toward each other and their opponents during important meets, rather than wasting energies during workouts.

In many sports, coaches perceiving that the stress of intersquad competition may be too great during workouts may suddenly one day present a program which is relatively unstructured and fun, rather than competitive and grim. A coach's directions to swimmers or runners to "simply swim (or run) an hour at your own pace," may have an emotionally uplifting effect that will facilitate their performances later, both during practices and during competitions.

Finally, the coach may correctly perceive that a forthcoming contest with a traditional rival may be imposing inordinate stress on the athletes. Healthy competitive urges may be subordinated by relatively unhealthy aggressions or hatred against traditional opponents that may prove detrimental to optimum performance. Steps may be taken by the coach to (1) lessen the threat of losing to their rivals, (2) encourage the athletes to see their rivals in human terms rather than as objects to hate, and (3) in other ways placing a forthcoming important contest into proper and reasonable perspective.

SUMMARY

Competitive behavior has been classified in innumerable ways. Individuals may compete against known or unknown standards, or against other people or groups. Competition may be for goals in which losers can share, or in which only one winner may emerge.

Data from studies in summer camps reveal that competition, if not well conceived, may lead to aggression. Moreover, these same studies indicate that often highly creative strategies must be employed to reduce intergroup hostility, anger that may have been produced by continued competition.

Orlick's study reveals that cooperative behaviors may be elicited and expanded if children are exposed to games in which cooperation is stressed. Thus, both cooperative and competitive behaviors may be molded in one or several ways.

Competition generally heightens activation, thus acting upon motor performance and athletic skills in ways similar to an audience or verbal exhortation to do better. Competition improves the performance of experienced athletes, in direct simple tasks and/or tasks that have been well learned. Conversely, competition is likely to disrupt new or complex tasks. Competitive behaviors that are relatively sophisticated are not usually seen in children under the age of 5. After that age, however, the child seems to be cognizant of mutually desired goals, and of the ability to achieve objectives. Competitive behavior in children is engendered by previous experiences in which they have been evaluated as successful. Competitive behavior, conversely, is blunted in children and youth when their initial exposures to achievement-laden situations have been negative, and in which they have failed.

Innumerable important questions have only been touched on in the available literature. For example, in the study by David Mettee (1974), the relationships between interpersonal liking and competition between high- and low-ability girls was studied. Further work is needed about the way competition either heightens or reduces interpersonal attractiveness, both of one's teammates and of one's opponents.

The initial work cited concerning the molding of cooperative behaviors in young children, as well as the manner in which aggression was reduced in the camp studies, seems to offer two fruitful lines of further study. More work of this type is needed.

The genesis of competitive behavior, speculated upon by Scanlan (1978) and others, has barely been explored. How the formation of achievement needs and self-esteem interacts with later competitiveness in youth is only one of the many questions that further work might illuminate.

The study by Dowell (1976) suggests that both athletes and nonathletes learned a competitive game strategy equally well. Thus, the argument that some kind of "competitive mind set" may generalize from various kinds of competitive situations could be disputed. The athletes in both cooperative and competitive situations performed equally well in the intellectual game with which they were confronted.

Finally, little is known about possible "accommodation to competition" effects on the part of experienced as contrasted to inexperienced athletes. Questions surrounding the circumstances that influence the ability of an athlete to accommodate positively to continued exposure to competition have not been explored thoroughly. Related to these problems is the question whether an athlete can accommodate to competitive effects in general, or whether such accommodations occur only within specific sports situations and do not transfer from sport to sport.

QUESTIONS FOR DISCUSSION

1. Discuss the definitions of competition offered in the text. Which one is most acceptable to you? Why?
2. What about the various types of competition presented? Can you give specific instances in sport of the categories of competition?
3. What conflicts might occur on a team in which both competitive and cooperative behaviors have to be exhibited within a relatively short period of time?
4. What psychologic and social conditions need to be present in order to have competition occur? Give examples using 5-year-olds playing in a sandbox, as well as adults playing handball.
5. Discuss the concept of "accommodation to competition," which may be experienced by more mature athletes?
6. What kinds of tasks have been employed by the psychologist to study competitive behavior? Do you believe that data from such studies are useful to the coach of an athletic team? If not, why? If the data are useful, how?
7. How may competition enhance skill or detract from skilled performance? Be specific about which skills may be enhanced in what sports and which may be impeded.
8. Discuss the concept of "perceived closeness" of one's opponent in the instigation and prolongation of competition.
9. Discuss how an individual's "competitive urges" may change from the ages of 5 to 55 years, within competitive sport.

BIBLIOGRAPHY

ALBERT S: Motivation properties of observed competition. *Proceedings of Annual Convention of American Psychological Association* VI (1971), 347–348.

ALDERMAN RB: *Psychological Behavior in Sport.* Philadelphia, Saunders, 1974, chap. 4.

ATKINSON JW: Motivational determinants of risk taking behavior. *Psychol Rev* LXIV: 6 (1957), 359–372.

AZRIN NH, LINDSLEY OR: The reinforcement of cooperation between young children. *J Abnorm Soc Psychol* LII (1956), 100–102.

BERGER BG: Factors within the sport environment affecting athletes' personalities: A conceptual approach. Paper presented at the Second Canadian Psycho-motor Learning and Sports Psychology Symposium, University of Windsor, October 1970.

BERNE EVC: An experimental investigation of social behavior patterns in young children. *University of Iowa Studies in Child Welfare* IV: 3 (1930).

BERRIDGE HL: An experiment in the psychology of competition. *Res Q* VI (1935), 37–42.

BLAKE RR, MOUTON JS: Overevaluation of own group's product in an intergroup competition. *J Abnorm Soc Psychol* LXIV (1972), 237–258.

———, MOUTON JS: Loyalty of representative to ingroup positions during intergroup competition. *Sociometry* XXIV (1961), 177.

BOND C: Some factors influencing the ability of secondary school boys in the performance of skilled activities under conditions of competitive stress. In *Fourth Annual Conference Report,* British Society of Sports Psychology, Loughborough College, April 1970.

BRUNING JL: The effects of various social factors on motivation in competitive situations. *J Soc Psychol* LXX (1966), 295–297.

BUHLER C: Die ersten sozialen Verhaltensweisen des Kindes in soziologischen und psychologischen Studien des ersten Lebensjahres. *Quell n Stud z Jugendk* V (1927), 1–102.

CARMENT DW: Rate of simple motor responding as a function of coaction, competition, and sex of the participants. *Psychonomic Sci* XIX (1970), 342–343.

CHURCH RM: The effects of competition on reaction time and Palmer skin conductance. *J Abnorm Soc Psychol* LXV: 1 (1962), 32–40.

CRATTY BJ: *Social Dimensions of Physical Activity.* Englewood Cliffs, New Jersey: Prentice-Hall, 1967, chap. 4.

DEUTSCH M: A theory of cooperation and competition. *Human Rel* II (1950), 129–152.

DOWELL LJ: Game strategy, apprehension of athletes and non-athletes in a competitive and cooperative learning environment. Paper presented to the AAHPER Convention, Anaheim, California (1976).

DUNN RE, GOLDMAN M: Competition and noncompetition in relationship to satisfaction and feelings toward own group and non-group members. *J Soc Psychol* LXVIII (1966), 299–311.

ECKLUND SJ: Competitiveness in boys as related to academic achievement and mother's achievement orientation. Unpublished doctoral dissertation, George Peabody College for teachers, 1970.

FERGUSON C: The effect of two competitive motivational conditions upon the improvement of rifle shooting scores. Unpublished Master's thesis, Texas Women's University, 1969.

FESTINGER LA: A theory of social comparison processes. *Human Rel* VII (1954), 117–140.

FIEDLER FE: The effect of inter-group competition on group member adjustment. *Pers Psychol* XX (1967), 33.

FORSYTH S, KOLENDA PM: Competition, cooperation and group cohesion in a ballet company. *Psychiatry* XXIX (1966), 123.

GAEBELIAN J, TAYLOR SP: The effects of competition and attack on physical aggression. *Psychonomic Sci* XXIV (1971), 65–66.

GALLO PS, McCLINTOCK CG: Cooperative and competitive behavior in mixed-motive games. *J Conflict Resolution* IX (1965), 68–73.

GRAVES EA: The effect of competition and reward on the motor performance of pre-school children. M.A. Thesis, University of Minnesota, 1934.

GREENBERG PT: Competition in children, an experimental study. *Am J Psychol* XLIV (1932), 221–248.

HARRES B: Attitudes of students toward women's athletic competition. *Res Q* XXXIX (May 1968), 278–284.

HEALEY TR, LANDERS DM: Effect of need achievement and task difficulty on competitive and noncompetitive motor performance. *J Mot Behav* 5: 2 (June 1973), 121–128.

HIGGS SL: The effect of competition upon the endurance performance of college women. *Int J Sports Psychol* 3:2 (1972), 128–140.

HIROTA K: Experimental studies in competition. *Japanese J Psychol* XXI (1951), 70–81. Abstracted in *Psychol Abstracts* XXVII (1953), 351.

HRYCAIKO DW: The effects of competition and social reinforcement upon perceptual motor performance. *J Mot Behav* 10:3, September 1978, 159–168.

HURLOCK EB: The use of group rivalry as an incentive. *J Abnorm Soc Psychol* XXII (1927), 278–290.

JOHNSON DW: Use of role reversal in intergroup competition. *J Pers Soc Psychol* VII:2 (1968), 135–141.

JONES EE, GERARD HB: *Foundations of Social Psychology.* New York: Wiley, 1967.

KAGAN J, MOSS HL: Stability of passive and dependent behavior from childhood through adulthood. *Childhood Dev* XXXI (1960), 577–591.

KOHLER O: Über den Gruppenwirkungsgrad der menschlichen Körperarbeit und die Bedingung optimaler Kollektivkraftreaktion. *Indus Psychotech* IV (1927), 209–226.

LEUBA CJ: An experimental study of rivalry in young children. *J Comp Psychol* LXVI (1933), 59–66.

LOY J: Competitive success in sports. Paper presented at the Research Section Symposium on Success in Sport, 83rd National Convention of the American Association of Health, Recreation, and Physical Education. St. Louis, March 30, 1968.

LUSCHEN G: Cooperation, association, and contest. *J Conflict Resolution* XIV (1970), 21–34.

MALLER JB: Cooperation and competition, an experimental study in motivation. *Teachers College Contributions to Education* 384 (1929).

MARTENS R, LANDERS DM: Effect of anxiety, competition and failure on performance of a complex motor task. *J Mot Behav* I (1969), 1–10.

MARTENS R, SCANLAN R: *Competition, A Working Reference List with Annotations.* Unpublished paper, Motor Performance and Play Research Laboratory, Children's Research Center, University of Illinois, Champagne, Illinois.

MARTIN LA: The effects of competition upon the aggressive responses of basketball players and wrestlers. Unpublished Doctoral dissertation, Springfield College, 1969.

MAY MA, DOOB LW: Competition and Cooperation. *Soc Sci Res Coun Bull* 25 (1937).

McCLINTOCK CG, McNEEL SP: Reward and score feedback as determinants of cooperative and competitive game behavior. *J Pers Soc Psychol* IV:6 (1966), 606–613.

McCUE BF: Constructing an instrument for evaluating attitudes toward intensive competition in team games. *Res Q* XXIV (1953), 205–209.

McGOWEN K. The effects of a competitive situation upon the motor performance of high anxious and low anxious boys. Master's thesis, Springfield College, 1968.

McMANIS DL: Pursuit-rotor performance of normal and retarded in four verbal incentive conditions. *Child Dev* XXXVI (1965), 667–683.

MEAD M: *Cooperation and Competition Among Primitive Peoples.* New York: McGraw-Hill, 1937.

METTEE D, RISKIND J. Size of defeat and liking for superior and similar ability competitors. *J Exp Soc Psychol* X (1974), 333–351.

MINTZ A: Non-adaptive group behavior. *J Abnorm Soc Psychol* XLVI (1951), 150–159.

MYERS A: Team competition, success, and the adjustment of group members. *J Abnorm Soc Psychol* LXV:5 (1962), 325–332.

MYERS AE: The effect of team competition and success on the adjustment of group members. Unpublished Doctoral dissertation, University of Illinois, Urbana, 1961.

NELSON LL: The development of cooperation and competition in children from ages five to ten years old: effects of sex, situational determinants, and prior experiences. Unpublished Doctoral dissertation, University of California, Los Angeles, 1970.

ORLICK TD: Sport in Red China, friendship first, competition second. *J Canadian Assoc Health, Physical Education, and Recreation* XXXIX (1973).

OWENS KL: Competition in children as function of age, race, sex, and socio-economic status. Unpublished Doctoral dissertation, Texas Technological College, 1969.

PARTEN MB: Social play among pre-school children. *J Abnorm Soc Psychol* XXVII (1933).

———. Social participation among pre-school children. *J Abnorm Soc Psychol* XXVII (1932).

PETRE RD, GALLOWAY, C: The effects of competition and noncompetition on performance of a motor task. *Psychonomic Sci* V (1966), 399–400.

PHILLIPS BN, DeVAULT MU: Evaluation of research on cooperation and competition. *Psychol Rep* III (1957), 289–292.

RARICK LG: Competitive sports for young boys: Controversial issues. *Med Sci Sports* I:4 (1966), 181–184.

RAVEN BH, EACHUS HT: Cooperation and competition in means-interdependent triads. *J Abnorm Soc Psychol* LXVII:4 (1963), 307–316.

RAVEN BH SHAW JI: Interdependence and group problem solving in the triad. *J Pers Soc Psychol* XIV (1970), 157–165.

Ross RC, Van Der Haag E: *The Fabric of Society.* New York: Harcourt Brace, 1957.

Ryan DE, Lakie WL: Competitive and non-competitive performance in relation to achievement-motive, and manifest anxiety. *J Pers Soc Psychol* I:4 (1965), 343–345.

Salusky AS: Collective behavior of children at a pre-school age. *J Soc Psychol* I (1930), 367–378.

Scanlan TK: Antecedents of Competitiveness. In Magill PA, Ash MJ, Smoll F (eds): *Children in Sport: A Contemporary Anthology.* Champaign, Illinois, Human Kinetics, 1978.

Shaw ME: Some motivational factors in cooperation and competition. *J Pers* XXVI (1958), 155–169.

Sherif, C: The social context of competition. Paper presented at the Conference on Sport and Social Deviancy in a session on extreme competition for children at the State University of New York at Brockport, December 11, 1971.

Sherif CW, Harris D (eds.): Females in the competitive process. *Woman and Sport: A National Research Conference,* AAHPER Series, Penn State: 2 (1972), 115–140.

———. Intergroup Conflict and Competition. *Sportwissenschaft* III (1972–1973), 138–153.

Sherif M, Sherif CW: *Groups in Harmony and Tension.* New York, Harper, 1953.

Smith SA: Conformity in cooperative and competitive groups. *J Soc Psychol* LXV (1965), 337–350.

Strong CH: Motivation related to performance of physical fitness tests. Unpublished Ph.D. thesis, State University of Iowa, 1961 (microcard); also in *Res Q* XXXIV (1963), 497–507.

Sutton-Smith B, Roberts JM: Rubrics of competitive behavior. *J Genet Psychol* CV (1964), 13–37.

Thomas EJ: Effects of facilitative role interdependence on group functioning. *Hum Rel* X (1957), 347–366.

Turner RH: Preoccupation with competitiveness and social acceptance among American and English college students. *Sociometry* XXIII (1960), 307–325.

Vaught GM, Newman SE: The effects of anxiety on motor steadiness in competitive and non-competitive conditions. *Psychonomic Science,* VI (1966), 519–520.

Von Bracken H: Mutual intimacy in twins. Types of social structure in pairs of identical and fraternal twins, *Character and personality*, 1934, 2, 293–309.

Voor JH, Lloyd AJ, Cole RJ: The influence of competition on the efficiency of an isometric muscle contraction. *J Mot Behav* I: 3, (1969), 210–219.

Wankel LM: Competition in motor performance: an experimental analysis of motivational components. *J Experimental Social Psychology*, VIII (1972), 427–437.

White RW: Competence and the psychosexual stages of development. In Jones MR (ed): *Nebraska Symposium on Motivation*, 8. Lincoln, University of Nebraska Press, 1960.

Whitmyre JW, Diggory, JC, Cohen D: The effects of personal liking perceived ability, and value of prize in choice of partners for a competition. *J Abnorm Soc Psychol* LXIII:1 (1961), 198–200.

Wickens DD: The effect of competition on the performance of tasks of differing degrees of difficulty. *Psychol Bull* XXXIX (1942), 595.

Wilson W, Miller N: Shifts in evaluations of participants following intergroup competition. *J Abnorm Soc Psychol* 2 (1961), 431–438.

Wittmore JC: Influence of competition on performance: an experimental study. *J Abnorm Soc Psychol* XIX (1924), 236–253.

Wrightsman L: Competition and cooperation in small groups. *Contemporary Issues in Social Psychology*, Part 9, 273–276.

Zajonc RB, Martin IC: Cooperation, competition and interpersonal attitudes in small groups. *Psychonomic Science*, VII (1967), 271–275.

5

Group Cohesion

Teamwork and similar terms in the sports literature imply that working together closely, thinking about one another, and other observable and emotional indices of positive group behavior contribute to team success. Since the turn of the century, behavioral scientists have also been interested in evaluating, observing, and otherwise dealing with concepts reflecting group cohesion. Often, researchers have used physical tasks in which groups participated. At times, their work has focused on motor activity itself, but for the most part their attempts have dwelt on various theoretical aspects of group behavior. They used easily measured physical tasks as conveniences, rather than as important central facets of their exploratory efforts.

Much of the information collected by social psychologists relative to group feelings and qualities reflecting cohesion has not been transmitted to coaches of athletic teams. Only a few texts published in the last 10 years have contained information of this kind, applicable to sport. Likewise, only a handful of studies dealing with group cohesion on teams have been published during the past 30 years, while the effect of group cohesion on team success has also received very little direct attention by researchers.

Despite these shortcomings, this chapter proposes to (1) illuminate basic concepts important to the study of group cohesion in sports settings, (2) relate this information to indices of team productivity, to winning and losing, and (3) outline helpful ways of enhancing group productivity on sports teams by considering the available findings.

The chapter has been divided into the following subsections: (1) a

87

discussion of the ways group cohesion can be defined and categorized, (2) a brief overview of the methods used to evaluate group cohesion and cooperative behavior, (3) various determinants of cohesion and group dissolution, including group size, in-group feelings of members, group success and failure, previous association, type of sport, as well as interpersonal attraction are examined, and (4) a review of the currently available literature dealing with relationships between cohesion on teams and their potential success. The chapter concludes with a summary and questions for discussion.

The contents of each chapter in this book have been selected arbitrarily. The concepts found in this and in the other chapters are not independent. Intergroup competition influences group cohesion, which in turn is likely to affect team effort. The "we feelings" on a team may be dependent on personality traits exhibited by team members. These might include anxiety, need for social approval, and the tendency to exhibit aggression. Thus, the topics covered in other chapters must be considered when reviewing the material that follows.

Rather than attempting to present unique material, the primary thrust of this chapter is to offer perspectives about "togetherness," reflecting the effect of mutual attraction of team members upon the relative success of the team's endeavors. An additional purpose is to suggest helpful ways researchers can add to the knowledge in this area of study.

Examining the Concept of Group Cohesion

Numerous definitions of the words *group cohesion* can be located in the literature. Essentially, these reflect something about the reasons groups form and stay together for at least a short period of time, about members' initial attraction to the group, and why people remain in groups. Golembiewski (1962), for example, suggests that the word *cohesiveness* applies best to small groups. He continues by stating that the concept of cohesiveness, "stick togetherness," or member attraction characterizes all small groups and differentiates them from other social units.

One of the most widely quoted definitions is that by Festinger (1968), who says that cohesion is "the total field or resultant of forces acting on members to remain in a group for its members." The other primary sources of membership attraction, according to Festinger, consist of the activities of the group and of the other group members.

Festinger is not alone in the formulation of definitions of group cohesion. A wide variety of terms from the narrative literature pertains to the way members of a group tend to "hang together." Stogdill (1963) uses the words *integration* and *morale,* for example. Integration he further defines as the tendency of the group to maintain its structure under stress. Hemphill and Westie (1950) use the word *viscidity,* referring to the capacity of the group to work together and to the group's ability to function as a unit in task situations.

Viscidity, however, does not necessarily imply that members are congenial toward one another. To denote warm interpersonal attractions and the degree of this attraction, Hemphill and Westie employ the term *hedonic tone.* This phrase relates to a variety of factors reflecting "pleasantness of group climate," geniality of the relationships between members, and satisfactions of group achievements. Thus, hedonic tone refers to conditions, emotional and otherwise, that determine whether a member likes the group and looks forward to meeting with it.

Other terms from the writings of social psychologists reflect the two divisions into which measures of group cohesion may be placed. These words include "morale," group compatibility, group satisfactions, group solidarity, and membership attraction. Thus, these words reflect the fact that group cohesion can be assessed by ascertaining the degree to which a group produces and/or performs efficiently regardless of interpersonal feelings and the emotions prevalent in the group, reflecting mutual attraction among members.

These emotions may at times be relatively independent of the quality of effort expended by the group. This second category has two subdivisions: (1) the feelings group members have about other *individual members* and (2) the feelings they project toward and about the *group as a whole.* The materials in the section that follows reflect these subdivisions and attempt to operationalize the ideas in the form of measurement techniques.

Assessing Group Cohesion and Cooperative Motor Performance

Several primary ways have been employed to evaluate group cohesion. The most common is the questionnaire. Another way of gaining insight into collective feelings of groups is to evaluate the performance quality evidenced, in contrast to the quality and nature of the group's verbal and social interactions. Performance modification, as a function of the interposition of a number of social-psychologic variables, is still another method to assess the outcomes of cohesive efforts.

The evaluation of group cohesion has always proved a difficult undertaking. Gross and Martin (1952) despaired of the various operational definitions of the term then used when they found little or no relationship among various measures of group cohesion. Eisman (1967) concurred with them, finding no significant relationships among five measures of group cohesion administered to fourteen college-age groups.

Despite these difficulties, researchers in the intervening years have forged bravely ahead. They have used projective tests of affiliation, questionnaires containing such questions as "Whom do you like?" "Whom do you like to work with?", as well as queries that purportedly reflect an individual's feelings toward the group as a whole. Among these questions might be, "How closely knit do you think your team is?"

The questionnaire used by Martens and Peterson (1971) in their study of intramural college teams has been employed extensively in sports, and contains questions similar to those listed above. Melnick and Chembers (1974) used a similar instrument in a more recent study of group cohesion in sport.

The measure of group cohesion, or of increased cohesion, obtained when using questions of this type is an average score reflecting the members' feelings about the team as a whole. The question "How closely knit do you think your team is?", for example, is scorable on a 1 to 9 point scale, from "very close" to "not at all."

A second type of measure used to determine group cohesion, or shifts in this elusive quality, is the number of mutually attracted or mutually chosen dyads present when friendship or work partner choices are requested of a group. Thus, in a group of twelve, there would be a low cohesion score obtained if only two members mutually chose each other as "attractive." On the other hand, the same twelve people would reflect greater group cohesion if responses on the same questionnaire produced five or six mutual choices of friends or desirable work partners.

Performance Tasks Reflecting Group Cohesion and Efficiency

The number of contests won has been a criterion frequently employed when assessing the productivity of a sports team and its internal cohesion. However, within research laboratories, in which variables are better controlled, a number of motor performance tasks have been utilized in studies over the past decades.

Several criteria should govern the selection and use of these tasks, according to Zajonc (1965). These principles include: (1) The task should be able to be analyzed relative to the influence of such variables as motivation, stress, load, practice effects, and the influence of various stimulus conditions. (2) The task should be quickly learned by most groups of subjects. (3) The effort should be able to be measured in units that reflect both group and individual effort and ability, and the experimenter should thus be able to evaluate each individual's contribution to the total performance effort by the group. (4) Zajonc also suggests that the task should permit the experimenter to manipulate the contribution of various group members, and the performance measure should be flexible enough to permit the experimenter to manipulate the feedback afforded individual performers, relative to its difficulty.

Landers, in a helpful survey, has applied these criteria to twelve performance tasks employed in studies of group effort during the past several years. This summary appears in Table 5-1.

It will be helpful to briefly explain some of the apparatus mentioned by Landers.

The rope pulling task, used by several researchers, measures pounds pulled collectively and individually, employing various kinds of strain gauges. This task will be referred to in another part of the text, dealing with group motives, as well as in another section of this chapter.

The table leveling task is a three-sided apparatus each corner of which contains a thumbscrew, permitting three subjects to independently lower or raise their corner. On each side is a carpenter's level, and thus various experimental arrangements are permitted, in which the subjects are "programmed" to compete or cooperate in the attempt to keep level a portion or all of the apparatus.

Both the *dial-a-maze* and the *motor maze* resemble commercially produced toys. In the latter, two people working separate vertical and horizontal line controls attempt, through their collective efforts, to manipulate the movement of a point (the intersection of two lines) through a prescribed pattern. The dial-a-maze is a modification of a game in which a board's tilt is manipulated by more than one person, in order to permit a ball to follow a course through a maze pathway. The two drawbacks inherent in these two instruments are that it is difficult to differentiate between individual and group effort, and that only two subjects may participate at a given time.

McLarney and Landers have used a pattern weaving task (Figure 5-1), consisting of three boards joined to form a triangle. Seven holes are drilled in each adjoining board, creating a hexagonal pattern. The task is to form various patterns, prescribed by the experimenter, by connecting strings through the holes. This is accomplished by passing a string through a hole, from one teammate to another, to the back of the board, at which point the process is reversed until the pattern is completed.

TABLE 5-1.

Task	Investigator	Potential for measuring individual inputs	Limits of group size for one task	Suitability for concurrently testing intergroup competition	Accuracy of measures	Potential for members to evaluate one another's performance	Experimental control of feedback to group members
Rope pulling	Cattell et al (1953) Wyer & Bedner (1967) Ringlemann (in Moede) (1927) Ingham (1973)	Fair	None	Poor	Fair–good	Fair	Poor
Ball & spiral	Carter et al (1951) Chapman (1957) French (1941)	Poor	3	Good	Fair	Poor	Poor
Table leveling	Crombag (1966) Raven (1963)	Poor	3	Poor	Good	Fair	Poor
Triad	Weick (1966)	Fair	3	Fair	Fair	Fair	Poor
Micrometer apparatus	Hall (1957)	Good	2	Fair	Good	Good	?
Dial-a-maze	Ryan	Fair	2	Good	Fair	Poor	Poor
Motor maze	Martens	Fair	2	Good	Fair	Poor	Poor
Motor steadiness	Laties (1961)	Poor	5	Fair	Fair	Poor	Poor
Rotary pursuit	Wegner & Zerman (1956)	Poor	4	Good	Good	Poor	Poor
Loco-motor maze	Chinoy (1954) Cratty (1963)	Good	5–8	Fair	Fair	Good	Good
Pattern weaving	McLarney & Landers	Good	3	Good	Fair	Poor	Poor
Group reaction timer (FKS Timing System)	Zajönc (1965)	Good	8	Good (4 vs. 4)	Good	Good	Good

Many unitary tasks which can only be scored additively could conceivably be scored in a conjunctive, disjunctive, or compensatory manner if the unit of analysis were two or more tasks being used simultaneously by different group members.
Many maximizing tasks are given only a fair rating for accuracy of measures, since the speed versus accuracy trade-off is a potential problem.

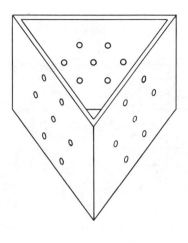

FIGURE 5-1. Reported by Landers, the pattern weaving task, showing apparatus and some of the patterns that may be formed by group effort.

Cratty in a number of studies, and Cratty and Sage in group studies, have employed what they termed a *locomotor maze* (Figure 5-2). The device permits members to evaluate one another's performance, to control feedback to participants, to assess intergroup competition, and to measure individual members' contributions to the total effort. The task consists of traversing, while blindfolded, a large pathway formed by pieces of plastic tubing placed waist high and about 3 feet apart. The performance criterion is traversal speed, and performers are not permitted to observe the pathway before traversing it. More will be said about this apparatus and the results of studies in which it was used when discussing primary and secondary group effort later in the chapter.

The pursuit rotor, often used in experimental work focusing on motor learning and performance, has been modified to encompass the evaluation of group effort. Wegner and Zeaman (1956), as well as others, have used a four-part handle on the stylus as shown in Figure 5-3, with which two to four individuals may cooperate while trying to keep the tip of the stylus on the rotating target placed on the pursuit rotor. The targets can be made to move at various speeds, and this task, while

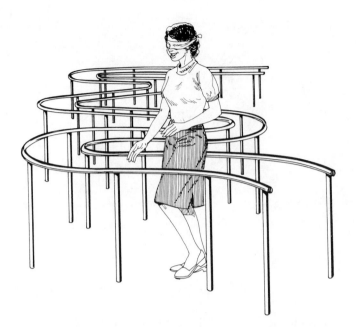

FIGURE 5-2.   The type of maze task used over the years in our
laboratory, employing blindfolded sighted college subjects. (Courtesy of Cratty BJ: *Movement and Spatial Awareness in Blind Children and Youth.* Springfield, Illinois, Thomas, 1971.)

producing a recording of group effort, does not permit the separation
of individual abilities when analyzing the data.

As shown, the four-way handle permits one, two, three, or four subjects to participate. A small spring in the bottom of the stylus permits
it to slide up and down easily, thus preventing any one subject from
exerting strong pressure on the turntable. The entire pursuit rotor is
shown in Figure 5-4.

Group dynamometer. An interesting device recording group force
was used in a study by Cattell, Saunders, and Stice (1953). Two steel
pipes, 1" by 30", were placed, one at each end of a dynamometer. The
group members, with canvas over their shoes, were asked to stand on
a heavily waxed floor. They were then given 30 seconds to get the
dynamometer handle as high as possible and were informed that this
was best accomplished by "jerking it." After 30 seconds, their score was
read to them. They were then asked to estimate their probable scores
in a second performance effort. This task was repeated in several ways,
asking the subjects to employ a variety of techniques.

Ball and spiral apparatus. A fascinating apparatus was used in studies by French, Crater, and Chapman, as well as by others, when assess-

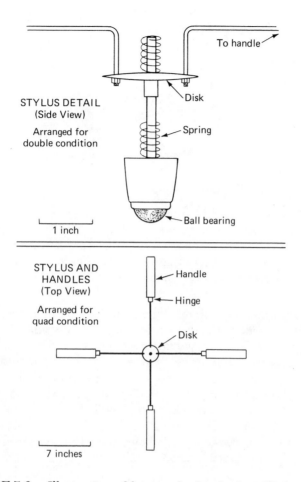

FIGURE 5-3.   Illustration of four-spoked stylus handle for pursuit rotor.

ing agents for the Office of Strategic Services during World War II. It consisted of a spiral ramp, made from a split garden hose, which wound around a wooden tripod. Three handles extended from the base of the tripod. A 1/4 inch diameter ball was made to "climb" up and around the spiral shaped ramp, as the subjects tried to manipulate the slant of the base while holding to the three handles. The steepness of the ramp made higher scores (the ball climbing higher) progressively more difficult. There were ten turns to negotiate. In Carter's experiment, there were 30 minutes given to obtain as high a score as possible. Modifications of this apparatus included the addition of three handles to the platform. At times, this apparatus was constructed so that the subjects

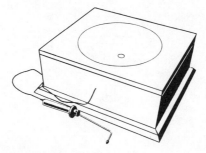

FIGURE 5-4. Rotary pursuit test. The subject tries to keep the stylus tip in contact with the target set near the edge of a revolving turntable. The score is the total time "on target" during the test period. (Courtesy of Fleishman EA: *The Structure and Measurement of Physical Fitness.* Englewood Cliffs, N.J., Prentice-Hall, 1964.)

were *unable,* under any circumstances and despite their best efforts, to make the ball ascend to the top. Under these latter conditions, the effort was made to study the individual's reactions to the stress of failure.

Purdue pegboard test, done cooperatively. In three studies in the 1950s, Comrey and his colleagues studied group performance using a Purdue pegboard test (Figure 5-5). The purpose was to determine if group effort was correlated to individual abilities when combined. The task evaluated discrete, alternating, serial-like responses of two people. One subject first placed a peg in a hole, while the second put a washer on the peg; the first again placed a collar over the peg, and finally the

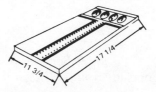

FIGURE 5-5. Purdue pegboard test. The examinee is required to place pegs in holes or to complete as many peg-washer-collar-washer assemblies as possible in the time allowed. Score is the number of pegs placed or the number of assemblies completed in the time period. (Courtesy of Fleishman EA.: *The Structure and Measurement of Physical Fitness.* Englewood Cliffs, N.J., Prentice-Hall, 1964.)

second subject placed a washer over the collar. A four-part assembly task was thus done cooperatively as described, as well as individually with one person performing all four operations. The results of this study are discussed elsewhere in the chapter.

Group reaction timer. Zajonc (1965) as well as others have used group reaction timers to evaluate group cohesion and cooperative behaviors. As shown in Figure 5-6, the apparatus permits up to seven subjects to be evaluated. They may be placed together or in separate cubicles. Usually, the subjects are expected, as quickly as possible, to turn off a light when it appears on their panels. One light, marked G, is a display to which the subjects respond as a group, while remaining displays provide feedback about the behavior of other group members. Each stimulus display also contains a "failure light" marked F. The apparatus permits analysis of individual as well as group effort. It also allows the measurement of either simple or complex reaction times, using single or multiple stimuli. Feedback on individual or group performance may be presented to a subject or withheld. In Zajonc's experiment, baseline data were obtained in about 10 minutes, with subsequent scores compared to the original baseline measures.

There have been numerous other "motor" tests and tasks employed by social psychologists over the years to evaluate group performance. A favorite has been puzzle making. Many of these require cognitive and perceptual qualities, with movement qualities contributing relatively little to the individual and group performance score. Weist, Porter, and Ghiselli (1961) used puzzle making as a task, for example.

In addition to the apparatus shown in Figures 5-5 and 5-6, during the past 20 years various projective tests have been employed, whose results directly and indirectly reflect the probable degree of group cohe-

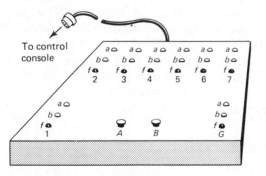

FIGURE 5-6. Group reaction timer. An illustration of individual working panels. *J of Exp Soc Psychol* I (1965), 71–88. "The Requirements and Design of a Standard Group Task."

sion. Shipley and Vernoff from Wesleyan University devised a modification of the Thematic Apperception Test in 1952. They used responses obtained as subjects were asked to inspect pictures and invent imaginative stories. A "need for affiliation score" was obtained, based on the subjects' responses.

As has been pointed out, often low to moderate relationships are obtained among the various indices of group cohesion. It thus appears that the scores acquired are influenced by group size, the length of association of group members, the nature of the task, and the measure of cohesion. In the sections that follow, attempts will be made to sort out the influence of these and other factors on the effectiveness of varying degrees of group cohesion seen on sports teams.

DETERMINANTS OF GROUP COHESION

Innumerable conditions and variables influence group cohesion. These may be divided into several categories, including relatively fixed conditions, such as the nature of the task, the personalities and needs of the group members, and such operational considerations as group size and the abilities the members bring to a performance situation.

In addition to these relatively stable qualities, there are a number of conditions that are more dynamic and vary over time. These include feelings about the objective measures of group success and failure, stresses imposed on the group, the clarity and acceptability of group goals, and finally the type and quality of leadership available, leadership which may only become apparent after a period of time.

An appreciation of the importance of these various factors may add to the technical and psycho-social "armament" of the coach. It could help him or her to become more sensitive to the forces that either bring the team together or tear it apart. Team members may also become more efficient upon considering these factors. More sensitive athletes may become better able not only to understand the motives of their fellow teammates more thoroughly, but also to form better and more sensitive impressions of their coaches.

The Nature of the Task

All sports do not require the same type of cooperative behavior among and between members. Golfers may compete at times out of sight of their teammates, while rowers must maintain rather close rhythm with their companions. On some teams, athletes have relatively the same role, as in cross-country skiing. On others, the skills are differentiated, varying from the minor differences seen on basketball teams to major differences in the skill requirements of team members of track and field groups.

It is important to carefully consider the nature of these differences in tasks and sports when surveying the later findings. The causes of group cohesion, productivity, success, failure, and dissension may vary, depending on the type of team interactions required in a given situation.

Steiner in 1972 proposed a helpful classification system for considering various types of sports teams with regard to the types of interactions taking place. Initially, Steiner suggests that an obvious division should exist between what he terms individual sports (or coacting sport) and teams in which the members must work closely in prescribed roles. In individual sports, Steiner suggests that an artificial score is obtained by adding individual efforts into a total.

Individual sports are further subdivided by Steiner to include those in which all-out effort is required, which he terms "maximizing tasks." These include tasks involving speed, strength, and the like. In contrast, as shown in Table 5-2, are individual sports in which success is measured in qualitative ways. Included on this list are such artistic endeavors as figure skating, gymnastics, and the like.

Steiner adds an additional two dimensions to his typology of sport: (1) "unitary tasks," in which all members perform in the same or a nearly similar manner, and (2) sports containing what he calls "divisible tasks." The latter involve members whose functions are differentiated in order to produce a final group effort. A three-dimensional look at what Steiner proposes is depicted in Figure 5-7.

TABLE 5-2.

	"Maximizing" (all-out effort)	"Optimizing" (esthetic judging)
Individual effort, combined "artificially"	Field performance in (athletics)	Gymnastics
		Diving
	Swimming	
	Shooting	Figure skating,
	Archery	free style
Close group effort prescribed by rules	Basketball	Gymnastics-modern
	Soccer (football)	Group synchronized swimming
	Ice hockey	

Consideration of Steiner's classification system might lead to several hypotheses.

1. It might be expected that greater group cohesion is necessary in sports, reflecting all-out effort in a team requiring close group effort and also in group situations in which optimizing aesthetic qualities are required.

2. Intrateam competition for perfection and achievement might be more tolerable in sport situations that require individual efforts (swimming, running, and the like) than in situations that require close and continued interaction during the course of the contest.

Steiner's classification system, however, does not precisely fit all sports. For example, one might conceive of a continuum reflecting the *degree* to which an individual must interact with other members of a team (Figure 5-8). Different sports might locate themselves at various points on such a scale. For example, golf and boxing require no physical interpersonal action in direct ways among team members. Swimming

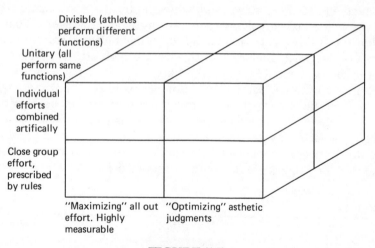

FIGURE 5-7.

and running contain relays, which require close cooperation, while other events in these same sports do not.

American baseball is another example of a rather mixed sport. Offensively, the players work more independently than is true on defense, in which close cooperation is needed particularly among members of the infield. At the extreme end of this kind of cooperation continuum are sports in which constant and close interaction is needed. Ice hockey, field hockey, soccer, football, and the like are examples of these. Thus, such a scale may appear as follows:

Boxing, weight lifting, wrestling, archery, etc.	American baseball, swimming relays, running relays, etc.	Soccer (football), basketball, ice hockey, etc.

←————————————————————————→

No direct physical interaction	Moderate direct physical interaction	Contunued and close interaction

FIGURE 5-8.

This continuum suggests several hypotheses. For example, at given times and in given sports, measures of affiliation, group cohesion, and the like may have important influences on the quality of athletic performance. At other times, in the same sport, measures of group togetherness may be relatively poor indicators of performance.

The degree to which the functions of team members are similar or different might also be projected on a similar scale (Figure 5-9) instead of viewed in the manner suggested by Steiner. In other words, some sports contain athletes whose functions are virtually identical, others prescribe roles for athletes that are slightly different, while still others have functions that are markedly different. The different roles of the players and the goalies in ice hockey and soccer, for example, represent activities within this middle range of the scale. This type of scale might appear as follows.

Landers (1974), in an attempt to classify sports groups with regard to psychosocial qualities, also assumes that different interactional requirements are likely to elicit different results when measures of group cohesion are compared to performance outcomes. He lists seven types of sports and sports functions in his typology. These include complementary tasks (officiating), conjunctive tasks (mountain climbing), disjunctive tasks (hiking, golfing), additive in series tasks (relays, doubles in tennis), and additive simultaneous tasks (crew, tug-o-war).

Archery, shooting, skijumping, etc.	American baseball, American football, soccer (football), ice hockey	

←————————————————————————→

Similar functions	Some similar, some dissimilar functions	Highly differentiated functions

FIGURE 5-9.

Research is beginning to indicate that different personality traits may be evidenced by various members of teams, depending on the positions and roles played. Leadership functions and roles may differ, depending on what position an athlete plays or what event is involved. Additionally, certain psychosocial characteristics of athletes may be similar, not because they are playing the same sport, but because they fulfill similar functions in different sports. These suppositions and similar hypotheses are examined in this and other chapters.

The major point here, however, is that certain sports and sports situations *by their very nature* impose different social and psychologic demands on participants. Thus, the success of the athlete and the team often hinges upon the degree of congruence required by the sport situation and the qualities the individual brings to it.

Illustrating this point is the recent study by Hatfield (1977). He found that athletes in individual sports were more likely to be tolerant of ambiguity, in contrast to team sport athletes who were less tolerant of situations that were not carefully structured. Moreover, when a matching of the individual's acceptance of ambiguity was congruent with the demands of the sport, more success was recorded than when this was not true.

When more data of this nature, illuminating match-ups between personal qualities and the social-psychologic demands of sports situations, are available, additional insights into this complex problem area should be forthcoming.

Group Interaction and Individual Abilities

In a series of studies carried out in the early 1950s, Comrey and his colleagues attempted to determine the ways individual performance contributed to two-man (and woman) efforts in a serial motor task (the Purdue board assembly task). In three studies, two questions were explored: (1) whether the best or worst performers influenced group performances more, and (2) whether either best or worst individual performance measures were more predictive of group performance.

Essentially, Comrey's findings resulted in a principle potentially important to coaches in several kinds of interactional sports. The findings suggest that whatever *personal motor* qualities individuals bring to a task, when two or more individuals attempt to interact in precise ways, the group quality may be most important. The ability to anticipate another's movements and time one's own actions to them may be at least as important as one's own performance qualities, independent of another person.

In the first study of the series, for example, it was found that only about 44 percent of the variance of the group scores could be predicted from inspection of the two individual scores that made up the total. In this case, the majority of the variance (66 percent) was attributable to what might be termed a group ability possessed by the subjects. In this same study, the contributions of subjects ranked both high and low in ability were not different when their actions were paired with those also working on the task.

A study by Gill (1977) has extended the findings of Comrey within the general problem area. She explored additional variables, such as ability differences in two-member performing groups, and looked at both high-and low-ability groups in a cooperative task. The task involved moving a ball through a maze by tilting the surface, using two individuals or one. Both average ability and differences in the ability of group members were predictive of combined efforts, although the correlations were not high.

Although it is obvious that more work is needed on this topic, particularly using tasks similar to those found on the athletic field, several implications seem valid. (1) The coach should exercise care when selecting starting team members. One should select players whose skills blend with those of their teammates, instead of becoming overly preoccupied with individuals who exhibit extraordinarily high levels of individual skills. (2) This principle seems particularly applicable to groups in which close team interaction is essential.

This kind of group quality appears to be more important when performing motor tasks than when the tasks require more thought than action. Wiest and his colleagues (1961), reflecting on the findings of Comrey, designed a study in which a jigsaw puzzle was used as a group task. Over half the variance in this task was attributable to the intellectual qualities possessed by each group member, in contrast to motor task performance when less than half the variance seemed "hooked in to individual performance."

These findings have potential implications for the coach. For example:

1. If it is true that some group performance quality is possessed by individuals, relatively independent of motor ability, players should be selected by referring to their individual skills only when they can perform alone in the sport. On the other hand, when the sport requires close coordination with others, skills specific to the sport are important to consider. At the same time, the coach should look carefully at those who seem to anticipate well the movements of others, and who time their movements and passes with the actions of their teammates.

2. Collective participation in cognitive tasks is likely to be correlated to

the intellectual abilities members bring to the group. Thus, the coach should involve team members in strategy decisions, particularly in sports in which tactics are important. Encourage collective thought among teammates concerning the way a game plan may be put into effect. Ask for and encourage the voicing of an athlete's intellectual impressions during the course of the game. At the completion of a contest, carefully weigh the athlete's comments. Collective intellectual input to groups represents what some psychologists have termed "resource input," data that are greater in larger groups than in smaller ones. Thus, some measure of "group think" is potentially helpful in sports in which intelligent decision making is a critical component.

Group Size

Many of the implications for sport based upon the size of the sports team must come from rather sterile laboratory experiments. For example, when studying the effects of group size, the experimenter may in rather methodologic ways vary the size of the group and study productivity, quality of interaction, member satisfactions, and the like. The coach, on the other hand, is bound within rules as to how many players he must use at a given time in a given sport.

Despite the shortcomings of laboratory data, there are potentially relevant findings that may be of help to the coach. For example, as a group becomes larger, several things begin to happen. Intellectual input becomes greater, more people know more things, and they are collectively in possession of more intellectual, perceptual, mechanical, verbal, and physical skills. Cratty and Sage (1964) found that individual performers who were not permitted to interact between the trials of a large maze task performed worse on subsequent trials compared to subjects who were permitted to exchange information about the task between trials.

However, as a group becomes larger, or on larger teams, there is a tendency for individual members to feel as though their individual contribution to the overall effort is a small fraction of the total performance. Thus, the discontent upon losing and elation because of winning, all things being equal, are likely to be less marked on larger teams than on smaller ones.

As a group increases in size and its physical efforts are focused on a relatively specific task, there is likely to be a loss of efficiency for two reasons: (1) Individual motivation may be less, as people feel they are becoming less important in the total effort. (2) At times, there is a built-in loss of efficiency for mechanical reasons. This is seen in rope-pulling tasks, when as more members are added they may not as easily coordinate their efforts, as was true when a smaller number were pulling.

There are other group size characteristics that can influence cohesion and performance. For example, a four-member group may form coalitions, with two members pairing off in some psychologic way "against" the other two. This kind of coalition may be less "fair" in a three-member group, as two may tend to "gang up" against the third, while a five-member group might also break up in two units, one containing three persons and the other two. This kind of effect, however, has not been studied extensively in smaller sports teams. Within business groups and those in factories, such behaviors are well documented.

In summary, Steiner (1966) suggests that group productivity as a function of size can be made into a formula by initially adding up such variables as resources available to the group, and comparing them to task demands. Subtracted from such an equation are losses due to faulty processes (social and otherwise). The final formula thus reads: Actual productivity = Potential productivity–losses due to faulty processes. These losses Steiner subdivides into those involving poor motivation, and coordination losses, referring to psychosocial rather than physical coordination.

Steiner's concepts of losses and productivity will be examined in more detail, with reference to studies in which physical performance has been employed and group size has varied. The tasks have used both larger and smaller muscle groups.

Wegner and Zeaman (1956) used the two and four "pronged" handle on the stylus with a pursuit rotor in their research, in which they varied the number of performers from two to four. They studied the effects of group size, but also varied their experimental groups so that some received initial practice under either group or individual conditions. Later in the experiment, the subjects exchanged conditions. Those practicing alone were paired with others, while those working with others performed alone. Thus, they elicited data reflecting the transfer of practice from group to individual performance conditions, and vice versa.

They found that: (1) The greater the number of subjects performing, holding the stylus at the same time, the better the performance level. However, performance was more variable when more performed, independent of how much practice the group members had had as individuals before combining their efforts. (2) Skill acquired during practice alone contributed as much to later practice in a four-member group as did prior practice in a group itself. (3) Skill acquired during practice alone contributed to skill exhibited when two were placed together to perform, but not as much as if prior practice had been gained with a partner. (4) Transfer was greater from practice alone to practice in groups than was the transfer occurring in the reverse direction.

The task they used was a highly precise one, requiring no physical effort. Thus, the data cannot be applied to many athletic situations without reservations and conditions. However, the findings do illustrate how group learning is different from individual learning, and how group cooperation may require skills different from those acquired alone. These findings suggest that in such sports as badminton, squash, and tennis, specific practice in doubles is important. Prolonged playing of singles may not be a good predictor of how well an individual will play with a partner.

Other tasks used in research efforts require physical power. There have been at least three studies, for example, in which rope pulling has been employed in group efforts to study changes in efficiency as group members are added or substracted.

In a study by Ringlemann,[1] data from a rope-pulling task illustrated a dropoff in efficiency as groups ranging in size from two to eight were employed. Ringlemann compared hypothetical group averages, if totals involving each individual's performance were combined, with the *actual* group pulling power. In one example, Ringlemann found that 63 kg represented an average individual effort. Thus, the potential efforts for groups of two, three, and eight people should have been 126 kg, 189 kg, and 504 kg, respectively. However, the actual group scores were 118 kg, 160 kg, and 248 kg.

Steiner (1966) has suggested that the magnitude of dropoff illustrated in Ringlemann's data is a function of the number of links between members of progressively larger groups. A group of two contains one link (between the members), while in a group of three, there were three links, connecting a and b, b and c, and c and a. Thus, in an eight-person group, there are 28 links. According to Steiner's calculations, the magnitude of the dropoff in the above experiment should have been 1, 3, and 28, respectively. The actual productivity of the groups was 0.87, 3.17, and 28, for the two-, three-, and eight-member groups. Steiner explains this discrepancy was due to sampling error, because of the relatively small number of groups used in Ringlemann's study.

In more recent research by Ingham, subjects pulled on a rope attached to a strain gauge. A decrease in individual efficiency of 7 percent was noted when up to three group members were added. After the group size reached six, the amount of inefficiency tended to level off.

[1]In the chapter by J. F. Dashiell in Murchison C (ed): *Handbook of Social Psychology* (Worcester, Mass.: Clark University Press, 1972).

In order to differentiate the influence of motivation ("I'll not pull so hard because others are helping me!") from actual pulling loss due to mechanical factors, these experimenters employed two groups in one experiment. One group was blindfolded and told that they were pulling in a group, while others (also blindfolded) were informed that they were pulling alone. Under both conditions, the subjects exhibited the same performance losses when they were *told* that more pullers were being placed on the rope and when more were *really* added. The results thus indicate that motivation may play an important part in a performer's "holding back" when more and more others are contributing to the total effort in a group task.

The amount of satisfaction and/or effort expended in a motor task may depend on the nature of the task. Using Steiner's classification system, Frank and Anderson (1971) found that increases in group size enhanced performance on a disjunction task (discrete responses, separate parts). However, increases in group size proved deleterious on tasks that were conjunctive. Tasks whose members performed simultaneously, therefore, seemed negatively affected by additions in group members, as was true in the rope pulling tasks.

The subjects in the Frank and Anderson study further reported that they perceived conjunctive tasks as less pleasant as the group size increased, whereas disjunctive tasks became more pleasant. This kind of report emphasizes the importance of motivation as a function of group performance in contrast to simple mechanical factors that may seem to be operative.

It is believed that these findings hold implications for the coach.

1. The larger the team, the more effort must be made to encourage group cohesion. In team sports requiring close and continued interaction, this is particularly important. But in individual sports the same effort should be made by the coach. Players should be informed of one another's goals and efforts, and of their total contribution to the team's score.

2. If the team suddenly becomes smaller, for example, a penalized player is removed, group efficiency may not necessarily diminish. Individual players may become highly motivated to work harder as they perceive their own roles as more important in the total group effort.

3. Information of the kind found in these paragraphs may also be helpful if related to the team members themselves. Their apparent losses of motivation as group size increases may be dealt with by the athletes themselves.

4. At times it should be attempted to reduce team sizes, so that substitutes have an opportunity to play rather than to sit out an entire season on the bench. Too many nonplaying reserves may heighten interpersonal hostilities on a team.

Previous Affiliation and Group Success

Numerous studies in industrial psychology have explored relationships among mutual liking, social interaction, previous affiliation, and group productivity. Fewer investigations, however, have been carried out using athletic teams. The findings of these studies have not always been in line with what common sense would predict. For example, groups that have affiliated socially, and who otherwise have been together for prolonged periods of time and in close ways, may not necessarily perform efficiently in tasks that require their close attention and are unlike the previous social relationships. The number of friendship choices in a group may not correlate with group productivity, for example.

Reflecting these findings are data obtained by Palmer and Myers (1955) on the interactions of radar crews. The degree to which members spent their free time together was negatively related to on-the-job success. The relationship held true whether or not the crew members were high- or low-status members of the three-man groups. The authors suggested that activities of human groups might be placed along a continuum, ranging from goals that are "natural" to those that are imposed.

They point out that activities of a group may be placed at various points along such a scale, from objectives sought entirely for the purpose of satisfying personal needs, to those imposed by others that have no relationship to what might be termed "personal need satisfiers." They concluded, therefore, that social compatibility and congeniality are related to group productivity only so long as the "natural" goals of group members are involved and the defined (imposed) needs are the same. However, if the defined goals usually imposed by an outside authority are at odds with those imparting member satisfaction (natural goals), a lowering of group productivity is the result.

It is likely that even on high level sports teams, members view the demands to win in different ways. Some conceive of the stresses of competitive sport in positive ways and in line with their natural needs, while others feel oppressed by the demands to achieve perfection. Thus, these differences comprise only one of the conditions which may result in conflicting findings when scores reflecting team cohesion on sports teams are contrasted with winning and losing.

Numerous studies carried out over the years substantiate the findings of Palmer and Myers. Hagstrom and Selvin (1965), for example, using a factor analysis, isolated nineteen measures of cohesiveness. These included "social satisfaction" and another dealing with the "instrumental" attractiveness of the group for its members.

Additionally, some groups, in sport and other aspects of life, are formed because people find themselves mutually attracted and want to satisfy their needs for social affiliation. A second reason groups form is to perform some kind of specific task in which mutual participation is necessary. The former kind of group is labeled a "primary group," while the second is sometimes called a "secondary group."[4]

Using a physical task, Cratty and Sage (1964) produced data in 1964 comparing the efforts of what they termed "primary" and "secondary" groups. The two groups, whose members performed independently, attempted to traverse, blindfolded, the large maze task that was described earlier in this chapter. The primary groups were recruited from two fraternity pledge classes, while the secondary groups were formed solely to perform the task at hand and had no prior social contact. The groups were permitted to interact socially between trials, which had been performed individually. An additional group, a secondary group, was not permitted to interact between trials. A blackboard was available so that the subjects' perceptions of the shape of the pathway could be discussed and drawn. It was assumed that a group leader might emerge, and this occurred as in each case one member of the group took the chalk and went to the blackboard to lead the discussion.

While both groups were superior to those performing alone, without any opportunity to interact, the performances of the secondary group were superior to those of the two primary groups. This was similar to the data from the study of radar crews. Observation and analysis of the interactions of the groups' discussions between trials revealed possible reasons for the results. For example, the secondary groups, having had no previous social association, had little to discuss except inferences and observations about the *task at hand.* They talked about the shape of the pathway, and how to place one's hands on the railings while moving through it blindfolded. One member, emerging as the leader, drew their collective impressions of the shape of the pathway on the blackboard. In various other ways, they aided one another to traverse the pathway faster and faster on succeeding trials.

After each trial, they initially determined who was to lead the discussion by finding out who had recorded the best time. This person's observations and techniques were apparently given more weight in the ensuing discussions than were those of slower-moving members.

On the other hand, the primary groups, composed of fraternity brothers, spent their discussion times in a number of ways, several of

---

[4]Chinoy (1954) has further pointed out that a primary group involves long-lasting friendships, and that members have value to one another, independent of whether or not they enable one another to meet some objective.

which were totally unrelated to the task at hand. They spoke of forth-coming social events, and often evidenced "social noise" unrelated to the task. At times, they did not discuss the maze problem at all between trials.

The preelected leaders of the primary groups, whose election had been based on whatever social or psychologic criteria were important in their fraternity, led the discussions, even when it was found that they were not the fastest maze travelers. These fraternity leaders seemed to resist others taking over their role, even in a performance situation unlike other task situations in which they had found themselves.

In sports teams, a neat dichotomy between what may be termed a primary group and a secondary group may be difficult to formulate. Bales (1953) has suggested that in groups a "swaying" relationship may occur. At one time, the group may value social qualities while at other times a premium is placed on winning, with a blunting of social-affilia-tive goals. The same swaying relationship can occur on a sports team and account in part for the diverse findings encountered when mea-sures of group cohesion are contrasted to performance and winning.

Investigations of the kind cited above, from a variety of sources including education and business, do suggest that there may be a ten-dency for "social noise" to interfere with performance of the task at hand. Thus, groups getting together primarily to meet affiliative needs, or within which affiliation needs grow strong, may become less effective as performing units than are groups oriented solely toward perfor-mance and achievement.

Though these findings suggest that teams whose primary need for being together is to perform well do indeed perform well, while those who simply wish to be together as friends may not do as well, in the real world of sport these contrasting motives may interact in rather complex ways. For example, as a team achieves success, team members are likely to begin to care more and more for one another. This tendency toward mutual liking is reflected in closer social affiliation and greater interper-sonal attraction both on and off the athletic field. As these social needs heighten, they may tend to blunt or otherwise reduce the initial need the group had for forming—to win games!

Thus, it seems that coaches should not become overly concerned about socializing team members as long as team performance remains high. At the same time, there is likely an optimum amount of interper-sonal tension, which if tolerated leads toward better performance. However, if it is exceeded, interpersonal tensions and hostilities may have a disrupting effect on the overall team effort.

Among the measures employed to determine the degree to which team members are motivated toward meeting needs for achievement, in contrast to needs for affiliation, is a device employed by Fiedler (1954). "Tapping into" what he terms "assumed similarity of differences," he scores whether or not individual team members perceive a small or a large number of psychologic and qualitative differences between teammates who contribute little in contrast to those who apparently contribute a great deal to the team's success. In general, if individual team members' perceptions of the better and poorer players are markedly diverse, it is assumed that the differences identify those who have high or low needs for achievement and performance success. Essentially, perceptions of large differences of this nature purportedly reflect a discontent directed toward the less able team members and a parallel distortion about the general worth of the better team members.

On the other hand, when reports from teams and individuals indicate that most perceive little difference between the less and more able performers, the responses are assumed to indicate that the individual (or group) has high needs for affiliation. The members of this latter group thus feel that their teammates are all "pretty good folks," whether they play well or not.

Using this measure, the coach with the help of a social psychologist can determine a great deal about the motivations of team players and about the group as a whole. Knowing whether or not an individual or team is performance or socially oriented is critical, and the information thus obtained could be employed in positive ways for all concerned.

Cohesion and Success on Sports Teams

Only recently have some of the questions and hypotheses raised on the previous pages been explored by researchers interested in sport. Much of the available data raises more questions, which need additional study.

For example, a study of team cohesiveness was carried out by Hans Lenk (1969), focusing on a German rowing team. This work revealed that despite marked intergroup conflicts, the crew won a European championship and received a Silver Medal in the 1964 Olympics.

According to the author, the evolution of interpersonal conflict actually paralleled performance improvement. The investigation, lasting over a period of 4 years, suggested that small groups containing relatively high levels of interpersonal conflict may still perform well. It is unclear, however, whether the rowing team performed well *in spite* of their conflicts, or whether interpersonal conflict and possible intrateam competition enhanced performance. It is also possible that coaching skills, physical abilities and conditioning, and facilities may have overcome the lack of cohesion seen in Lenk's data.

Findings of this nature have also been forthcoming in studies of bowling teams by Landers and Luschen (1974), rifle teams by McGrath (1962), as well as in basketball teams by Fiedler (1952), Grace (1954), and Melnick and Chembers (1974). Thus, in individual, small group, and team sports, measures of group cohesion are not necessarily related to team success.

In contrast to these findings, innumerable studies, primarily employing athletes in team sports, have indicated that cohesiveness and effective team performance are positively related. Long (1972) and Seagrave (1972) found that greater cohesiveness was present on successful basketball teams, as well as on soccer and rugby teams, than was present on track and field and baseball teams.

In the same year, Guy Arnold and John Petley studied the cohesiveness of high school basketball and wrestling teams. Both of these studies also showed that success parallels high measures of group cohesiveness. Dan Landers and his colleagues (1971) also found that high school basketball teams evidenced high levels of "togetherness." Similar findings have been found by Walters (1955) studying bowling teams, by McIntyre (1970), Stogdill (1963) and Trapp (1953) using football teams, by Essing (1970) and Veit (1973) using soccer teams, as well as by Bird, Slepicka (1975), and Voss and Brinkman (1967) with volleyball teams.

The data from these studies may reflect correlational inferences rather than causation. That is, it may be hypothesized that with continued success teams become more cohesive, rather than that a given level of cohesiveness *causes* performance success. Bakeman and Helmreich (1975), studying cohesiveness and performance within underseas laboratories, postulated this same hypothesis.

To summarize the divergent findings, the relation of cohesion to performance success may be caused by (1) the different measures of cohesion available, (2) differences in the make-up of teams, (3) differences in the tasks required of various teams, (4) inability to disengage causal relationships between cohesion and performance, (5) different competitive levels, which may not be comparable, and (6) differences in stability and make-up of the groups studied.

One answer to some of these problems is to engage in a longitudinal study of a sports team, regularly assessing cohesion and comparing the data obtained to performance success and failure. An initial attempt at doing this is represented by studies by Martens (1971), using intramural college teams of moderate ability. Surveying 144 teams, it was found that:

1. Teams who evidenced high levels of affiliation were less successful, but the members evidenced more satisfaction with their seasons than did those who evidenced low or moderate levels of affiliation.

2. During a season, motivation toward the achievement of interpersonal affiliation on successful teams did not change significantly.
3. A successful team season was marked by increased postseason cohesiveness.

Martens' approach is laudable, and when followed up using high-level national and international sports teams, could produce helpful data. While it is possible that athletes in independently performed sports do not need to evidence the same high levels of cohesion as do team members, the data are unclear at this point. Martens' sample included 144 teams who were together primarily to satisfy social needs and who had experienced varying degrees of previous affiliation. Thus, generalizing from these data to teams at higher competitive levels does not seem warranted.

Several studies, carried out in various parts of the world, point to another interesting facet of the problem of cohesion-performance relationships on sports teams. Attempts have been made, usually using sociometric data reflecting friendship choice, to discover whether the affiliation of certain team members is reflected in how they play. Simply stated, it has been attempted to ascertain whether good friends on teams tend to pass to each other more than do players who are not close friends.

It is usually assumed that when friends pass to friends more than would be desirable, the team will do poorly. In general, this finding is upheld at lower levels of competition. At higher levels, however, the relationships between friendship and the manner in which players physically interact are not pronounced. Members of national and international levels teams are apparently not swayed by friendships when playing to win in important contests. More sophisticated studies of this nature seem called for, and the data should prove enlightening.

IMPLICATIONS FOR THE COACH

Formalizing implications for the coach for the understanding and possible modifications of team cohesion is a somewhat tenuous undertaking. For the team, like any working group under stresses that vary over time, is psychosocially an extremely dynamic situation, in a constant state of flux. Thus, the initial implication the coach should keep in mind when attempting to understand and deal with the "we" feelings on a team is that changes are likely to occur. Modifications in the nature of the competition, the membership of the team, as well as the occurrence of unseen personal problems among team members are likely to unbalance and strain the human relationships in the group, which may have been closely interwoven and productive. The coach should assess the group situation, using a flexible and open "mind set," being sensitive and open to changes in interpersonal relationships that may fluctuate from day to day, from competition to competition, and even from moment to moment.

Additionally, the coach should not expect, or even demand, complete social tranquility. At times, more successful teams evidence an optimum amount of interpersonal tension, negative feelings that may flow from the more able to the less able team members. And while the exaggeration of these feelings may certainly prove detrimental to performance, their presence to a moderate degree should be tolerated. It can indicate that the team members really care about how things are going and about their personal and the group's performance.

One reasonably well-documented principle in the annals of the social-psychologic literature is that certain groups, and pairs of people possessing certain mood tendencies and personality traits, function well together. On the other hand, other individuals possessing other traits may not mix well, and conflicts are more likely to occur when they are placed under stress to perform well. But clearest of all are findings indicating that individuals within close physical proximity seldom exert neutral effects on one another. The mere physical presence of two or more individuals is likely to elicit change in those associating, as well as in the overall group tone. For the most part, individuals who are relatively similar in psychologic make-up, motives, and attitudes toward life (or who perceive themselves to be) tend to understand one another better and to get along. That is, people tend to understand, accept, and thus like best those who are psychologically similar to themselves.

Thus, the coach should attempt at times to achieve optimum "mixes" of individuals on the team, to pair athletes during practices, games, and when planning living arrangements who will complement each other and contribute to each other's emotional well-being. The too-tranquil athlete may be paired with a verbose coach as a counselor, for example, while roommate selections, when traveling and practicing, may be carried out with careful judgment, rather than being arrived at random. Constant attention to the principle of selective pairing can enhance group cohesion, reduce excess interpersonal and group stress, and otherwise contribute to optimum team and individual performance.

Group cohesion may often be facilitated by the formalizing of team committees. Various aspects of team discipline may be the responsibilities of this kind of group. When carried out, they may make the members feel important as decision makers in situations that are often perceived as authoritarian, dictatorial, and relatively devoid of a great deal of "we feeling."

It is important in this context to (1) initially make it quite clear what functions these authority committees have and then (2) to *really permit* the committees to exercise the responsibilities assigned to them. Demoralizing in such a situation is *sham democracy,* the purported giving of authority and then the blunting or reversal of decisions as difficult situations arise. If a coach really wants a committee of team members to provide a portion of the decision making, he should uphold their decisions, or the results could be negative.

The membership and use of these committees should be considered with some care. Their decisions could markedly affect the team morale, and thus the number and the type of judgments they are permitted to make may vary according to their maturity and experience. Judgments about playing or not playing, about team membership itself after some transgression may have taken place, can have more than momentary influence on the athletes involved. Decisions of this nature may have a lifelong effect on the athlete. Thus, the constitution of and responsibilities assigned to a team committee should be carefully thought out.

The advantages of the presence of team committees include: (1) They give more athletes "a hand" in the decision-making process, and thus perhaps make the players feel that the team is truly theirs; the effects can be motivating. (2) Negative decisions involving breaches of team rules emanating from a committee of peers may somehow cushion the effect on the players, and result in a sharing of the responsibility that would normally be borne by the coach. Peer pressure in this form, if well used, may have a positive effect on team morale, individual discipline, and overall group behavior.

The cohesion of a team is important to its ultimate success. Although at times close warm friendships are not always necessary to good team performance, players must act and interact in socially helpful ways, and in turn this kind of interaction often results in good team performance. A team of constantly fighting players requires a great deal of coaching energy to settle the squabbles, energy that may be diverted from the important work of teaching skills and conditioning the team.

The cohesion of a team can be both felt and measured. It is thus the responsibility of the coach to improve team togetherness, using practical and specific methods. Theoretically, the job is made more difficult among teams in an individual sport (swimming, track and field, etc.) whose membership is rather large, while there is greater likelihood that group cohesion may be good (or that lack of cohesion can do the most harm) among groups of athletes on teams whose roster is relatively small (i.e., basketball).

Usually, the smaller the group the more likely each member will feel that what he or she accomplishes will make a real difference in the outcomes. The larger the team, the less likely it will be that a single member will believe that he or she is contributing anything of importance to the overall success. Therefore, it is often hard to promote "we feelings" among larger teams in larger individual sports, while it is sometimes less difficult to promote cohesion in sports teams with smaller rosters.

A good method for promoting team cohesion is for the coach to make a special effort in team meetings to indicate to *each* member that his or her personal contribution is important to team success. The coach should be perceived by the players as a "social traveler," relating to and moving up and down the status hierarchy represented by the team's better and less able players. Special attention should be paid to the physically less gifted athletes, and in meetings their time and efforts should be placed in context and the worth of their energies should be made clear to all. Often, less gifted athletes will either surprise the coach with their ability and/or expend extra effort when it is needed. They are more likely to do this if their potential contributions are acknowledged prior to competitions.

An effort should be made to illustrate to all players that the team's star performer is not accorded special privileges, and in many ways is no more important than the less able members. If special privileges are extended to the more able, team morale and group cohesion may suffer. Temporarily or permanently suspending an athlete transgressing team rules should be done if necessary, whether or not he or she displays excellent athletic skills.

Simple tallying methods may also be used to determine relationships between group cohesion and friendship patterns, and team performance. For years, teams in Eastern Europe have been scrutinized to determine who interacts with whom in rather direct ways on the playing field as related to who likes whom. The technique, which involves the careful recording of who passes to whom during the course of the contest, may be the responsibility of a student manager. When it is noted that (1) good friends seem to pass to each other more than would have happened by chance, (2) there are patterns of passes independent of what would be termed "good team play," and/or (3) certain members of the team seem to be neglected (they do not get the ball very often despite their obvious attempts to "get open"), measures should be taken.

If after being presented with the collected evidence, if the offending players do not rectify their behavior in games, they may be withdrawn from competition to think over how they may be blocking overall team success. Such data, obtained both on the court and by using sociograms (who are your first and second best friends), often give clues as to why certain players are unhappy and why the team is not winning as often as possible. Evidence of this kind, presented diplomatically, can improve team cohesion to a marked degree. However, in high-level teams, it is becoming increasingly apparent that close relationships in physical interaction in the contests do not correspond to social friendship patterns.

It could be argued that the most important job of the team sport coach is to select a group of players that represents an ideal psychologic-social mix, and one whose skills can get the job done. An individual's skill level when on his own may not be the same as it is when that same skill must interact with the skills, running speeds, and unique characteristics of others. The ability to time one's own movements with those of others may be more critical in the overall performance of a team than the skill level of each individual.

The ideal team may *not* be composed of people who possess the best individual skills, but rather consist of a group of athletes whose combined skills are best. The coach, according to this premise, must constitute the team of those who are ascendant and whose achievement needs for their own success are high, together with others who are willing to subordinate themselves for the good of the team. Thus, putting together an "ideal" team is not a simple problem of evaluating the material on an individual basis, but of ascertaining what people will work best together.

SUMMARY

The concept of group cohesion is reflected in a number of terms heard in the locker room, including teamwork, spirit, and morale. The measurement of group cohesion is carried out through projective tests, using questionnaires as well as viewing performance outcomes.

Athletic teams evidence various needs for cohesion, depending on the roles each member is called upon to fulfill. Some athletic tasks are highly individualistic, while others require the close cooperation of others. Still other sports require a combination of highly integrated and independent skills. Thus, conceivably the needs for cohesive efforts vary from sport to sport, and even from task to task within given sports.

Further complicating the problem is the indication that within individuals and in groups, motives promoting group cohesion and social affiliation often conflict with those revolving around performance excellence. For the most part, successful teams may subordinate needs for affiliation to needs for excellence, although this finding varies according to the level of competition. At this writing, longitudinal studies of this kind of problem have involved teams at rather low levels of competition, such as intramural teams in college.

Group cohesion and the feelings members have about a group are influenced by previous affiliation, the group size, and the reasons for group formation. Larger groups, while containing more physical and intellectual resources, may tend to blunt members' feelings about their unique contributions to the team's success. Feelings of this nature need to be counteracted by the coach.

The innumerable forces impinging upon a sport team create stresses, which may at first bind the team together but if continued are likely to tear it asunder. The sports climate is socially and psychologically complicated, and contains the feelings of people, as well as their competencies and perceptions of competition. Thus, participation on a sports team is a somewhat perilous one. However, athletic competition, and the "we feelings" discussed in this chapter, may be among the more positive experiences in the life of a child, youth, or adult. It was the intent when compiling the material for this chapter to help the reader perceive ways in which participation in sport may be as fruitful as possible, while reducing the number of stumbling blocks to happiness to a minimum.

QUESTIONS FOR DISCUSSION

1. What qualities may increase the cohesion of a team?
2. How is group cohesion evaluated? What are the limitations of the presently available instruments? What are their strengths?
3. How, and for what reasons, might a team's cohesion change during a competitive sports season?
4. How might group cohesion influence performance both negatively and positively? Cite specific examples of each condition.
5. What qualities should measures of group cohesion possess?
6. Discuss Steiner's classification system in sport, and the implications of the typology relative to group cohesion in various sports.
7. Discuss the concept of "group motor qualities" as expounded by Comrey's research. How might this concept influence the selection of players on two-person performing units, on teams with five to eight members?
8. What are the relationships between group size and group cohesion? What special problems may be encountered when trying to engender "we feelings" on larger vs. smaller athletic teams?
9. How does adding members to a performing group both enhance and detract from performance?

10. How does previous affiliation influence group cohesion? \
of previous affiliation are most likely to enhance performa
athletic team? What kinds of previous association are like
help, or even to detract from performance?

BIBLIOGRAPHY

ALBERT RS: Comments on the scientific concept of cohesiveness. *Am J Sociol* LIX (1953), 231–234.

ARNOLD GE, STRAUB F: Personality and group cohesiveness as determinants of success among interscholastic basketball teams. Unpublished report, School of Health, Physical Education and Recreation, Ithaca College, Ithaca, New York, 1972.

ARNOLD G: Team cohesiveness, personality traits, and final league standings of high school varsity basketball teams. Master's degree thesis, Ithaca College, Ithaca, New York, 1972.

BAKEMAN R, HELMREICH R: Cohesiveness and performance covariation and causality in an underseas environment. *J Exp Soc Psychol* 11 (1975), 478–489.

BALES RF: The equilibrium problem in small groups. *Working Papers in the Theory of Action.* New York, Free Press, 1953, 111–116.

—— *Interaction Process Analysis.* Reading, Mass., Addison-Wesley, 1950.

—— Adaptive and integrative changes as sources of strain in social systems. In Hare AP et al (eds): *Small Groups.* New York, Knopf, 1966.

BERKOWITZ L: Group standards, cohesiveness and productivity. *Hum Rel* VII (1954), 509–519.

BIRD AM: Team structure and success as related to cohesiveness and leadership. *J Soc Psychol* 103, 1977, 217–223.

—— Development of a model for predicting team performance. *Res Q* 48:1 (March 1977), 24–31.

CARTER L, HAYTHORN W, MEIROWITZ B, LANZETTA J: The relation of categorizations and ratings in the observation of group behavior. *Hum Rel* IV (1951), 239.

CARTWRIGHT D: The nature of group cohesiveness. In CARTWRIGHT D, ZANDER A (eds): *Group Dynamics.* New York, Harper & Row, 1968.

CATTELL RB, SAUNDERS DR, STICE GF: The dimensions of synality in small groups. *Hum Rel* VI (1953), 331.

CHAPMAN LJ, CAMPBELL DT: An attempt to predict the performance of three-man teams from attitude measures. *J Soc Psychol* XLVI (1957), 277–286.

CHINOY E: *Sociological Perspective.* New York, Random House, 1954.

COMREY A: Group performance in manual dexterity task. *J Appl Psychol* XXXVII (1953), 207.

—— DESKIN G: Group manual dexterity in women. *J Appl Psychol* XXXVIII (1954), 178.

—— DESKIN G: Further results in group manual dexterity. *J Appl Psychol* XXXIX (1955), 354–356.

—— STAATS CK: Group performance in a cognitive task. *J Appl Psychol* XXXIX (1955), 354–356.

COOPER R, PAYNE R: Personality orientations and performance in football teams: leader's and subordinates orientations related to team success. *Organizational Psychology,* Group Report No. 1, University of Aston, Department of Industrial Administration, January 1967.

CRATTY BJ, SAGE JN: Effect of primary and secondary group interaction upon improvement in a complex movement task. *Res Q* XXXV:3 (October 1964), 265–271.

CROMBAG HF: Cooperation and competition in means-interdependent traits: a replication. *J Pers Soc Psychol* IV (1966), 692.

DASHIELL JF, MURCHISON C (eds): Experiental studies of the influence of social situations on the behavior of individual human adults. *Handbook of Social Psychology.* Worcester, Mass, Clark University Press, 1935.

DION KL: Cohesiveness as a determinant of ingroup and outgroup bias. *J Pers Soc Psychol* XXVIII:2 (1973), 163–171.

DOWNING J: Cohesiveness, perception and values. *Hum Rel* XI (1958), 157–166.

EDWARDS H: *Sociology of Sport.* Homewood, Illinois, Dorsey, 1973.

EISMAN B: Some operational measures of cohesiveness and their interrelations. *Hum Rel* 12 (1967), 183–89.

ELIAS N, DUNNING E: Dynamics of group sports with special reference to football. *J Sociol* 4 (1966), 388–402.

EMERSON M: Mount Everest: a case study of communication feedback and sustained group goal-striving. *Sociometry* 3 (1966), 213–227.

ENOUCH JR, MCLEMORE SD: On the meaning of group cohesion. *Southwestern Soc Sci Q* 48 (1967), 174–182.

ESSING W: Team line-up and team achievement in European football. In KENYON GS, GREGG TB (eds): *Contemporary Psychology of Sport.* Chicago, Athletic Institute, 1970, 349–354.

FESTINGER L: Informal social communication. In CARTWRIGHT D, ZANDER A: *Group Dynamics.* New York, Harper & Row, 1968, 182–191.

FIEDLER FE: Assumed similarity measures as predictors of team effectiveness, *J Abnorm Soc Psychol,* 49 (1954), 381–388.

FIEDLER F et al: *The Relationship of Interpersonal Perception to Effectiveness in Basketball Teams.* Urbana, Bureau of Records and Service, University of Illinois, 1952.

FRANK F, ANDERSON LR: Effects of task and group size upon group productivity and member satisfaction. *Sociometry* 34:1 (1971), 135–49.

FRENCH JRP: The disruption and cohesion of groups. *J Abnor Soc Psychol* XXXVI (1941), 361–77.

GILL DL: Individual member abi lities and group motor performance in compet ition. In LANDERS DM, CHRISTINA R (eds): *Psychology of Motor Behavior and Sport,* II. Champaign, Illinois, Human Kinetics Publishers, 1977.

GOLEMBIEWSKI RT: *The Small Group.* Chicago, University of Chicago Press, 1962.

GRACE H: Conformance and performance. *J Soc Psychol* 40 (1954), 233–237.

GROSS N, MARTIN WE: On group cohesiveness. *Am J Soc* 57 (1952), 554–62.

HAGSTROM WO, SELVIN HC: Two dimensions of cohesiveness in small groups. *Sociometry* 28 (1965), 30–34.

HATFIELD FC: Effects of interpersonal attraction and tolerance-intolerance of ambiguity on athletic team productivity. In LANDERS DM, CHRISTINA R (eds): *Psychology of Motor Behavior and Sport,* II. Champaign, Illinois, Human Kinetics Publishers, 1977.

HEMPHILL JK, WESTIE CM: The measurement of group dimensions. *J Psychol* 29 (1950), 325.

KAGAN J, MUSSEN PH: Dependency themes on the TAT, and group conformity. *J Consult Psychol* 20:1 (1956), 29–35.

KLEIN M, CHRISTIANSEN G: Group composition, group structure and group effectiveness of basketball teams. In Loy, J. and Kenyon, G.: *Sport, Culture and Society.* London, MacMillan, 1969, 397–407.

LANDERS DM, CRUM TF: The effect of team success and formal structure on interpersonal relations and cohesiveness of baseball teams. *Int J Sport Psychol* 2 (1971), 88–96.

LANDERS D, LUSCHEN G: Team performance outcome and cohesiveness of competitive co-acting groups. *Int Rev Sport Sociol* 9 (1974), 57–69.

LENK H: Top performance despite internal conflict. In LOY JW, KENYON GS (eds): *Sport, Culture, and Society*. New York, Macmillan, 1969, 393–397.

LONG GRANT: Cohesiveness of High School Baseball Teams, Completed Research in Health, Physical Education, and Recreation, AAHPER, Washington, D.C., M.S. Thesis, Southern Illinois University.

LOTT AJ, LOTT BE: Group cohesiveness and interpersonal attraction. *Psychol Bull* 64 (1965), 259–309.

LOTT BE: Group cohesiveness: a learning phenomenon. *J Soc Psychol* 55 (1961), 275–86.

LOY JW, KENYON GS: *Sport, Culture and Society*. London, MacMillan, 1969.

LOY J, McPHERSON BD, KENYON G: *Sport and Social Systems*. Menlo Park, Calif, Addison Wesley, 1978, Chapter 3.

MARTENS R: Influence of participation motivation on success and satisfaction in team performance. *RQ* 41:4 (1970).

—— The influence of success and residential affiliation on participation motivation. *J Leisure Res* 3:1 (Winter 1971), 53–63.

—— PETERSON J: Group cohesiveness as a determinant of success and member satisfaction in team performance. *Int Rev Sport Sociol* 6 (1971), 49–59.

MARTENS R, LANDERS D, LOY J: *Sports Cohesiveness Questionnaire*, 1972.

McGRATH JE: The influence of positive interpersonal relations on adjustment effectiveness in rifle teams. *J Abnorm Soc Psychol* 65 (1962), 365–75.

McINTYRE TD: A field experimental study of cohesiveness status and attitude change in four biracial small sport groups. Ph.D. in Physical Education, 1970. College Park, Pennsylvania State University.

MELNICK MJ, CHEMBERS MM: Effects of group social structure on the success of basketball teams. *RQ* 45 (March 1974), 1–7.

MEYERS A: Team competition, success and the adjustment of group members. *J Abnorm Soc Psychol* 65 (1962), 325–32.

MURRAY C: Motor performance, size and the dyadic system. *Percep Mot Skills* 29 (1969), 531–534.

MYERS A: Team competition, success, and the adjustment of group members. *J Abnorm Soc Psychol* 65:5 (1962).

NIXON HL: *Sport and Social Organization.* Indianapolis, Indiana, Bobbs-Merrill, 1974.

—— Team orientations, interpersonal relations, and team success. *Res Q* 47 (October, 1976), 429–435.

—— An axiomatic theory of team success. *Sport Sociol Bull* 3 (Spring, 1974), 1–12.

PALMER FH, MYERS TI: Sociometric choice and group productivity among radar crews. Paper presented at the American Psychological Association, San Francisco, 1955.

PETERSON JA, MARTENS R: Success and residential affiliation as determinants of team cohesiveness. *RQ* 43:1, 64–75.

PETLEY J: The cohesiveness of successful and less successful wrestling teams. Research Project, Ithaca College, Ithaca, New York, 1973.

RAVEN B, REISTSEMA J: The effects of varied clarity of group goal and group path upon the individual and his relation to his group. *Hum Rel* 10 (1957), 29–44.

SAGE JN: Effects of incentives and primary and secondary group interaction on learning a complex maze. *Percep Mot Skills* 29 (1969), 71–74.

SEAGRAVE JO: Comparison of group cohesiveness in club and varsity athletic teams for men. M.S. in Physical Education, Washington State University, Pullman, Washington, 1972.

SHEPHERD C: *Small Groups. Some Sociological Perspectives.* Scranton, Pennsylvania, Chandler, 1964.

SHERIF M, SHERIF C: *Groups in Harmony and Tension.* New York, Harper, 1953.

SHIPLEY TE, VERNOFF J: A projective measure of need for affiliation. *J Exp Soc Psychol* 43 (1952), 349–56.

SINGER J, SHOCKLEY VL: Ability and affiliation. *J Pers Soc Psychol* 1:1, (1965), 95–100.

SLEPICKA P: Interpersonal behavior and sports group effectiveness. *Int J Sports Psychol* 6 (1975), 14–27.

SMITH GJ: The concept of group cohesion and its significance in physical education and athletics. Paper presented to the Sociology of Sport Section, CAHPER, Convention, Victoria, British Columbia, 1969.

SNYDER EE: Athletic dressing room slogans as folklore: a means of socialization. Paper presented at the American Sociological Association Meeting, Denver, Colorado, 1971.

STEINER ID: Models for inferring relationships between group size and potential group productivity. *Behav Sci* 4 (1966), 273–83.

STOGDILL RM: *Team Achievement Under High Motivation*. Columbus Bureau of Business Research, College of Commerce and Administration, Ohio State University, 1963.

STRAUB WF: Team cohesiveness in athletics. Unpublished paper, School of Health, Physical Education and Recreation, Ithaca College, Ithaca, New York.

TRAPP WG: A study of social integration on a college football squad. In *Proceedings of the 56th Annual Meeting of the College Physical Education Association,* Washington, D.C., 1953, 139–141.

VANDER VELDEN L: Relationships among member, team, and situational variables and basketball team success: a social-psychological inquiry. Unpublished Ph.D. dissertation, University of Wisconsin, 1971.

VIET H. Some remarks upon the elementary interpersonal relations within ball games teams. In KENYON S (ed): *Contemporary Psychology of Sport.* Chicago, Athletic Institute, 1973, 355–362.

VOS K, BRINKMAN W: Success en choesie in Sportgroepen. *Sociologiesche Gids* 14 (1967), 30–40.

WALTERS CE: A sociometric study of motivated and non-motivated bowling groups. *Res Q* 26 (1955), 107–112.

WEGNER N, ZEAMAN D: Team and individual performances on a motor learning task. *J Gen Psychol* 55 (1956), 127–42.

WIDMEYER WN: When cohesiveness predicts performance outcome in sport. Unpublished Ph.D. dissertation, University of Illinois, 1977.

WIEST WN, PORTER LW, GRISSELLI EE: Individual proficiency and team performance. *J Appl Psychol* 45:6 (1961), 435–40.

WOLMAN BB: The impact of failure on group cohesiveness. *J Soc Psychol* 5 (1952).

ZAJONC RT: The requirements and design of a standard group task. *J Exp Soc Psychol* 1 (1965), 71–88.

6

The Athlete's Motives in a Social Context

This chapter presents ideas about the way variables in the social context interact with the motives of an individual participating in sport. Further, the discussion contains inferences concerning how the athlete perceives various kinds of social evaluation and how these perceptions in turn may modify feelings about performance and actual performance.

Among the primary threads running through the cloth composing the chapter are the following: (1) How the athlete conceptualizes about success and failure, past, present, and future. (2) The ways an athlete's perceptions of personal competence are influenced by his or her feelings about the abilities of teammates. (3) The ways future goal setting and effort expended are influenced by feelings about personal efforts and abilities, as well as by the individual's perceptions of the efforts and abilities of teammates.

An important assumption in the following material is that an athlete is not a passive performer, unable or unwilling to evaluate the consequences of, and reasons for, success and failure. Rather, the athlete *actively thinks* about *why* he or she may be doing well or poorly in a given situation, then adjusts future aspirations and effort expended.

If the coach, or team psychologist, understands the reasons athletes formulate for their successes or failures, the quality of interactions between performers and their mentors will be enhanced. That is, the coach should realize that the athlete is not only acting as his own coach, but also much of the time also serves as his own psychologist.

Some of the ideas and models to be discussed have only recently been formulated. Additionally, there have only been a few studies that apply these new ideas to sport. However, the concepts these new theories contain are provocative and important, and for this reason their implications are worthy of consideration in both a practical and a theoretical context.

Historical Background

One of the earliest statements related to the topics under consideration came from the German Hoppe (1930), who suggested that a person's feelings of success are not dependent on the attainment of some absolute score or measurable performance level, but upon whether or not the person reaches some hoped-for goal. Thus, the "closeness" of an *actual performance* to the *performance expected* is a most important consideration when people define success or failure to themselves or others.

These basic ideas prompted numerous studies in the 1940s and 1950s, dealing with such topics as "self-estimation" and "aspiration level."[1] Typically, the researchers asked their subjects to first estimate how well they thought they could perform on a given task, and then to perform the task. The skills were usually unfamiliar to the subject, and were usually motor skills.

The scores obtained in these studies included: (1) differences between future estimations, and actual performance levels attained, (2) whether or not the performer adjusted estimates upward or downward and why, and (3) the relationships between directions of shifts upward and downward after success and failure.

Several variables were explored as influencing the subjects' goal-setting behaviors. These included the personality traits of the performers, past success and failure (either real or manufactured by the experimenter), and social conditions.

A most important implication in this early work was that the performer is an active participant in the process of performance evaluation. It was observed that the subjects thought about and tried to ascertain the reasons their performance was good, acceptable, or poor.

Two other forces in the 1950s, in the behavioral sciences, prompted further research about how people react to success and failure in competitive situations. The first was the trend reflected in increased interest in, and expansion of, "cognitive theory." This general theoretical approach assumes that people think about the results and future conse-

---

[1]This research is discussed in Cratty BJ: *Social Dimensions of Physical Activity.* Chapter 3, "Aspiration Level." Englewood Cliffs, New Jersey, Prentice-Hall, 1967.

quences of their behavior, and do not react mindlessly to people, problems, and situations.

A second trend that influenced the building of new models relative to human motivation was the interest created by Atkinson and others, who began to look into what were termed achievement needs. As explained in Chapter II, Atkinson and those who followed his lead assumed that the need to exert mastery over a task was an extremely important influence upon human striving, goal setting, and effort expended both in daily activities and in achievement-laden situations.

Further, these theorists assumed that achievement situations invariably involved social comparisons. How well an individual is doing in some task is contrasted to performance standards, both by the performer and by others. In various task situations, the individual high in achievement needs will select goals and performance standards intermediate in difficulty, in which there is about a fifty-fifty chance of success. This phenomenon is recorded in a 1974 study of motor performance by Roberts as well as by others within other task orientations. Furthermore, Weiner and others in the early 1970s began to speculate that cognitive judgments about causality mediate between level of achievement needs exhibited and performance itself.

Causal Attribution Theory

By the late 1960s and early 1970s, model building had become more refined. Researchers began to focus more and more on the interactions between perceived success and failure, goal setting, and performance outcomes. They also attempted to ascertain what *causes* people to be attached to success and failure in achievement situations, and to formulate lists of factors that influenced success and failure, according to performer speculations. These causes were at first proposed to include luck, ability, task difficulty, and effort. Thus, it was assumed that individuals, when confronted with performance situations, acted as amateur psychologists. They tried to ascertain just *why* they had done well or poorly.

Furthermore, attribution theorists began to construct scales on which one might place the various causes for success or failure. One was termed "external-internal." This scale assumes that some causes might be considered within the performer, while others may be external to the performer. Examples of internal causes were ability and effort, while external causes included luck, task difficulty, and the effort or ability of opponents.

As more attention was paid to these speculations, other dimensions appeared in the writings, reflecting new continuums upon which causes for success or failure might be placed. Next to emerge was a scale reflecting causes that are considered stable; these include ability, task difficulty, and the like. Unstable causes, at the other end of the same scale, included effort and luck. Still a third dimension was added to the model, suggesting causes that were both intentional and unintentional. Table 6-1, from Rosenbaum's work, illustrates the interaction of these three dimensions, together with examples of some of the causes that may be placed within each of the eight categories.[2]

Thus, causal attribution theory makes allowances for personal, individually oriented causes, and for social causes of perceived success or failure. The latter can include stable or unstable effort of others on the team, teammates' abilities, and the effort and abilities of opponents.

The answers to three primary questions were sought by researchers exploring these theoretical models. These queries were: (1) What are the causes people believe influence their success and failure? How might one classify these causes? (2) How are these causes formulated by the performer? What conditions occurring before performance influence people's opinions of why they did well or poorly in a given task? (3) How do the causes people formulate for performance fluctuations influence future success, failure, and effort expended in subsequent performance situations?

Research dealing with causal attribution is still in its infancy. Scholars are just beginning to struggle with the weighting of more than one cause a person may formulate to explain success or failure. Precise definitions of success and failure are also being actively explored.

The situational nature of causal attribution poses other conundrums.

TABLE 6-1.   A three-dimensional taxonomy of the perceived causes of success.

	Intentional		*Unintentional*	
	Stable	*Unstable*	*Stable*	*Unstable*
Internal	Stable effort of self	Unstable effort of self	Ability of self	Fatigue, mood, fluctuations in skill of self
External	Stable effort of others	Unstable effort of others	Ability of others; task difficulty	Fatigue, mood, fluctuations in skill of others

SOURCE: E. Rosenbaum, *Unpublished Ph.D. dissertation*, U.C.L.A., 1972, p. 21.

[2]More recent work by Elig and Frieze postulates additional dimensions, including "mediate" causes, interests, desires, and moods, which trigger an indivdual's formulations of causes.

For example, attempts to determine whether causes formulated by a person after failure on an examination will be similar to those formulated after failing to do well in a tennis game are important. Temporary mood states and individual differences in personality are also being studied as possibly influential on the selection of causes for success and failure.

As will be seen in the following section, this rich theoretical "playground" has barely been tapped by those interested in motivation in athletics.

Causal Attribution and Sport: Preliminary Findings

Most aspects of causal attribution theory can be applied to sport and to athletes. Sport is a highly charged, achievement-laden situation, one in which an individual or a group performance is compared not only to the performance of others, but also to absolute standards of height, speed, distance, and time. These precise criteria often possess worldwide status, and are thus highly visible.

Additionally, there are usually uncertainties as to outcomes, as an athlete or team embarks on a competition. Thus, preperformance and postperformance judgments are virtually always engaged in both by athletes and interested others.

Most studies in which athletes have been subjects have resulted in data that parallel those collected in other types of achievement situations. However, at times the results are not as clear-cut as one might like. Martens (1971), for example, found that there were no differences in the effects of praise and reproof on the motor performance of young boys when they attributed their performance to internal (personal) or external (others') controls.

However, for the most part, successful athletes, as is true of people successful in other endeavors, attribute their success to internal causes, which are both stable and unstable. Frieze, McHugh, and Duqui (1976), for example, found that athletes attributed success to individual and team effort (internal and external causes that were relatively unstable), as well as to the severity of the training to which they were exposed. In this same study, transitory feelings of being either "high" or "low" prior to competition were also mentioned by the subjects as important to their winning or losing.

The results of another study of spectators attending soccer matches, conducted by Mann (1974), raises an interesting point. The data underscored just how situationally specific the formation of causal attributes may be. For example, fans from the winning team's district attributed the team's success, which they had enjoyed vicariously, to superior play (internal causes). In the same study, between 25 percent and 65 percent of the fans backing the losers believed that the lack of success experienced by *their* heroes was due to external causes (luck, poor officiating, etc.).

Although criticized by some as merely echoing common sense, attribution theory, when carefully considered, affords rather detailed insights into the nature of human motivation and thoughts that influence motives. In summary, the available data suggest that: (1) People attribute success and failure to a variety of causes, not all of which are accounted for within currently available models. (2) The frequency with which people attach success and failure to various causes may not only be situationally specific, but also may fluctuate according to relatively transitory occurrences. The weather, losing and winning, temporary mood of the performer, as well as the effort and feelings projected by opponents are likely to cause changes in the reasons people attach to winning and losing in sport.

Certain findings, however, tend to hold up within a variety of situations. These include (1) Effort and ability (internal causes) are usually perceived as the most important determinants of success and failure by successful people and teams. Moreover, successful people, even when losing, are not likely to easily change their feelings about causal attributes. They tend to continue to believe that losing is their own fault, rather than circumstances or the efforts and abilities of others. (2) Luck is used as an excuse for failure or success more often by less successful people. Thus, external causes are more likely to be used as excuses for performance success or failure by those who fail more than they succeed. (3) Successful performers, when not winning on a few occasions, may attribute their momentary losses to relatively unstable events (their own lack of effort or the superior effort of opponents). Thus, they view their causes for failure as "things," which can easily be changed in future competitive encounters.

IMPLICATIONS FOR THE COACH

Many of the ideas expressed in this chapter may not be new to the perceptive coach. Indeed, attribution theory has been criticized as simply reflecting common sense. Thus, if the coach has examined not only his own motives but those of the athletes with whom he is dealing, he has no doubt come up with many of the concepts discussed. Finding excuses for losing or winning is an almost continuous pastime for both athletes and coaches.

What has been attempted, both by attribution theorists and by the writer, has been to arrange in a formal manner the ways people think about success and failure. It is hoped that the discussion will invite further thought. This final part of the chapter will attempt to illustrate how concern about the causes people assign to success and failure can be employed in practical ways to optimize athletic performance, and to understand the motives of competitors in sport.

The implications of the preceding materials will be discussed within a time dimension, consisting of precompetition considerations and post-competition implications. In addition, within each of these periods of time, two primary dimensions of attribution theory will be discussed, causes residing on a stability dimension and causes residing on a scale described as "locus of control" (external or internal to the competitor).

Precompetition

Prior to a competitive season, or before a specific event, several considerations should be kept in mind relative to the causes athletes may attach to possible future success or failure. Initially, it should be assumed that the athlete *is* thinking about one or more causes for success or failure, and may be attempting in advance to find an "out" for losing.

It should not, however, be assumed that the causes the athlete is voicing are truly those he or she is conceptually pondering. A common occurrence involves an athlete's decrying the fact that he or she either feels bad or has an injury. This kind of behavior may have real causes (there *may* be an injury present), or the athlete may be searching for an acceptable external (but transitory) cause for possible failure. Thus, the athlete lays the groundwork for nothing but success. For if there is a loss, it can be blamed on the prevoiced problem, while if there is a win, the athlete has overcome adversity.

Furthermore, the athlete may be quite concerned about relatively stable internal or external causes for possible failure, including lack of ability and/or the ability of the forthcoming opponent(s). A competitor who is apparently searching for external causes for failure prior to a contest is probably anxious, while one who dwells on relatively stable attributes of opponents as well as himself is probably displaying less precontest anxiety, and an emotionally mature and realistic outlook. Thus, the coach should listen closely not only to the content of the athlete's verbal behavior, but for other signs that indicate just how the athlete is thinking about forthcoming competition and failure or success.

There *are* times when a coach must prepare a team, or individual, for the fact that ability may not be adequate to produce a win. That is, relatively stable internal or external causes may really prevent a triumph. In this case, it may be helpful for the coach to aid the individual or team to define success in realistic terms, perhaps to redefine success overall. That is, the guiding mentor may help the athletes to formulate definitions for winning that may be different than those previously held. It may not be destructive for the coach to tell a group of swimmers, or track and field athletes, that success may include exceeding their personal best efforts and posting a given team score, rather than defeating an obviously superior team manned with better personnel. Thus, the mental health of the athlete(s) may be best served by letting them know that the coach perceives the dimensions of their actual abilities, and their best effort may be forthcoming if they receive this kind of counseling. If mature at all, the athletes already know their abilities in a given situation.

Prior to competition, the coach may also need to help athletes avoid distorting external causes for possible defeat ("Our opponents are too tough!"). The forthcoming opposition may not actually be as formidable as the athlete(s) believe. If this situation should arise, the coach should attempt to determine whether the athlete is merely *voicing* the belief that the opposition is superior, in an effort to lay blame for possible defeat on external rather than to internal causes, or whether the athlete (or team) *really believes* that winning is beyond them, despite their best efforts.

Most of the time, during precompetition exhortations the coach concentrates on a variable which is modifiable, and classified as unstable by attribution theorists—effort. "Try harder," the coach will tell the team, "and you will win." During this same precompetitive period, the coach will deprecate the role of external and unstable factors, luck and poor officiating, although at times he will dwell on the unstable and external factor of the opponent's effort ("*They* will be trying hard").

The more sensitive coach, however, might give attention to subtle factors operating in the pregame situation related to the formation of causal attributions by his team members. These notions include: (1) Not all the athletes are thinking alike about the causes of possible success or failure. (2) A given athlete may be thinking about more than one cause for possible outcomes of the competition. (3) What an athlete may be voicing may not be a true reflection of thoughts.

Thus the coach, rather than limiting himself or herself only to group pep talks, should approach each athlete prior to the contest and ask such questions as, "How do *you* feel about what is going to happen?" The answers may lead the coach to deal in depth with an athlete's motivational framework in positive ways.

During the anxiety-ridden precompetition period, the coach who communicates best with athletes, and who receives the most valid answers in return, is likely to be one who has continually passed an "honesty test" informally given by all athletes to their coaches. An honest coach, many athletes feel, is one who does not consistently either underrate or overrate opponents in attempts to "fool" them into winning. An honest coach is one who accurately assesses the real ability of his or her own athletes and helps them to set reasonable, achievable goals, whether that includes winning or reaching some personal best.

An important part of how the athletes view the coach and his or her attempts to deal with their motives prior to a game or contest revolves around how they have been prepared both physically and psychologically. Much of the success in any athletic contest, as everyone well knows, comes about because of preparations made well *before* the contest. Mindless and last-minute exhortations to "try harder and you will win" are likely to fall on deaf ears of the more sophisticated contemporary athlete of any age.

Following Competition

Immediately following competition, the causes an athlete attaches to success or failure may differ from those formulated in a more serene context a day or two following the event.[3] Some of the time an athlete or team, just after losing a game, will blame transitory and unstable external causes for defeat (bad luck, officiating, the ball bounced funny, etc.). However, after having time to reflect, together perhaps with counseling from coach and friends, they may change their minds and attribute the loss to factors within themselves, which are either stable or unstable (ability or effort).

Also, a few days after a defeat, a talk by the coach may aid an athlete to correctly perceive that more than one cause may have contributed to lack of success, including perhaps not only the superior ability or effort of an opponent but his own lack of effort or even of ability. While attribution theorists often classify personal ability as a stable cause, most coaches are aware that with proper training methods, apparently stable ability may be changed over time.

[3]The modification of causal attributes over time has not been dealt with extensively by theorists at this point, to this writer's knowledge.

It is also true that in an athletic competition an athlete or team may meet a single opponent more than once, and that an opponent is also constantly in the process of formulating reasons for success or failure. Thus, the more perceptive coach, or team psychologist, can help athletes try to determine how their opponents may have perceived reasons for success or failure during initial confrontations, and how the reasons formulated by the opposition can be somehow used against them in future contests. For example, their opponents upon winning initially may perceive that they have won through superior ability, rather than because of lack of effort of the opposition. The coach may suggest: "Your opponents, having defeated you once, will tell themselves that you just weren't good enough (a stable and external attribute), whereas it is likely that you lost because you did not try hard enough (an unstable attribute). Thus, if you try harder next time you might win, because of both your real ability and their complacency."

Following a winning or successful contest, the athlete may formulate reasons for success that may be harmful or helpful psychologically in future competitions with the same or a different opponent. It again may be the task of the coach or team counselor to aid the athlete to make realistic assessments about success, and armed with this realism, enhance the chances for future success. For example, it may be true that the success of an athlete was due to a unstable attribute, lack of effort on the part of an opponent. Thus, if the athlete believes that his or her ability (an internal and stable factor) was the reason for winning the first time, he may be less prepared for a rematch when next confronting the same opponent, who may try even harder when next they meet.

Additional Considerations

A number of additional factors should be kept in mind when attempting to untangle the numerous variables that determine how athletes view victory and defeat. For example, mediating causes may be present in the athlete's emotional make-up, moods and traits that trigger either realistic or unrealistic reasons the athlete formulates for winning or losing. With penetrating discussion, the competitor may reveal just why he or she seems to decide on certain causes.

The athlete may, for example, although at the pinnacle of physical ability, believe that he or she is not good enough to win much of the time. Thus, the athlete may decide that when winning does occur, it is due to an opponent's good luck, his own good luck, or to the opponent's lack of effort, rather than to his or her actual abilities. To use the language of the attribution theorist, the athlete may attribute victory to unstable and stable external causes, rather than to stable internal causes.

On the other hand, the athlete may have a distorted sense of his or her own abilities, and thus view failure as due to bad luck, superior or unusual effort by opponents, or other external uncontrollable causes, rather than to his own inferior abilities and/or lack of effort.

"Mediating causes" for distortions in the formulation of causes for success and failure may be temporary mood states, triggered by personal problems. It is important for the coach or team counselor to be aware of these problems, which may affect not only the causes formulated but also actual defeat or victory. Indeed, revelation of personal problems may come about because the coach listens closely to distortions in causes the athlete attaches to winning and losing efforts. Relief of the problem usually results in more realistic appraisals of personal defeat and victory. Thus, the coach should not only attempt to determine the reasons behind the athlete's feelings about victory and defeat, but also to ascertain the reasons behind the reasons!

SUMMARY

This chapter has illustrated now an individual's judgments about the reasons for success and failure affect future performance and helped the reader formulate helpful ways to deal with information postulated by causal attribution theorists and the principles they advocate.

Attribution theory contains several postulates, including: (1) People act as their own psychologists, postulating reasons that influence their success and failure on tasks. (2) These reasons, or causes, may be arranged on several scales, including reasons which are internal or external to the individual, causes that are stable or unstable, intentional or unintentional. Furthermore, it is assumed that more successful individuals attribute their success to relatively stable internal causes, while the less successful attribute failures and successes to less or more stable external causes.

Within these theoretical assumptions, the reader has been encouraged to seek implications helpful for working with the motivational make-up of athletes. These assumptions have included: (1) The athlete is not a passively performing organism, but a thinking being who constantly reflects about why he or she is winning or losing. (2) At times, the coach may aid the athlete to formulate productive and realistic reasons for success or failure, reasons that may later result in optimum performance. (3) Each athlete, because of unique emotional make-up, present problems, and past successes and failures, is likely to formulate a personal list of causes for success or failure. (4) More than one cause may be attributed to either a successful or unsuccessful confrontation. (5) An awareness of these variables makes the coach a more productive counselor and motivator of those in his or her charge.

QUESTIONS FOR DISCUSSION

1. How does cognitive theory relate to the discussion of motivation in Chapter V?
2. Trace the history of attribution theory.
3. What are the basic assumptions underlying attribution theory? Upon what continuums are perceived attributes projected by this theory?
4. What shifts in attributions might occur after winning vs. after losing? What differences in attributions might be found if successful vs. unsuccessful athletes and teams were polled?
5. What meanings might a coach derive from the findings that apply attribution theory to sport? How might he or she attempt to mold the perceptions of athletes in positive ways, after success and failure experiences, relative to causes of inferior vs. superior performance?
6. What kind of attributes of consistently successful people generally apply to their performances? What kind of attributes are consistently voiced by the less successful individual?
7. Are the reasons voiced by people those which are actually believed by them to have influenced success or failure? Discuss.
8. How might concepts within attribution theory be applied to athletes prior to a contest? After a contest?
9. What kind of situational and personality variables are likely to influence voiced attributes for winning or losing experiences?

BIBLIOGRAPHY

CRATTY BJ: *Social Dimensions of Physical Activity.* Englewood Cliffs, New Jersey, Prentice-Hall, 1967.

ELIG T, FRIEZE IH: A multi-dimensional scheme for coding and interpreting perceived causality for success and failure events: The CSPC. *JSAS Catalog of Selected Documents in Psychology,* 5:313 (ms no. 1069), 1975.

FRIEZE IH, MCHUGH M, DUQUIN M: "Causal Attributions for Women and Men and Sports Participation, paper at the American Psychological Association, Convention Washington D.C., 1976.

HEIDER R: *The Psychology of Interpersonal Relations.* New York, Wiley, 1958.

HOPPE F: Erfolg und Misserfolg. *Psych Forsch* 14 (1930), 1–62.

KELLEY HH: Attribution theory in social psychology. In Levin D. (ed): *Nebraska Symposium on Motivation* 15, Lincoln, University of Nebraska.

MANN J: On being a sore loser: how fans react to their team's failure. *Aust J Psychol* 26 (1974), 37–47.

MARTENS R: Internal-external control and social reinforcement effects of motor performance. *Res Q* 42: 3, 307–313.

PASSER MW: Perceiving the causes of success and failure revisited: a multidimensional scaling approach. Unpublished doctoral dissertation, UCLA, 1977.

ROBERTS GC: Effect of achievement motivation and social environment on risk taking. *Res Q* 45:1 (March 1974), 49–55.

ROSENBAUM RM: A dimensional analysis of the perceived causes of success and failure. Unpublished doctoral dissertation, UCLA, 1972.

ROTTER JB: Generalized expectancies for internal versus external control of reinforcement. *Psych Monogr* 80 (1966), 1–28.

WEINER B, RUSSELL D, LERMAN D: Affective consequences of causal ascriptions. In Harvey JH, Ickes WJ, Kidd RF (eds): *New Directions in Attribution Research*, 2. Hillsdale, New Jersey, Erlbaum Press, 1978.

WEINER B, KUKLA A: An attributional analysis of achievement motivation. *J Person Soc Psychol* 15:1 (1970), 1–20.

7

Group Motives and Aspirations

Questions dealing with the motivation of athletes are among those most frequently asked by coaches during their confrontations with behavioral scientists. At times, their queries are answered with candor, but the information offered is not usually undergirded by data obtained within the athletic environment.

Moreover, the questions themselves often lack precision and perspective. For example, statements that search for a single athlete's motives often ignore the fact that a group's (the team's) motives may be different from those of a single athlete. Coaches' questions regarding motivation are many times actually attempts to gain information about how to activate or arouse athletes. Motivation is the study of why people do what they do; often, coaches are intent on discovering how to make athletes try harder, a concept that usually involves heightening activation levels.

Numerous operational and situational variables may influence group motivation, factors that are not always under the control of the coach. For example, in the study by Goldberg and Maccoby (1965), the stability of the group membership was studied as influential of group productivity. As might be expected, it was found that groups that were more stable and engaged in continual interaction performed more effectively than did groups with a constantly changing membership. The same principle may hold true among teams whose membership remains relatively stable.[1]

[1]Chapter IV, "Changes in Team Membership and Team Composition," in Cratty, BJ, Hanin, Y: *The Athlete and the Sports Team,* Love Publishing Co. Denver, Colorado, 1980, deals in detail with interpersonal problems among teams whose membership changes.

The forces, circumstances, and variables that influence goal setting, motivational structure, and aspirations of *individuals* seem at times to act in different ways within a *group of athletes.*

Research dealing with motivation comprises approximately one-third of the available scholarly literature in psychology and social psychology, with the remaining two-thirds almost equally divided among learning and perception. Surprisingly few studies, however, have focused on group motives. In the 1960s, however, a few programs of research were initiated focusing on the group and its motivational dynamics. Some of the questions this research raised, as well as the answers it produced, have relevance for athletic teams.

As described in the previous chapter, during the 1950s and 1960s there was a gradual evolution of thought, stemming from early studies of aspiration level and arriving at various cognitive determiners of motivation and effort, as represented by attribution theory. During these years, physical tasks were often employed when individuals' motives were evaluated. In studies by Smith (1941) and by Clarke and Clarke (1961), for example, motor performance criteria were employed. Smith used football playing time, while Clarke and Clarke used a grip-strength test.

Numerous questions remained, however, concerning how groups engage in assessing their own motives and in formulating reasons for performing well. These include such questions as: Is a group simply a sum of the parts (individuals)? Can a sport team's motivation and achievement be surmised simply by adding the scores from individuals? Or is the whole different from the sum of the parts? Do groups behave in different ways than do individuals when they perceive themselves

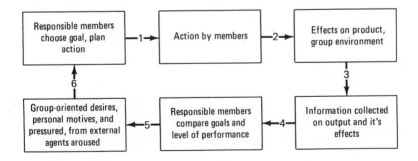

FIGURE 7-1.
Zander (1971), p. 5.

failing to meet or exceed expected norms? Do groups and individuals react in the same or in different ways to success?

A beginning can be seen in the work of Alvin Zander and his co-workers, carried out in the 1960s. Initially, Zander tried to find out how motives of group members, self-assessments of group productivity, and various external factors interact to form what he termed "group oriented desires." Using a "feedback model," Zander suggested that most important is the fact that a group's assessments of its efforts are related to the degree of correspondence between perceived performance and previous goal setting, rather than to any objective and fixed performance levels or criteria. Thus, Zander was influenced by Hoppe (1930) and others interested in goal setting, aspiration level, and achievement needs of individuals.

If differences between goals set and actual performance are too large, Zander hypothesized, adjustments in group aspirations are likely to be made, including: (1) future group aspirations will be lowered, (2) the group will try harder during subsequent efforts, or even (3) the group will reject actual performance levels attained, an emotional and perceptual distortion seen in the dynamics of individuals as well as groups. These processes have been diagrammed by Zander in Figure 7-1.

An even more elaborate representation of Zander's basic ideas may be represented in Figure 7-2.

Zander has also represented the way the group goal for a member and that member's goal for himself or herself may interact (Figure 7-3). In this model, Zander suggests that there are at least two sets of properties: on the left, variables involving the individual member's goals, and on the right, the group goals. He thus infers that researchers must recognize variables and problems lying within each of the four boxes. Data from Zander's experiments, using these models, appear in his book *Group Motives* (1971).

Measuring Group Motivation
and Aspiration Levels

At times, sport psychologists have employed questionnaire methods to evaluate group morale in teams and group motivation. Some of these are described in *The Athlete in the Sports Team* (1980) by Cratty and Hanin. Zander, however, employed a task in many of his studies which was an interesting modification of one used earlier by Rotter (1942) and others.

In the device shown in Figure 7-4, Rotter had his single subject push a ball bearing up an inclined groove, using the stick. It was intended to come to rest within one of several numbered, scooped-out half-circles. Thus, over- or underestimations could be corrected for on subsequent trials by pushing harder or softer, as seemed called for.

Zander's efforts to evaluate group aspiration and goal setting were carried out by considerably enlarging the device shown, so that up to six subjects could be made to work together in various ways, pushing

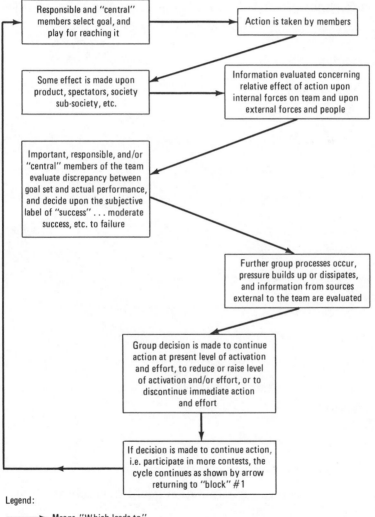

Legend:

———▶ Means, "Which leads to"...

FIGURE 7-2.   Group decisions and motives.

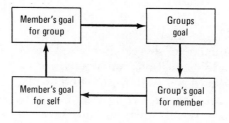

FIGURE 7-3.   Relations among individual and group goals.
From Zander (1971), p. 5.

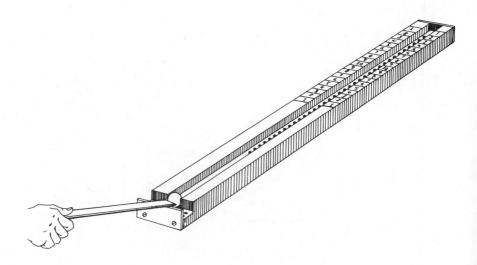

Figure 7-4.   View of the aspiration board with subject poised to
roll the steel bearing.

Rotter, *J Exp Psych*, V. 31, 1942, Level of aspiration as a method of
studying personality), 31 (1942), 413.

a larger ball up an expanded ramp. The ramp was 12 in long, while the pole used to push the ball was a 6-in aluminum rod, which could be grasped by three to six subjects.

In a fascinating group of experiments, subjects were informed that they were to take part in studies focused on a special ability termed "teamwork in muscular control." It was further explained to them that teamwork occurs in many contexts including flying an airplane, running a computer, and playing on a professional ball team. Among the variables imposed upon the subjects included spuriously "wiring up" the handle in order to "detect" the exact effort expended by each boy subject, manipulating the amount of information each team received about what was a reasonably good score, and the like. Usually, ten trials were permitted with a possible score of 50 attainable. Group scores, and guesses about subsequent trials, were recorded and compared to individual scores obtained as team members worked alone on the task.

In a series of studies by Zander and his co-workers, both objective as well as subjective data were recorded. For example, informal notations were made concerning the degree and kind of verbal interactions that transpired during and between trials. When aspirations and estimates were either met or failed to be met, these also were recorded. At other times, group scores were announced at intervals (after every trial or series of trials). An interesting use was made of *consensus feelings* about what the group might be expected to do, in contrast to the accuracy of the performance measures later expressed.

Zander and his colleagues also studied individual and group goal setting, in contrast to performance, by obtaining records of charity fund-raising efforts by individuals in various parts of the United States. They looked at the way these kinds of goals (estimates of how much could be collected in the future) were influenced by past efforts. Zander's assumptions concerning group motives were also based on how projected sales quotas of beer salesmen were related to their actual sales records.

One could speculate that the laboratory task described, as well as the other measures used by Zander, are dissimilar from tasks found in athletics. However, data collected in the three contexts described tended to be similar in nature. Thus, these experiments may reflect rather common qualities influencing group motivational states, which are consistent despite modifications in task, and generalizations from these studies to the sports arena may not be too far-fetched.

Zander found both similarities and differences in the way groups and individuals react to performance and goal setting, and in general reflect motivational tendencies. For example, he found that: (1) Both individuals and groups adjust goals upward after success and downward after failure in similar ways. A difference was seen, however, in the tendency for groups to be slightly less likely to revise estimates of future performance downward after failure. The group, in contrast to individuals, tends to resist reacting to failure. These findings held true whether the group consisted of three or five members. (2) The averages obtained from group members individually, when asked to predict performance, closely approximated those of the group estimation taken collectively in the ball-pushing laboratory task. (3) There is more consistency among groups in the way they raise aspirations upward after success than in the way they lower estimates downward after failure. That is, a group can be more counted upon to raise goals after success than they can be to lower aspirations after failure. Again the group seems to resist perceiving a single failure experience as critical.

To explain these and other findings, Zander has formulated two postulates: (1) As practice and goal setting takes place, a group's feelings about the possibility of success (POS) rises. (2) As a group fails to meet expected goals and finds a task more and more difficult, scores reflecting probability of failure also increase. Or as Zander phrases it, their subjective probability of failure (SPF) increases.

Furthermore, group satisfaction is greater when success has been achieved on a task perceived as difficult than when a group has been successful in a task they believe to be easy. Finally, the tendency for groups to fail to lower scores as quickly after failure as do individuals is explained by Zander as an attempt by the members to keep at a minimum negative feelings within the group. As would be expected, negative feelings are not as marked after a group has failed at a task they perceived as difficult, than after it has failed at what was perceived as easier.

Zander's findings are similar to those from a study by Emerson (1966), evaluating social-psychologic interactions within a group attempting to climb Mount Everest in 1963. Both Zander under laboratory conditions and Emerson evaluating field data found that a group's motivation and goal setting remain high if two conditions are present: (1) the goal of the group is absolutely clear to all concerned, and (2) they perceive their chances of reaching the goal are neither too easy nor too difficult.

This tendency toward seeking and setting intermediate and attainable goals has been noted in the chapter dealing with individual motivation. It is reflected in Zander's data, as well as in findings by Emerson that studied the goal setting of the leaders in the Everest expedition. He found that the leaders tended to keep group morale and motivation high by (1) making the more easily traversed trail to the top seem slightly more difficult than it actually was and (2) by suggesting to the members that the more difficult line of ascent could be traversed with effort, and was not as insurmountable as some might have thought. Thus, with this intermediate goal setting, group success is followed by heightened group self-esteem and self-respect.

In an effort to answer questions about the "whys" of individual achievement need formation in groups, Zander suggests that several variables are important:

1. How the individual perceives the group's needs for achievement as a totality. For example, Zander falsified average achievement need scores of groups and found that spurious information of this type molded achievement expectations of individuals.

2. Degree of conformity of achievement needs was also found to be greater after success than after failure. That is, individuals seem to react in a more unpredictable and variable way to group failure than to group success.

3. Challenging tasks seem to elicit more uniform aspiration levels and achievement needs than do tasks that are less challenging.

This final statement reflects an interest several researchers in this country and abroad have had in the nature of the uniformity of achievement needs among group members as related to performance success.

Klein and Christensen (1969) have found that athletic teams whose members uniformly evidence high levels of aspiration usually outperform those whose members evidence uniformly low levels of aspiration, as would be expected. More important, however, their data reflect that the team whose members evidenced variability of achievement needs (some with high and some with low) generally outperformed teams whose members evidenced uniformly high achievement needs.

Data of this nature have several possible practical implications for the coach. In general, it indicates that the coach might search for combinations of closely interacting sports teams in which all do not perceive themselves as stars. A sports team should be composed of supporting players as well as those who need to constantly exhibit their talent. Someone must pass to the talented forwards in hockey and soccer, and subordinate their success to the more visible success of others, and of the total team. Coaches of some of the more successful teams in the United States tend to follow this general rule of team selection, looking for subordinate as well as ascendant players, independent of physical ability traits.

External Influences on Group Goal Setting

Group aspirations and team achievement are engendered not only by dynamics within the group itself but also by a variety of external social conditions.

It has been hypothesized, for example, that the reluctance of groups to lower their estimations after failure is due to group pressures or social pressures to succeed. Additionally, pressures from the social perceptions of other teams in a league can influence group aspirations, goal setting, and motivation.

Reflecting this were findings from one of Zander's ball-rolling studies, intended to determine how comparative processes influence group goal setting. The subjects were given information concerning the "average score" (a fictitious one) obtained by other groups in the task, just before each trial and just before they chose their next performance goal.

Two experimental conditions were present in the study. (1) One group was told that an unreasonably high average score was being achieved by all the groups (over 40 out of a possible 50). The groups were thus under pressure to achieve under unfavorable competitive conditions. (2) A second group was informed that the group average was unrealistically low (about 30 out of a possible 50). Thus, this second group continued to make estimates and perform under favorable conditions, and thought they were doing well.

A comparison was then made between the two groups determining how they tended to raise and lower goals after both success and failure experiences. It was found that the group who performed under favorable conditions (thinking they were exceeding group averages) tended to reduce the differences between their future estimations and their actual performance scores. On the other hand, the group facing unrealistically high, manufactured averages more often tended to raise their goals after success and lower them after failure. Thus, these experimental groups, as may be true on athletic teams, tended to react more to failure and success when they felt themselves at a disadvantage than when they were comfortable and happy with their level of performance. Further work using athletic teams would seem needed to confirm these assumptions in the field, however.

Observer Goals and Group Aspirations

An important source of stimulation on group behaviors is the way observers behave and otherwise interact with performers in a group. Zander (1965), using high school boys performing the ball-rolling task, studied a portion of this kind of phenomenon. Using observers, Zander gave the teams false information concerning the watcher's expectations. In one case, he stated that the observers thought the team should do better than they were doing. A second group of teams was informed that their observers thought the groups were doing better than they thought possible.

Contrasting goal-setting behaviors has potential implications for athletic teams relative to the spectator effect.[2] Groups whose efforts were apparently being evaluated favorably tended more to raise their expectations after success. This was done even though observers' expectations were not reflected by the group's actual performance in over half the trials.

On the other hand, the groups who were evaluated negatively most of the time bested their observers' low goals. But the negative evaluations had a dampening effect on team goal setting. The latter groups were less likely to raise aspirations after success, while the groups who were evaluated positively by observers tended to resist lowering their goals after failure.

In the sports world, it is likely that spectator expectations have an effect on team goal setting. If a team perceives its efforts as being viewed negatively, goal setting may be blunted. A team who feels that "their" fans are truly behind them may resist lowering aspirations after a loss, and will also tend to persist in high goal setting even though the expectations set for them by others may not be reached all the time.

Experiments have also been carried out by Zander and others in which shifts in group motivation and goal setting have been studied, while real and manipulated opinions of groups external to those performing are inserted at various times during performance. The contexts of these studies are not the sports environment. In general, however, their findings may be summarized as follows:

1. Central and important members of groups are highly conscious of social pressures related to goal setting and are particularly sensitive to the social pressures present after failing performances are recorded.

2. Observers present in the same rooms, from whom negative estimates of a group's performance emanate, do not increase levels of aspiration. Thus, this kind of negative situation elicits more actual success as performance is continued and tends to exceed spectators' expectations.

3. The reverse also seems true. When observers voice high expectations, they generate high aspirations. However, in this situation there is a greater likelihood of failure, as actual performance does not reach either the group's level of aspirations or the goals voiced by spectators.

Transposing these findings to the sports world, it is possible that fans who generate high expectations for an athletic team may have a negative effect on team morale, as the team is less likely to match fans'

---

[2]This audience effect is also discussed in detail in Chapter VIII.

expectations to actual performance. Conversely, teams whose fans are not as enthusiastic about their possible success may experience more success under conditions that are not as pressure-ridden.

Furthermore, the research data indicate that if observers' expectations are reasonable, the group is more likely to be influenced by them than by norms set within the group for its own performance. On the other hand, expectations by observers that are perceived by a group as unrealistic encourage members to rely upon norms generated within the group, rather than becoming influenced by standards voiced by nonperforming spectators.

Overall, several conditions together influence group goal setting. These variables are relatively independent of one another, even though their effect tends to be additive. They include: (1) the attractiveness of rewards offered by spectators and observers, (2) whether the standards voiced by observers are false or realistic, (3) the congruence of the expectations of observers to the actual performance of the group, and (4) the satisfaction of the group members with their performance as reflected in the behavior of spectators.

The Motive to Avoid Failure

The need to avoid failure has been identified as an important subtopic in the extensive literature dealing with achievement needs. Generally, it is assumed that an individual who works hard because of the threat of failure is not as likely to achieve as much as one who strives to achieve success. At the same time, the need to avoid failure, and/or to avoid negative social judgments for one's effort, is a powerful incentive.

Athletic teams may also strive under the pressure of this negative motive. They may find themselves near the bottom of standings, for example, and work hard late in the season to finish better than last place. They are thus trying to avoid failure rather than attempting to achieve what may be unattainable—success, winning the league.

Data from the study of groups and their possible needs to avoid failure have been similar to data from studies in which individuals' motives have been scrutinized. For example, several studies have found that groups usually prefer to work under conditions that engender success rather than those that seem to prevent failure. In other words, the achievement of success seems to be a more dominant motive both in groups and in individuals than the need to avoid failure.

Individuals who are working hard to prevent failure are more likely to prefer group situations than those working alone. Anxiety-ridden individuals thus appear to gravitate toward company when competing, rather than performing by themselves. Thus it could be surmised that: (1) Individuals who are motivated to achieve success are more likely to gravitate toward individual sports than toward team sports. (2) The reverse may be true on the part of individuals who fear failure; they may prefer team to individual sports. However, these and other hypotheses about the need to avoid failure need further attention by researchers before definitive statements can be made with regard to athletics and athletes.

Motives for Group Success and Individual Needs for Success

Some research findings have made it increasingly apparent that there are personal preferences which indicate that people are either oriented toward achieving success for the group in which they participate or work hard to achieve personal success, relatively independent of the group. That is, some individuals value success from a rather selfish standpoint, while others seem to subordinate personal feelings and strive for group success.[3]

Zander and others have studied this kind of problem. In some studies they have contrasted the behaviors of individuals who strive for personal success and those who value group success. Other research has compared groups made up of individuals with a personal success motive and groups made up of people who value group success. The questionnaire used by Zander to classify people is on page 149. Each question forces a choice between satisfactions gained from team membership and personal feelings of achievement. It is interesting to note the number of questions which seem to relate to motor skills or sport.

Obviously, many variables may determine the degree to which an individual dwells upon personal vs. group achievement. Among these, according to Shaw (1960) and others, are: (1) the share individuals may perceive they contribute to the possible success or failure of the group, (2) the importance or "centrality" of the individual in the group, and (3) whether or not the task is likely to elicit anxiety. In this final instance, people usually prefer to subordinate themselves within a group situation and to identify with group success or failure.

[3]A chapter devoted to value systems is found in Cratty and Hanin: *The Athlete in the Sports Team*, 1980 (Chapter VIII, "Individual and Group Value Systems)," Denver, Colorado: Love Publishing Company.

Personal Preference Inventory

In the following questions, you are asked to choose between two things on the basis of your own personal preference. Answer each question by putting a check mark in the box beside the alternative which you most prefer. There are no right or wrong answers, so give the answer that suits you best.

1. If I had an important project to do for class and had a choice, I would rather
   _____ work on it with a few others as a group project
   _____ work on it on my own

2. I prefer to
   _____ do things on my own
   _____ do things while working with others

3. I think I generally am most efficient when
   _____ I work with a group
   _____ I work by myself

4. If I had to choose between them, I would prefer to be
   _____ the pilot of a single-seater military plane
   _____ the pilot of a military plane with a crew on board

5. If I were on the track team, I would rather
   _____ run as a member of the relay team
   _____ run in an individual race

6. I prefer to do my homework
   _____ alone in a room
   _____ in a room with others present

7. If I wanted to learn to play the guitar, I would rather
   _____ join a combo of beginners
   _____ practice at home in my room

8. If I were a medical research worker looking for the cause of a disease, I would like to
   _____ be a part of a team that makes an important discovery
   _____ make an important discovery on my own

9. When I play tennis or Ping-Pong I like
   _____ to play against another boy in a singles match
   _____ to join another boy in playing against two others

10. In sports, I like to take part in
    _____ team games like football, basketball, baseball, etc.
    _____ individual sports like wrestling, golf, swimming, or track

11. When there is a job to do, I get more satisfaction out of
    _____ getting my share done on my own
    _____ doing my share while working with a bunch of people

12. I find that I learn more
    _____ when I am a member of a student group planning a report for the class
    _____ when I plan my own report for class

Among the other findings obtained by Zander when using the questionnaire was that 65 percent of those completing the form indicated that they preferred to work for their own success, rather than for the success of a group. Little work has been done in the United States, using this kind of questionnaire, with sports teams. However, it could be surmised that the coach of an individual sport would have less of a problem with individuals having highly self-centered motives, as contrasted to the coach of a team sport attempting to work with those similarly inclined.

Among work groups or on athletic teams, some members become convinced that they are more competent that others. These individuals generally evidence more interest in the group and work harder for group success than do the less competent. The study of "feelings of competency" was carried out by Zander, using the ball-pushing task. The rod contained a series of wires and an impressive set of indicators at various points along its length where the subjects gripped the large instrument. This equipment, the subjects were informed, gave the experimenters a "clear picture of the competencies of each member." This purported competency was spuriously transmitted to each subject after the trials.

It was found that the feelings individuals had about group success depended on the perceptions they had about their own importance to the group. In sport, this "centrality" is often a function of the type of game played and the position the player occupies. More central players gain greater satisfaction when winning, work harder and more often than peripheral players, and equate their personal effort with the quality of the total group output. At times, these central members will subtly manipulate group goals to include those that are difficult (and thus worthwhile) but attainable.

Other findings obtained when using Zander's questionnaire have potential interest to the coach and athlete. For example, it was found that: (1) People with high needs for achievement and low needs to avoid failure (who are self-confident) are more likely to work for personal goals and not for group goals. (2) Those with high achievement needs would rather work in central than peripheral roles in groups. (3) Subjects who differed in their needs for affiliation did not seem to differ in their preferences for group work in which they would be rewarded, in contrast to working as individuals for the subsequent rewards. It therefore seems that the need to receive credit for success as an individual, or as a member of a group, is independent of the need simply to *be* with other people.

These findings hold up, even when experiments have been manipulated to give apparent success to those who need to achieve success or to avoid failure. Failure (manufactured) by those who have high achievement needs does not dissuade them from further striving through individual efforts. Manufactured success in those who manifest high needs to avoid failure does not significantly alter their preferences for subordinating individual efforts to group outcomes.

IMPLICATIONS FOR THE COACH

In general, the coach should expect that the group's motive, goal setting, and fluctuations in aspiration level will tend to be influenced in the same ways, and by similar social-psychologic forces, as those of individuals. Thus, success leads teams to set higher goals and to heighten aspiration, while the reverse is true when failure is continually encountered.

Most likely, the way the coach interacts with individuals in dispensing social rewards will be reflected in the way the total group reacts to praise or derision. At the same time, however, the team as a whole is less likely to evidence fluctuations in aspiration level as great as those in individuals following success (or the coach's appraisals of success) and failure.

The coach, however, may be in a position to aid team members to appraise themselves realistically and to set goals which are realistic and attainable. For example, the coach may find that as the team gains experience in competing together, members are more and more likely to evidence marked feelings about subsequent goal setting. Thus, the coach should expect the group feeling to heighten, for the group to react more intensely when they or others make estimations about future contests and competitions.

Moreover the coach, like leaders of other work groups who performed under stress, may heighten the team's success by giving them an accurate idea of the difficulty of the task. Distortion in either direction, stating that the coming competition is overly difficult or easy, is likely to lessen the team's appetite for the contest as well as lower their satisfaction with success. For the most success to be felt by a team, the coach should (1) ascertain the *real* strength of forthcoming opponents and (2) help the team believe that the task of overcoming them is difficult, but achievable.

The data discussed also have implications for dealing with a team after failure. More individual attention to players will probably be necessary after failure than after success. That is, after losing, members of groups are likely to evidence mood shifts than after winning.

The coach may also act as a buffer for external influences on the team's goal setting, the sports fans. If, for example, the team feels inordinate and perhaps unrealistic pressures to win, they may be less likely to satisfactorily adjust their goals downward after a loss than if no audience pressure for success was present. Thus, the perceptive coach may, if he thinks fan expectations prior to a contest are unrealistic, aid the team to perceive correctly just what future success might consist of. That is, success may be construed as achieving the team's optimum performance. If the team accepts this version of success and is able to cast off unrealistic influences of fans with the coach's help, their feelings after contests in which they did not win may be more emotionally healthy, upon which more positive attitudes may be constructed during the remainder of the season.

Realistic goal setting by the coach, with the help of the team, should also lead to fewer and less marked shifts in aspiration after both failure and success experiences. That is, the team as a whole, like the individual, is less likely to markedly shift aspirations upward after success, and downward after failure, if prior to the competition realistic group aspirations have been set and agreed on by all.

The group data reviewed also indicate that the coach may have to pay special heed to the emotional needs of his athletes during the final part of a less-than-successful season. That is, during this time in the competition, the team may be working to avoid failure (to not finish last in the standings) rather than to achieve success. This kind of negative striving is likely to be accompanied by heightened levels of anxiety, and thus may contribute to further losses rather than to optimum performance.

The data obtained by Zander suggest that the central and more competent figures on a team may appear as self-centered rather than group-oriented. At times, the coach may take exception to such an attitude, yet it seems inevitable and in line with expected findings. The central and more competent team members are likely to be achieving more for their own success than the group's success, and to take greater satisfaction when group winning takes place. It is obvious that the mannerisms of these central figures are likely to cause more "social dissonance" among athletes in team sports than in individual sports. In the latter case, both coach and team players seem more likely to tolerate an all-star attitude than are members and coaches of a sport requiring a close team effort.

At the same time, these central athletes should not be crushed by the coach. They do tend to work harder, and to be more important in overall success, than are the more peripheral individuals. Rather, the star should be encouraged to excel, work hard, and contribute to not only his or her own personal satisfactions but to the group effort. At times, the remainder of the team may have to be given special help to understand this apparently arrogant attitude on the part of one or more of the members.

SUMMARY

The chapter has summarized data dealing with group motives. The primary focus has been on the research program by Zander in which a motor task, participated in by three- to six-member teams, has been used to evaluate group motives in various ways.

Zander's theoretical framework includes references to achievement needs and to the need to avoid failure. In general, his research indicates that groups behave in much the same way as do individuals, when goal setting and when reacting to failure and success. However, the group is more likely to be resistant to negative evaluations by observers, as well as apparent failure in a task, when attempting the task (or another task) again. The group as a whole is less likely to adjust goals downward after failure.

Groups, like individuals, tend to set intermediate goals if their achievement needs are high. Additionally, leaders of groups will tend to adjust group goals to intermediate levels in order to obtain the most work from members. As would be expected, success in difficult tasks is highly prized by groups, in contrast to success in tasks perceived as easy.

Satisfaction with group goals will depend on whether or not the individual has high achievement needs, and the degree to which the individual perceives himself as a central member of the group with some degree of influence on the group's performance. Less competent group members and/or those with the fear of failure are more likely to adhere to group goals than are the more competent or those with high achievement needs.

Throughout the chapter, inferences were made relative to coaching and to the athletic team in general. However, these inferences will become valid only with the production of research specifically focused on the sports world, which at this point is lacking.

QUESTIONS FOR DISCUSSION

1. How do group motives differ from those of individuals? How are they similar?
2. What information in the chapter might be of interest to a coach of a winning team toward the end of the season? Of interest to a losing coach at the same time in the season?

3. What might a team be like whose membership includes many who are working to avoid failure, rather than to achieve success?

4. What effects do negative evaluations of others have upon a team that has achieved success *vs.* a team which has avoided failing?

5. What might be the negative outcomes emanating from fans who expect an average team to do extremely well in competition?

6. What might be the advantages and disadvantages to an average team whose fans do not expect even average performance in competition?

7. How do central, important members of sports teams react to questionnaires that attempt to ascertain whether they are more interested in group *vs.* individual goals and efforts?

8. What implications can you draw from the information in the chapter for the coach of an individual sport? For the coach of a team sport?

9. How is group motivation evaluated? Can you think of other ways, in an athletic context, than those cited in the chapter?

10. What findings from the experimental data cited might be applied to sports teams? What data might not be applied with validity to sport?

BIBLIOGRAPHY

ATKINSON JW, FEATHER NT (eds): *A Theory of Achievement Motivation*. New York, Wiley, 1966.

BRYAN JF, LOCKE EA: Goal setting as a means of increasing motivation. *J Appl Psychol* 51:3 (1976), 274–277.

CLARKE HH, CLARKE DH: Relationships between level of aspiration and selected physical factors of boys aged nine years. *R Q* 32 (1961), 12–19.

COWEN J: Test anxiety in high school students and its relationship to performance in group tests. Unpublished doctoral dissertation, School of Education, Harvard University, 1957.

CRATTY BJ: *Social Dimensions of Physical Activity*. Chapter 2, "Aspiration Level." Englewood Cliffs, New Jersey, Prentice-Hall, 1967.

———, HANIN, Y.: *The Athlete in the Sport Team*. Denver, Colorado: Love Publishing Company, 1980.

ELIAS N, DUNNING E: Dynamics of group sports with special reference to football. *Br J Sociol* 4 (1966), 388–402.

EMERSON RM: Mount Everest: a case study of communication feedback and sustained group goal-striving. *Sociometry* 3 (1966), 213–227.

GOLDBERG MH, MACCOBY EE: Children's acquisition of skill in performing a group task under two conditions of group formation. *J Pers Soc Psychol* 2:6 (1965), 898–902.

HOPPE E: Erfolg und Misserfolg. *Psych Forsch* 14 (1930), 1–62.

KLEIN M, CHRISTENSEN G: Gruppenstruktur and Effektivität von Basketballmannschaften (Group composition, group structure and effectiveness of basketball teams). In Gunther L (ed): Kleingruppenforschung und Gruppen in Sport. Köln, Westdeutscher Verlag, 1966 (translated and reprinted in Loy JW, Kenyon GS (eds): *Sport, Culture and Society.* New York, MacMillan, 1969).

MARTENS R: Influence of participation motivation on success and satisfaction in team performance. *R Q* 41:4 (1970), 510–520.

————. The influence of success and residential affiliation on participation motivation. *J Leisure Res* 3:1 (Winter 1971).

McCLELLAND DC: Toward a theory of motive acquisition. *Am Psychol* 20:5 (1965), 321–333.

MURRAY HA: *Explorations in Personality.* New York, Oxford University Press, 1938.

RAVEN BH, RIETSEMA J: The effects of varied clarity of group goal and group task upon the individual and his relation to his group. *Hum Rel* 10 (1957), 29–44.

ROTTER JB: Level of aspiration as a method of studying personality. *J Exp Psychol* 31 (1942), 410–422.

SHAW DM: Size of share in task, and motivation in work groups. *Sociometry* 23 (1960), 203–208.

SMITH CH: Influence of athletic success and failure on the level of aspiration. *R Q* 20 (1941), 196–200.

WEINER B: *Theories of Motivation: From Mechanism to Cognition.* New York, Random House, 1972

ZANDER A: *Motives and Goals in Groups.* New York, Academic Press, 1971.

————, MEDOW H: Individual and group levels of aspiration. *Hum Rel* 16 (1963), 89–105.

————, MEDOW H, EFRON R: Observers' expectations as determinants of group aspirations. *Hum Rel* 18 (1965), 273–287.

8

Aggression in Sport

Aggressive behavior is not unique to a single species, nor is it limited in time, or to specific nations or regions. Aggression and hostile reactions are instrumental in the "sorting out" that stratifies members of animal communities. Aggressive hunting behaviors of our primitive ancestors are antecedents of strivings that find contemporary outlets in intellectual, commercial, and artistic endeavors by modern man.

Aggression and hostility were concerns of the ancients, as they attempted to formulate rules for compatible living, documented in the earliest records of civilization. Within the past decade, interest in human aggression has prompted a number of studies from laboratories of social psychologists, as well as countless writings of ethnologists, cultural anthropologists, psychiatrists, criminologists, and others interested in this fascinating and often dangerous component of the personality. More recently, psychologists and social psychologists interested in sport have focused their attention on aggressive behaviors in athletes, fans, and coaches.

Aggression is not always an obvious social phenomenon. An individual, for example, may engage in a good deal of aggressive behavior directed inward, toward himself. Some would argue, however, that even self-directed aggression is instigated to a large degree by social variables.

For the most part, aggression has rather pointed and important social connotations. Individuals or groups many times produce conditions that instigate or magnify aggression in people. Aggression may also imply hostility initiated by one member of a group against one or more persons. Thus, the study of aggression is and has been a legitimate part of the study of social psychology.

A search for a definition of aggression in the literature produces more questions than answers. For example, is aggression synonymous with the inflicting of injury? One of the early definitions by Dollard, Dobb, and their colleagues (1939) implied that the two concepts are closely intertwined. May one be aggressive with a look or gesture only mildly suggestive of dislike, as has been suggested by Scott (1968)? Must physical contact occur in order to be counted as an aggressive act, or may the voicing of a *threat* to do harm be enough? Some of the leading scholars writing on this subject differ in their answers to these and similar queries. One authority even suggests that aggressive behavior is simply a magnification of intellectual, work, and/or verbal behaviors.

Another difficult question, in life, politics, and sport, is what constitutes an optimum amount of aggression. What are desirable levels, and when are these levels exceeded? In some sports, for example, it is usually implied that some optimum level of aggression has been exceeded if the athlete's performance is impaired in some way.

Some contemporary work by sport psychologists in several countries has focused upon problems that might be termed "probability" research. They have tried to "tease out" the variables that lead to high probabilities of aggression in sport competitions. The measures of aggression have ranged from hostile verbal exchanges, to fights, to the number of fouls committed.

Another dimension of this problem area is the suggestion that various sports differ in both the amount and the nature of aggression for their optimum execution. In a previous text by the author a scale was formulated representing this variation. The following diagram attempts to depict varying degrees and types of aggression and additionally shows sports that purportedly fall at various points on the continuum. A modified version of this diagram appears below in Figure 8–1.

Degree	Direct aggression encouraged	Limited aggression	Indirect aggression	Aggression vs. objects, apparatus	Little observed aggression
	┼	┼	┼	┼	┼
Examples	Boxing, American football, Thialand kick boxing	Basketball, soccer	Handball, tennis	Golf, apparatus gymnastics	Ice skating, free exercise

FIGURE 8-1. A scale depicting varying amounts of aggressive behavior in sports.

Thus, in analyses contained later in this chapter, the relationships and interpretations should be interpreted with reference to this type of scale.

Some of the answers to questions about aggression are not found in neatly stacked research journals. Rather, they depend on the philosophy of coach, athlete, or athletic administrator. Coaches differ, for example, as to how much aggression an athlete should display. They are not in agreement as to whether an athlete should stay just within the rules, or whether the rules should be "bent" to some degree. However, in the sections that follow, some tentative answers to the following queries will be attempted, conclusions that are beginning to emerge in the presently available literature.

1. What causes excess aggression in sport? What constitutes optimum, as well as excessive, aggression?

2. What variables or factors, taken together or operating individually, tend to optimize the probabilities that aggression will occur?

3. What type of individual differences are seen in the temperaments of athletes who are aggressive, in contrast to those who remain self-controlled during athletic competitions? What personality traits, if any, are related to aggressive tendencies? What maturational and sex differences seem related to aggressive behaviors in sport?

4. What type of intellectual machinations are likely to elicit or suppress aggressive behaviors? How do the perceptions of situations, of one's opponents, influence the probabilities that aggression will occur? How does an individual's perceptions of the victim of aggression influence aggressive behavior?

5. What is the nature of immediate, in contrast to delayed, retaliation to an aggressive act? What other time dimensions exist within the cause-effect chain of aggressive and retaliatory behaviors?

6. What conditions, training, or other factors tend to reduce or otherwise ameliorate hostile acts, in life and in sport?

7. Whare are the relationships between competition, frustration, and subsequent aggression in sport and in other situations?

In order to examine these and related questions, the material that follows has been divided in the following manner. Initially, various theories of aggression are examined. Next, the chapter contains a large section delving into the causes of aggression. Situational variables, pre-performance conditions, and individual physical and psychologic factors are examined. Woven into this part of the discussion are brief explanations of the ways aggression and hostility have been measured. A third section contains a review of the limited data reflecting the way fitness, arousal-activation, and physical activity may interact with hostile behaviors. A fourth section contains the results of studies dealing with aggression and sport. The conditions that seem to heighten aggression in both athletes and fans are discussed in this part of the chapter. The final part of the chapter discusses how aggression and hostility can be dealt with in positive ways by coaches, athletic administrators, and athletes.

DEFINITIONS AND THEORIES

Definitions

In earlier reviews of the subject, the definition often cited is that by Dollard and his colleagues (1939), which suggests that aggression is "any sequence of behavior, the goal of which is to do injury to the person toward whom it is delivered." Many writers since that time have emphasized the intent of the aggressor, not solely whether actual harm is inflicted or not, in their attempts to define this elusive term. Moreover, the recent research also attempts to ascertain motives, as studies have focused upon how the victim assesses the aggressor's motives when formulating reasons and possible plans for retaliation.

More recent scholars have divided the term into "reactive aggression," in which there is a conscious attempt to injure a person or persons, and "instrumental aggression," a form frequently found in sport, in which the attempt is made to secure some reward or achieve some goal in a forceful manner, without any malice directed toward another person.

In a similar classification system, Berkowitz and Feshback (1970) also proposed that there are two different kinds of aggression: *instrumental aggression,* behavior aimed at securing rewards other than human suffering, and *hostile aggression,* whose sole aim is to inflict injury. Later in this chapter, the perceptions of sportsmen who receive aggression are discussed. However, usually more hostile reactions will emanate from a victim who perceives that hostile rather than instrumental aggression is being employed, even though the behavior of the aggressor may be remarkably similar in two situations.

Committing an aggressive act may have many outcomes for the aggressor, including material rewards as well as the improvement of social status. Wishing to degrade an opponent may be as powerful a motive as are material rewards that may rest upon victory. Thus, Bandura (1973) further expands the definition of aggression, as he includes not only behavior that may inflict personal injury and destruction of property but also acts that may injure another psychologically. Moreover, he suggests that to fully understand aggression one must consider both behavior that injures another and the *social judgments* made by the victim. These in turn determine which acts are felt to be physically and/or psychologically injurious.

Johnson (1972) also views aggression as a multidimensional concept. At one point, he asks if aggression *can* be defined, considering a myriad of human situations to which observers might attach the term. In sport situations also, a variety of aggressive behaviors may be seen, from excessive aggression, in the form of a fight in football, to psychological aggression reflected in insulting remarks to an opponent before or after a contest. Hard hitting, within the rules of boxing or American football, is also considered aggressive, but most would label it *instrumental.*

In the discussions that follow, the reader may attempt to match the principles and findings presented with various sports situations. The term *aggression* should be viewed in a flexible manner, reflecting behaviors that are often situationally specific.

Theories of Aggression

Since the turn of the century, scholars have attempted to formulate theories and models to explain the causes and effects of human hostility and aggression. Some of these explanations fall within the theoretical models covered in the first chapter of the book. The more viable models of aggression, however, seem to be in a constant state of flux. Many are refined continually as contemporary data illuminate, in more and more detail, the causes of and outcomes of human aggression.[1]

Freud (1920) first wrote that aggressive behavior is the result of the blocking of either pleasure-seeking or pain-avoiding behavior. In later writings, aggression was conceived of as an inborn drive, rather than the result of the frustration of strivings for pleasure or avoidance of pain.

This instinctual approach prompted Freud (1950) to adopt the pessimistic view that aggression is unavoidable in humans, and that thus it is relatively fruitless to attempt to reduce or eliminate it. He did suggest, however, that the development of emotional ties between people could lessen its impact, as could regulatory devices, including discharging of aggressive impulses through vigorous and "harmless" sport.

Even among his more avid supporters, Freud's ideas about aggression won few accolades. It was simply not credible to most that inborn impulses constantly prompt people to strive toward their own destruc-

---

[1]The subject of animal aggression has been reviewed by John Scott and Roger Johnson, as well as others, and will be dealt with extensively here.

tion. Experimenters also began to find that aggressive behavior could be prompted by innumerable conditions and situations, and also reduced in various ways, thus weakening the instinctual argument advanced by Freud.

Frustration-Aggression Hypothesis

One of the more popular theories of the 1940s and 1950s was first proposed by Dollard and his colleages in 1939. Although they borrowed ideas from Freud, they rejected the concept of aggression as an expression of a death wish, or the idea that instincts prompted aggressive behavior. Instead, they linked aggression to various psychologic "events" which, to them, apparently preceded most aggressive acts. The primary reason for aggression, they proposed, was frustration.

This argument gained the attention of researchers in the two decades that followed, and they probed into a variety of frustrating conditions, while studying the outcomes relative to aggression. Their findings began to illustrate that:

1. Frustration is not always followed by aggression.
2. Not only is frustration difficult to quantify and define, but it also appears in many forms and is partly a function of how a single individual views a situation.
3. Whether or not an individual reacts to frustration by exhibiting hostile behavior may be due to one or more of many variables, including the personality of the one frustrated, the type of frustration experienced, and even the measure of aggression employed. The favorite measure (now deemed unethical) was the administration of real or sham electric shocks to an actual or a "sham" victim. The measure of aggression was often the intensity of the shock the aggression "gave" to the victim, on a 1–10 or 1–20 scale.

Some have theorized that competitive sport, by its very nature, produces frustration. Someone must inevitably lose in a competitive situation. Thus, frustrated losers are always aggressive, it has been reasoned. However, since common sense experience suggests that losers are not always aggressive in obvious ways, the frustration hypothesis is further weakened, according to many observers.

Studies in sport and other areas of life have continued to reflect the preoccupation of some researchers with this theory. Rocha and his colleagues (1976), for example, found that children of 5 and 6 years of age exhibited physical, verbal, and "interference" aggression when competing, as well as when high levels of reward were present. Even more recently, they presented a case study in which a child experiencing a frustrating childhood began to emulate a boxer and engage in fistfights with adults to form an aggressive-like outlet for her frustrations. Further work of this nature, delving not only into childhood but also into the nature of contemporary sport situations that are frustrating to athletes (the end of a game in which the favored team is losing), should not cancel out the frustration-aggression hypothesis, but should result in more precise statements than are presently found in the literature. It is obvious that sometimes frustration does indeed cause aggression (or at least is followed by it). Thus, the problem becomes (1) to ascertain why frustration does not always lead to obvious aggression, (2) to determine what preconditions have made frustration more intolerable to an individual who aggresses, and (3) to find out what other variables combined with frustration tend to heighten the chance that hostility will occur. Figler's (1978) study of "aggressive response to frustration," among athletes and nonathletes, is a step in the right direction.

Layman (1968) suggested that frustration is likely to elicit what has been termed "reactive aggression," while failing to cause instrumental aggression. Contemporary reviewers of the frustration-aggression hypothesis suggest that its simplicity limits its contribution to the understanding of this facet of human behavior. Some say the theory is an "interesting historical milestone" in the continuing attempt to understand aggressive behavior. However, as reflected in some of the previously cited studies, it is a foundation upon which more sophisticated research has come to be based.

Instinctual Theories of Aggression. Similar to Freudian concepts of human aggression, the instinctual approach to aggression is based on observations made in animal communities, particularly those inhabited by primates. The primary popularizer of the theory was Lorenz, the ethnologist, in *On Aggression* (1966). It was further illuminated by the playwright Ardrey in the same year.

The model supposes that man's aggressive tendencies are inborn instinctual mechanisms inherited from animal ancestors, behaviors that resulted in their survival as individuals and as a species. These instincts are purportedly based on the maintenance of territory, fighting behaviors necessary for survival and similar devices seen in the personality of various subhuman species.

Writers supporting this view further assume that man's aggressive drives are more dangerous than those seen in the animal communities because:

1. Humans possess the means to annihilate themselves in ways more efficient than the fangs and horns used by animals.

2. Animal evolution also tends to propagate built-in aggressive-inhibiting responses, which are sometimes lacking in humans. Often, sham battles are engaged in by animals, in which no real harm can occur, as the status hierarchies are established.

3. Man seems to be the only animal who at times possesses the means and the intent to exterminate at least a portion of his own species.

Like many instinctual theories, the model proposed by Lorenz is circular. To state that man is aggressive because he possesses aggressive instincts is to explain little. This theory also contains the notion that exhibiting aggressive behaviors that are less than destructive to human life (i.e., sport) may provide a catharsis.

However, the research data reflecting attempts to explore the purported cathartic or cleansing effects of aggressive acts through sport lend little support to this line of reasoning. Even Scott, whose studies of animal behaviors and aggression are classics, suggests that while play and sport may reduce aggression, sport exists for reasons other than the displacement of aggressive instincts in man.

Only a few studies have produced data that support the catharsis hypothesis with regard to participation in and viewing of sporting competitions. Johnson and Hutton (1955), for example, found that measures of aggressive feelings obtained from a projective test (tree-house-person) in eight wrestlers, taking 4 to 5 hours before the first intercollegiate match of the season, were greater than apparent feelings projected by them the morning after competition. The heightened aggression before the match, the writers suggested, was connected with possible feelings of guilt, paralleling the anticipated aggressive sport. This aggression was thus hypothesized as intrapunitive in nature, or aggression directed toward themselves rather than their opponents.

More numerous studies support the hypothesis that sports participation may heighten aggressive tendencies. Husman in 1954 also administered a projective test to boxers (The Thematic Apperception Test), and found that aggression increased during a season. Innumerable studies of aggression in children have illustrated that attempts to reduce aggression through the use of aggressive and vigorous play therapy have the opposite effect. Aggression is often heightened under these circumstances. In most cases, however, the children in the studies had not been previously angered or frustrated, which is often the case in athletics.

More hopeful have been studies in which means other than aggressive exertion have been employed to reduce aggression. These strategies, discussed elsewhere in the chapter, have included using a mirror to help people see themselves aggress, teaching individuals to aggress within game limits, and teaching children to control their frustrations when losing. The effects of exercise and fatigue as possible reduce aggression will be covered elsewhere in the chapter.

Social learning theory. Over the past 15 years, a flexible and comprehensive theory of behavior has been advanced and expanded on in the experimental literature. A primary proponent of this model is Albert Bandura, who described it in *Aggression: A Social Learning Analysis* (1973). This model encompasses a wide variety of determiners of human aggression. Further, the theory delineates the forms which aggressive behavior may take and the way hostility may vary from situation to situation, and in different people.

The theory contains the following postulates.

1. Simple instinctual drives cannot account for the variety of aggressive behaviors triggered by a variety of circumstances. Similar aggressive behavior may be caused by different conditions, and conversely a single condition or event is likely to cause many different kinds of aggressive reactions.

2. Patterns of behavior can be acquired by observing the behavior of others. These "modeling effects" are more marked when the model is perceived as having social power, and the viewer identifies with the model. In numerous experiments, researchers have studied modeling effects on aggressive behaviors of both children and adults.

3. First new modes of behavior are tentatively explored, and then effective ones are retained while less successful ones are discarded.

4. Thus, social learning is based on the assumptions that patterns of responses are learned and their maintenance and elaboration depend on rewarding circumstances, by observations of positive results, by positive social evaluations, and by the intellectual evaluation of the results of the behavior. Bandura thus combines behaviorism with cognitive theory, as he suggests that cognitive processes have an important control function in the initiation and propagation of behaviors.

In the world of sport, these assumptions suggest that the athlete's immediate and past social experiences, more than his innate physiologic drives, influence the degree of aggressiveness manifested. As the athlete consciously evaluates the results of his aggressive efforts (instrumental as well as hostile), he formulates new plans of action, which may or may not include hostility. He may eliminate hostility and aggression from his behavior or modify the form they may take.

Overview

Rosen (1957) has pointed out that any viable model of aggression should include three important dimensions: (1) A delineation of "an aggressive motive, dealing with the strength and direction of aggression." (2) Anticipation of the consequences of aggression and concern with the possible aftermath of an aggressive action. (3) "Action readiness," or the degree to which the individual will act in an aggressive manner and the variables that seem to contribute to this kind of "mental set." The more flexible approaches to aggression contain provisions for Rosen's criteria.

The section that follows attempts to illuminate causes for aggression. As will be seen, there are few data directly from sport and from athletes. Thus, the reader should transpose ideas to the gymnasium and athletic field, with some reservations.

CONDITIONS ACCOMPANYING HUMAN AGGRESSION

It is proposed to inspect and analyze findings that may shed some light upon the possible causes of, and conditions that accompany, aggression and hostile behaviors of various kinds. Three primary subdivisions make up this section:

1. Predisposing factors, including long-term social conditions such as family history, as well as short-term factors including possible modeling effects. Also are included a look at the arousal-activation state the individual may bring with him or her to situations that may trigger aggressive reactions.
2. Situational factors, including the victim's perceptions of the potential or actual aggressor, as well as the aggressor's perceptions of the victim.[2] Such variables as success and failure, frustration, social contagion, competition, and victims' perceptions of their retaliatory capacities are also examined.
3. Various postaggression variables, including cognitive assessments of the reasons why the aggressive act took place.

The Social Setting and Its Influence on Aggression

Smith (1973) has chronicled frightening examples of hostile outbursts in sport. Smith's survey points out the important role of the total societal context on the likelihood of violence and excess aggression, instigated

[2]Interesting verbal and behavioral interactions between aggressors on sports teams and teammate "victims" are discussed extensively in Cratty BJ, Hanin YL: *The Athlete in the Sports Team,* in Chapter VII, "Interpersonal Communication," Denver, Colorado: Love Publishing Company.

by fans and by players alike. Among the causes cited for hostility during and after games are:

1. The presence of ethnic, religious, national, or other cleavages.
2. The unavailability of alternative avenues of protest for purported grievances.
3. The unavailability of appropriate targets to which responsibility can be attached for wrongs done to athletes or to teams.
4. The rapid communication of hostile beliefs and incidents through the media.
5. The accessibility of objects for attack, including vulnerable officials and less-threatening players.

Among the violent outbursts in sports reviewed by Smith are several that seemed to precipitate wars. These included the collective violence between a Jewish sports club and an Austrian police sports club in 1947, the soccer official who was beaten to death by players and fans in 1948 in Buenos Aires, and the referee who was beaten until unconscious in 1954. The 1964 Lima-Argentina game in Lima, Peru, followed by a riot that resulted in 292 fatalities, was also discussed, as was the 1969 Honduras–El Salvador "soccer war" involving riotous outbursts in three World Cup soccer games in June of that same year. These games were followed by the severance of diplomatic relations between the two countries.

Violence and undue aggression in sports participation, both by fans and participants, is not confined to specific parts of the world. Smith outlined probable causes for the violence associated with English soccer during the 1960s. Overly volatile fans, both at home and on the Continent, often became so aggressive that troopers were called out to restore order at provincial borders.

These cases, as well as more recent incidents, make a strong case for the fact that collective violence by fans and athletes is influenced not only by the immediate circumstances, but also by long-standing political, economic, religious, and regional and national stresses and strains that may have existed for years.

Predisposing Factors: Child-Rearing

Chapter II contained a discussion of the kind of predisposing child-rearing practices likely to instill hostility in children and youth. Overly harsh or highly permissive methods of rearing children, particularly suppression or tolerance of aggression on their part, are both likely to produce overly hostile children. For example, Feshback (1970) suggested that there was no variable as strongly related to aggressiveness in children as the amount of physical punishment that had been administered by the parents. A description of this highly aggressive parent, resorting to punishment of a physical nature, is often seen in the autobiographies of professional athletes published in the United States during the past two decades.

McCord and Howard (1961), Gordon and Smith (1965), and Bandura and Walters have produced data that seem to point to the following summarizing statements: (1) Aggressive boys seem to come from parents who are rejecting, fight among themselves, and undermine each other's values. (2) Parents who are inconsistent in their guidance produce frustrated, aggressive children. (3) Less aggressive children seem to stem from family environments that emphasize warmth, consistency, and respect. (4) Moderately aggressive youngsters are from families who are warm and nonthreatening, but who also evidence some nonconformity, and whose controls are not always consistently administered.

A study by Smith (1972) contains information bearing directly on the problems of social conditions and sanctions that may mold aggressions of children in sport. Smith analyzed what he termed "normative violence" in ice hockey, defined as behavior occurring within a "tolerable normative range." Smith contrasted this with two other types of violence in sport: prohibited or illegitimate violence, and a single hostile outburst seen in group behavior and involving fan and athlete.

In a methodical manner, Smith carefully recorded the violent reactions in numerous hockey games, and attempted to determine just what group of people seemed to most influence the boys' tendency to become violent during games. It was found initially that violence would occur if a boy was attacked or otherwise threatened, or dominated by another player in the game.

In interviews with 83 players, the frequencies with which the boys' perceptions of their "reference group's" sanctions for assaultive behavior on the ice were tabulated. It was found that mothers and fathers had different effects than nonplaying peers. The peer group displayed the most vocal support of violent behaviors in the games, while the mothers were the most passive toward violence. The father, in general, believed that violence was all right if the child was initially aggressed against.

The fathers, however, viewed "rough play" negatively, including boarding or cross-checking that could result in penalties, and fights. It is uncertain whether the fathers' disapproval of excess violence stemmed from moral reservations, or from the fact that such behavior often results in the assessment of counterproductive penalties.

The players viewed their nonplaying peers as most eager to observe violence in any form. Smith states that "most of them [nonplaying peers] came to the games just to see someone get killed." Smith's ideas, if extended to other sports and other age levels, could have an important impact on knowledge in this field. They might also produce helpful strategies to reduce violence in sports in which the likelihood is high that two or more players will "face off" against each other.

Another study by the Ministry of Community and Social Services in Canada, focusing on ice hockey violence, reveals another important group among the potential instigators to violence in sport. This 1974 study pointed out that one of the primary causes of excess violence (defined in this work as "the unlawful exercise of physical force") is professional players whose behaviors serve as negative models for impressionable boys. The report states: "It is not surprising that virtually every boy playing hockey is profoundly influenced by violent examples portrayed in the National Hockey League."

The report also contains a statement reflecting the attitude of a Canadian coach who is a mentor of a youth team. He is quoted as saying, "All I have ever told my players at any level is *stand* your ground. If there is going to be a fight you get the first shot." The writer of the report contrasts this coach's statement with one obtained from the "great Russian coach Tarasov":

> Courage means the ability to stay out of a fight. I know just how hard it is to contain yourself, how unfair it seems when you have to calmly take it from some overstrung athlete. I know just how hard it is to hold yourself back from paying him back in kind, but real courage calls for self-control and patience.

The issues raised by this report are critical ones in relation to aggression and violence in sport. From a developmental standpoint, children early in their careers are exposed to contact and semicontact sports. It is contingent upon coaches to teach them to control aggression and to exercise self-control. Lessons about the differences between instrumental and hostile aggression should be taught. Concepts of this nature will be particularly reinforced if parents, coaches, community organizers, and the children's own peer groups are also helped to gain positive attitudes about aggression in sport.

The Effects of Aggressive Models

The situations above described the effects of children modeling their behavior after adult hockey players. In this kind of field observation, it is difficult to control the duration of exposure to such models, as well as other variables that might have influenced the children's hostility.

However, in numerous laboratory studies over the past 15 years, efforts *have* been made to look in detail at rather short-term predisposing factors that conceivably can influence aggression and hostility.

Numerous studies in the 1960s and 1970s have demonstrated how viewing models of aggression molds subsequent aggression. Numerous variations of the type of model and of opportunities to be aggressive, as well as of the time the subject has been exposed to the model, have been employed.

For example, Hicks (1965) studied the relative effects of both peer and adult models of each sex on aggression in children. Both short- and long-term influences were measured. It was found that male peers had the most immediate influence in shaping children's aggressive behaviors, while adult males had the most lasting effect.

Both an actual model and films have been used in such studies and the effects contrasted. In general, the findings have suggested that viewing aggression, particularly if the aggressor is identified with by the subject, will cause immediate aggressive responses to be elicited in children, youth, and adults. In contrast, nonaggressive models, according to Baron (1971), have the reverse effect. Subjects observing them tend to exhibit less aggression. The latter finding has some relevance for the way a less than tranquil coach may behave in front of a potentially aggressive athlete or group of fans during critical competitions.

Subtle variables have also been studied in this type of context. Baron (1976) found that lowering his subjects' body temperatures with a cool drink tended to reduce aggression, while Scheier (1974) found, as have others, that if an individual is placed in a position to see himself being aggressive (using a mirror), the amount of aggression is reduced.

The implications of these and similar studies for the athletic team and its members are not always clear. For example, there appear to be few, if any, studies in which the intent was to modify aggression in a real athletic setting by prior exposure to either an aggressive or nonaggressive model. Observation and common sense suggest that the tendency for a team member to fight, or otherwise exhibit violence in excess of the rules, tends to become greater if he has just witnessed a previous act of aggression perpetrated by a teammate, or by an opponent against one of his peers. The tendency to become violent might become greater if the observed violence of an opponent is either rewarded by gaining some advantage in the game or not punished by the referee or other official. Aggression, if successful against a teammate with whom a player identifies highly, is also likely to produce retaliatory violence.

Perhaps in the future, a systematized picture of the way player violence and extra-aggression is initiated and then sustained, in a game and during a season, will emerge. Such a study should illuminate these various modeling effects and result in a probability picture of what variables acting together heighten chances for violence to occur.

Activation and Arousal

Several investigators, including Zillman (1970) and his colleagues at the University of Indiana, have tried to isolate the way arousal-activation levels influence aggressive behaviors. One of the primary strategies has been the introduction of varying amounts of physical exercise. For the most part, these studies have limited themselves to a short-time period—6 minutes is typical.

Zillman (1972), in a study typical of several, found that after exercise, aggression was heightened. He concluded that a heightened arousal level at times combines with cognitive assessments of prior arousal-producing activities to elicit greater levels of subsequent aggression than would be present within a lower arousal state. Willingness to deliver an electric shock was used as a measure of aggression, while blood pressure was the measure of activation employed.

Although the time periods involved in these studies have been rather short, time between the initiation of arousal and the measurement of subsequent aggression has ranged in most from 2 minutes 30 seconds to 6 minutes. Thus, the question of what may trigger aggression by an athlete rather late in the game might be difficult to ascertain upon inspection of these findings and methods. One clue has been provided by Zillman and his colleagues (1974). They found that aggressiveness increased significantly, in subjects exhibiting medium and low levels of fitness, after the exercise effects had worn off. Thus, moderate fatigue in the less fit may add stress that can heighten changes for aggression. This subject obviously needs further study.

When subjecting these ideas to field tests, it is important to ascertain whether aggression caused by activation via exercise is due to the exercise alone, or to some personal or psychologic insult the player feels might have been directed toward him or his teammates. Thus, one could advance the following postulates relating exercise-activation to both physical and psychologic insults in game situations. (These statements are in obvious need of experimental verification.)

The hypotheses have been arranged in the order of the likelihood they will produce aggression at a later time, from those least likely to those highly likely to cause hostile reactions.

1. Activation via exercise, unaccompanied by any physical or psychologic insult emanating from another.
2. Activation by witnessing or receiving a personal or group insult.

3. Activation through exercise, plus witnessing or directly experiencing a physical or psychologic insult.

Other variables to consider within such a context include: (1) the athlete's physical condition. A more fit athlete may be better able to control his level of activation following arousal-producing situations. (2) The degree to which the athlete feels he or she can successfully be aggressive against those who aggressed against him or her. (3) The length of the time interval interposed between the initially arousing conditions and the athlete's subsequent opportunities to be aggressive. (4) The level of arousal maintained during the time interval between the instigating act (or activation) and the possibility of aggressing. (5) The level of activation initially experienced by the athlete as the result of aggression or insult.

SITUATIONAL FACTORS

In addition to variables occurring before the onset of aggression, a number of factors, conditions, and situations occur almost simultaneously with the act of aggression. Among these are the potential aggressor's perceptions of the potency of his victim and whether the potential aggressor feels that he will experience failure or success as the result of the aggression. Whether the attack is being reacted to in concrete or symbolic ways is important, as are the number of onlookers and the feelings in the group that may be present as an aggressive act occurs. Finally, the aggressor's perceptions of his *own* retaliatory capacities are critical to consider.

Perception of Opponent-Victim

There are several kinds of opinions a potential aggressor may formulate about a potential victim, which in turn may or may not trigger aggression and control the level of aggression initiated. These include whether or not the victim is likely to retaliate, the level of aggression that may have been previously exhibited by the potential victim, as well as a most important variable, the perceived attitude of the victim if aggression takes place.

The 1967 study by Epstein and his colleagues produced the expected results. Using the usual "shock-giving" apparatus, they found that significantly more aggression is leveled against a victim who has first aggressed in a manner that seemed punitive and hostile than one whose behavior had been perceived as instrumental aggression.

If the victim seems too able, as seen in the work by Shortell and Epstein (1970), aggression may be postponed, or declined entirely. In its place will appear feelings of suppressed aggression, accompanied by anger.

Greenwall and his colleagues (1973) dealt with the problem of perceived intent of attacker and retaliation. They found that if the aggressor was perceived as wishing to produce injury, the amount of punishment was not important. If the attacker was perceived as engaging in aggression in a nonpersonal way, even though the attack (shock administered) is great, retaliatory anger will not be high.

Findings of this kind may account for the tendency of some experienced players in contact sport to ignore their opponents. They keep "poker faces" and avoid eye contact with opponents when striking them. Thus, the aggressor seems less likely to later receive aggression from a former victim. Kauss (1975), in a study of an American football team, found that more experienced players viewed their opponents less personally and more dispassionately than did less experienced players. The latter seemed to need to hate their opponents in order to play well. This finding relates to those described earlier in laboratory settings, when victim and aggressor paired off in various ways.

The way people react to aggression, and the strength of their retaliatory efforts, may be caused by their own levels of "residual aggression." In an interesting study of 8-year-old boys, Peterson (1968) found that boys who consistently exhibited low levels of aggression tended to inhibit aggression when they expected retaliation. Boys who exhibited high levels of aggressive behaviors tended to be more aggressive when retaliation was expected. This general level of aggression may be a function of the boys' inherent psychologic make-up, or be caused by some "role" they expect others require them to play in aggressive situations.

Findings from a 1971 study by Baron indicate that young adults may be more circumspect in their evaluation of potential retaliation by victims than are children. He found no differences in subsequent aggression following conditions that purportedly convinced potential aggressors that retaliation would be high in contrast to situations in which youths were led to believe that less aggression would be forthcoming.

In this same study, however, whether or not the youths were exposed or not exposed to an aggressive model had an effect upon the aggression they displayed. Thus, this study indicates that modeling effects may be a stronger incentive to later aggression than forming cognitive inferences concerning whether the aggressor is capable of retaliation. In this and numerous similar studies, important personality variables that potentially influence results were not evaluated or controlled for.

The influence of the perception of the victim's ability to retaliate has not been systematically studied within a sports setting. It would seem to be a fruitful field for exploration.

Game Location and Social Contagion

Two studies have recorded the incidence of fouling in soccer-football in order to study aggressive behavior. Their findings reveal that home team athletes display less aggressive behavior than do members of visiting teams. The greater aggression on the part of visiting teams, both researchers speculate, represents the tendency of the visitors to consciously attack not only the players in front of them, but in indirect ways to unconsciously aggress against the usually unfriendly spectators.

Berkowitz (1963) and his students studied aggression in college students after they watched fight films. Although aggressive tendencies were heightened, the direction of the aggression seems to be selective, rather than generally expressed. More aggression was leveled against men than against women. Other studies have produced results that suggest aggression against an inanimate object or against an individual who did not aggress against you is far less satisfying than "taking it out" directly on the person who was initially aggressive.

Aggressive behavior is contagious. A chain of behaviors may begin when one aggressive act is accomplished, according to Wheeler and Caggiula (1966). Berkowitz has suggested a "completion model" of aggression, pointing out that once aggression is started there is often engendered in observers an urge to complete, to "get even," in a way that will permanently terminate the chain of hostility that has started and been built up.

Audience effect on aggression was studied by Baron (1971). Sixty males were first angered and then presented with opportunities to be aggressive toward their tormentors under each of three conditions: (1) with no audience present, (2) in front of an audience who had seen them angered initially, and (3) with an audience who had not witnessed the first transgression.

The results of this experiment are not what one might expect. Under the audience conditions, the potential aggressors remained relatively calm. The experimenters suggested that the presence of an audience tended to blunt aggression. It is questionable whether the same result would have been seen in a sporting arena filled with avid fans.

Although there are few studies in which athletes have been used as subjects to study aggression, an exception is one by Zillman, Johnson, and Day (1970). It was found when nonathletes, non-contact-sport athletes, and contact-sport athletes were provoked by a confederate, the nonathletes displayed more aggressiveness than did both athletic groups. Zillman and his colleagues attribute this finding to the possibility that the athletes had acquired superior ability in coping with provocation under competitive circumstances. The effect, however, may be partially counteracted by inherent aggressive tendencies in athletes who participate in contact sports, who proved more aggressive after provocation than did non-contact-sport athletes. Thus, the following equations may be viable, and on completion of additional research their precision may be improved.

1. Nonathletes + provocation + little experience handling provocation = relatively high levels of aggression exhibited.
2. Contact-sport athletes + provocation + experience that has enabled them to practice inhibiting aggression +high aggression level due to psychologic needs or traits=intermediate amounts of aggression when provoked.
3. Non-contact-sport athletes + provocation + experience in handling provocation + personal traits resulting in aggression inhibition = little aggresssion exhibited.

Personality and Aggression

Many have felt that the personality traits of potential aggressors are important variables to study. Since World War II, many psychologists have focused their attention on measures and models that attempt to delineate "the aggressive personality."

In 1952, for example, Thibaut and Coules asked each of their subjects, organized into two-man groups, to write their initial impressions of their partners. On this basis, the subjects were classified as either friendly or hostile. The subjects had had no previous association. This type of measure is reflective of what is termed "manifest hostility," or the amount of hostility an individual will consciously be aware of. More recently, measures of hostility have been paired with personality trait scores, and have included the previously mentioned tendency to deliver electric shocks to adversaries.

Rosen (1957) theorized that there were three aggressive patterns seen in people consisting of:

1. *The overly aggressive person.* This is an individual characterized by weak internal restraints against expressing impulses, and who uses direct aggression as a goal. Thus, he or she is motivated to injure another person either physically and/or psychologically, and evidences little concern with the long-term consequences of direct ag-

gression. This type of individual will tend to act aggressively under even mild conditions. Scheier has suggested recently that this type of individual is low in guilt feelings after showing aggression.

2. *The overly inhibited person.* This individual has strong restraints against expressing impulses. He or she does not develop the intention to retaliate toward others, and may be characterized as one who engages in "deflected aggression," choosing paths other than those leading directly toward an agent or situation that is frustrating.

3. *The intermediate person.* This individual possesses moderate internal restraints and does not regard others' efforts to influence him as typically aimed at "doing him in" or "beating him out of things." However, if he discovers that direct aggression is instrumental in preventing him from achieving some goal, he may aggress in turn.

Rosen bases his assumptions on inventory data obtained from 60 children from 12 to 14 years of age. Observational data were also employed.

Numerous other researchers have attempted to ferret out the aggressive personality and the variables that contribute to this syndrome. Hokanson and Gordon (1958), for example, also used a scale of "manifest hostility."

As work has progressed on this topic, researchers have become increasingly sophisticated in their control of variables that may interact with personality traits identified. For example, Fishman (1965) researched the "need for approval" trait as it interacted with aggressive behavior under varying degrees of frustration. Among her findings were that subjects with high need for approval manifested a continued elevation in arousal (measured by blood pressure changes) following aggression. On the other hand, subjects low in need for approval evidenced a decline in arousal after frustration and subsequent aggression.

Along this same line of investigation was a study by Lipetz and Ossorio (1967), who examined the relationships among authoritarianism, aggression, and status. Among their findings were indications that those high in authoritarianism aggressed more against equal status aggressors than did those low in authoritarianism. Low authoritarians were more aggressive than were those high in authoritarianism toward higher status aggressors. The findings from this and subsequent investigations of personality and aggression illustrate the subtle interaction of a variety of traits, conditions, and perceived abilities of those aggressed against, as well as of the aggressors themselves.[3] Scheier and his colleagues, for example, found that when the aggressor's self-esteem was

[3]There are discussions about interactions between aggressors and their victims on sports teams in Cratty BJ, Hanin YL: *The Athlete in the Sports Team,* Love Publishing Co., Denver, Colorado, 1980, Chapter VII, section on "Oppressors and Victims."

altered by giving him vivid feedback about how he looked while aggressing, aggression tended to subside.

As sport psychologists and social psychologists become adroit, they will likely become able to integrate more and more variables into their studies of aggression and personality. Most important, as suggested by Kauss (1975), is to study situational measures, mood states, and stable personality traits when forming a picture of the total athlete and his or her tendencies to perform well, fail, aggress, and otherwise function in the emotional context of sport. This kind of complete assessment also requires projective tests, as well as formal and informal interview data. Using these measures it may become possible in the future to label an athlete as aggressive or nonaggressive in nature. But to be scientifically accurate and fair to the athlete, it would seem more useful to determine just what conditions, situations, and pressures are likely to make him or her become aggressive or remain calm.

Cognitive Determinants of Aggression

"Cognitive mediators" constitute another important type of variable likely to influence aggression. If one accepts the premise that athletes and others engage in intellectual-evaluative processes prior to, during, and following aggressive acts, it is further logical to assume that these thoughts influence the probabilities, intensities, and onset as well as the suppression of hostile behavior in sport and in other aspects of life.

The work of Zillman (1970, 1972) and his colleagues, previously cited, hinges upon assumptions formulated by Schachter, who proposed a two-factor theory of emotion. This model suggests that a person may not only become emotionally aroused, or at least changed, as reflected in physiologic measures, but also in various ways *evaluates* the meaning of the changes experienced. Subsequent action, or inaction, depends not only on the actual level of arousal experienced, but also on the individual's thoughts about the meanings of the changes experienced.

Conceptualization of the intent of the aggressor undoubtedly provides an important influence on the probability of future aggression. Important evaluative decisions thus take place as the aggressor contemplates the results of aggression recently engaged in, as well as the consequences of withholding aggression in a critical situation.

Ryan's (1970) study of the effects of vigorous physical activity on the lowering of aggression also contains inferences related to conceptual activity. His findings include the observations that "vigorous motor activity" (pounding on a block) did not lessen aggressive tendencies, and that there was no simple "drainage" of these hostile tendencies due to physical activity. He concluded that most indivuals aggressed against probably feel most relieved by retaliating not against inanimate objects, but against the frustrator, against the real instigator of aggression against them. The victim knows that a locker, block of wood, or the family dog, while available to be kicked, are not truly the objects or people who should have retribution directed their way. Most satisfying, apparently, is retaliation toward the actual instigator of a noxious act, a judgment formed by the *conceptual processes* of the victim.

Based upon a cognitive model, the schematic in Figure 8–2 has been constructed to explain the interaction of situational, cognitive, and emotional factors prior to, during, and following an aggressive act. According to the diagram, the probability of the instigation of aggressive behaviors is based on the interactions of societal factors, together with variables immediate to the situation, which are evaluated by a victim and a potential aggressor. These, together with the transitory and stable mood states of the individual, combine to either cause, delay, or prevent aggression.

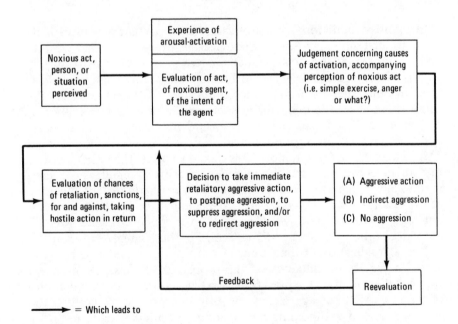

FIGURE 8-2. A model depicting the interaction of situational, cognitive, and emotional (physiologic arousal) factors in the instigation of aggressive behaviors.

AGGRESSION IN SPORT

Aggression in sport at times reaches monumental proportions. Concern about this problem prompted an international gathering in Belgium in 1977. Representatives from over fourteen European governments were present, together with leaders from fifteen international sports federations and six international organizations of other types. Their discussion focused on the nature of the problem, as well as steps that might be taken to reduce the incidence of violence in sport, both among athletes and among fans. Further, their concerns revolved around the international implications of aggression in games between teams from one or more countries.

Their deliberations brought to the surface questions, and few answers. The same is true of the research data obtained at this point. But these are beginnings, and helpful ones.

Two useful studies, for example, have been carried out by obtaining data from aggressive acts occurring in soccer-football. The data from the two studies, based on number of fouls committed, produced similar findings. The more ambitious of the two investigatons tabulated fouls in more than 1800 games, and was published in the German publication *Sport Sciences* in 1971. Its author, Volkamer, assumed that the team is a microscopic version of society itself, and therefore contains the frustrations, rewards, and possible interactions seen in other societal groups. His findings included the following:

1. Losers commit more fouls than do winners. He hypothesized that the frustration of losing may have produced this difference.

2. Teams playing on a visitor's field commit more fouls than do those playing on their home field. The author suggests that this is indicative of displaced aggression by the visitors toward the often hostile and nonsupportive crowd.

3. Fouls are less frequent when a large number of goals are scored than when only a few points are on the scoreboard. Volkamer assumes that this is because frequent changes in score elicit less frustration and tension than when a few points are scored infrequently. Thus, on the basis of this and other assumptions Volkamer seems to accept the frustration-aggression hypothesis discussed in Chapter I and in this chapter.

4. Teams lower in standings commit more fouls than those higher in the standing. He further found out that lower ranking teams show more aggression, even when winning a game.

5. When a higher ranking team and a lower ranking team play, the higher ranking team commits more fouls. He ascribes this finding to

a reflection of the "law of the pecking order" seen in animal studies, in which aggression of higher ranking members toward those lower in rank is more likely to be condoned.[4]

Further provocative findings from this helpful study were that when teams from the extreme levels (high and low in the standings) played, more fouls were committed than when teams from among the middle ranks met. He attributed this to a more "controlled environment" present when evenly matched teams compete. Additionally, Volkamer found that the closeness of the score related to the number of fouls committed. Games that were extremely close, as well as those not closely contested, evidenced fewer fouls than games moderate in competitive intensity. He suggested that in the closely fought games, players were careful about needlessly expressed fouls, which led to penalties against their team.

Although Volkamer points to several problems when using a simple "foul count" as a measure of aggression, he concludes that aggression in sport is sociologically and psychologically normal in athletic teams. He lists four main variables influencing the incidence of fouling,[5] including (1) whether a team is in front of a friendly crowd, (2) whether differences in scores are great, (3) whether the opponent's rank is at the upper, middle, or lower part of the standings, and (4) whether the team is losing or winning.

A study by Lefebvre and Passer (1974) also employed soccer-football and used fouls as a measure of aggression. Although not as extensive as that by Volkamer, this second investigation displayed a good deal of theoretical and statistical sophistication. Fouls committed in 240 games by teams in the first and second divisions of the Belgian National Soccer Association were compared. The researchers predicted that more fouls would be displayed by players of the visiting team, by players in the more important first division, and by players in danger of losing. In general, their findings supported these assumptions, and thus the data are consistent with those obtained by Volkamer.

In opposition to one of their primary hypotheses, however, Lefebvre and Passer found that the less adroit players in the second division fouled more than did those in the first division. Thus, it was assumed that ineptitude, rather than the intent to aggress, may lead to fouling. More creative research on this topic might try to divide fouls caused by awkwardness and those caused by overly aggressive behavior.

---

[4]Studies in the U.S.S.R. of hostile comments from team member to team member also have indicated that hostility in verbal form tends to "flow" downward within the status order.

[5]A foul can be evidence of inept play, rather than of aggression; it can also be one of a chain of hostile acts within a game situation.

The latter two researchers, in the discussion of their findings, were careful to assign no causative interactions to the situations surveyed. They do, however, offer helpful directions for additional research. They suggested, for example, that further studies might correlate the number of spectators, and their proximity to the playing field, with fouls committed by visiting and home teams. These kinds of data, they suggest, plus measures of the importance of the contests obtained from players, might reveal other causative variables. Passer and Lefebvre recommended that athletes be exposed to "frustration training," which might result in fewer instances of hostile aggression while retaining the instrumental aggression required in many competitive sports.

IMPLICATIONS FOR THE COACH

When attempting to understand and to deal with aggression, the coach is confronted with several types of problems:

1. Attempting to determine in advance what athletes are likely to exhibit excess aggression in competitions.
2. Ascertaining just what game and contest behaviors constitute optimum *vs.* excess aggression.
3. Trying to predict what situations are likely to bring on excess aggression from a team.
4. Attempting either to calm an overly aggressive athlete (or team) or to arouse an athlete (or team) to exhibit more aggression so that performance increases in quality.

In order to meet and deal with these problems, the coach can take various courses of action. For example, when dealing with a new team composed of a large number of athletes, special attention to scores and impressions gained from a thorough psychological work-up is likely to aid in prediction of athlete(s) who may exhibit too much aggression under competitive stress. Inspection of an athlete's autobiography may also help predict those who may be overly aggressive or who may not exhibit sufficient aggression when needed.

The coach should consider in advance of each team sport contest, and individual sport in which direct aggression is involved, just what conditions are likely to be met that may "set an athlete or team off" and elicit too much aggression. Not only should the coach make this kind of judgment individually, but his or her conclusions should be transmitted to the team members. This should be done so that the individual athlete may be better able to control excess aggression in situations likely to elicit it. It should be pointed out to athletes that exhibiting excess aggression has not only negative moral connotations but also practical drawbacks. The team, or team member, who is too angry usually commits an unusually large number of rule infractions, and thus does not contribute in a positive way to team and individual success.

A thorough knowledge of an athlete's motivational and value system also permits the coach to ascertain just who may (1) need help in the optimum expression of aggression when called for, and (2) help the coach to relieve some athletes of possible negative feelings after expressing a correct amount of aggression.

Information about how cognitive mediators mold aggressive behavior should lead the coach to help an athlete realize that the amount of aggression he or she is likely to exhibit at a given time is determined by personal interpretations of situations and of the people involved; it is not "knee-jerk" retaliatory behavior. Thus, if an athlete or team seems to exhibit undue hostility toward another team or individual, individuals can be helped to perceive that too negative feelings in advance of a contest may "push them over the edge" during the stress of competition and lead to unhealthy expressions of aggression.

Although frustration does not automatically bring about aggressive behaviors, it is at least an important contributor to aggressive tendencies in sport, as in other aspects of life. Thus, the perceptive coach may attempt to reduce frustrating conditions to which athletes are subjected, in order to forestall unusual amounts of aggressive behavior on teams. For example, one of the more frustrating experiences athletes are put through is that of being continual substitutes. Indeed, it is not unusual to see frustrated substitutes incur unusual numbers of fouls when they are at last permitted to play in a game during its final minutes. Helping substitutes deal with this problem, by arranging extra games and otherwise giving them as much playing time as possible, are some of the ways these negative feelings can be reduced.

An athlete who after starting for some time is suddenly reduced to a substitute role is likely to exhibit too much aggression during both practices and games. Here again, the coach should attempt to deal with the situation in a positive way, both through personal conferences and with the help of a psychologist if one is available.

The coach of younger athletes may need to reduce aggression and aggressive tendencies in his or her charges by trying to blunt the effects of aggressive models to which youngsters are exposed. The coach should try to reduce the impact of fighting among professional athletes seen on television and should also personally provide a controlled model by maintaining composure during "tight" game situations.

It appears helpful to provide team members with some of the information contained in this chapter. If the athletes themselves are aware of conditions, including their own heightened levels of action, that are likely to set them off, they may personally prepare themselves to deal with sports situations in controlled and useful ways.

The exhibition of too much aggression in sport cannot be predicted with the precision of a chemical reaction, but both athletes and coaches should be aware in advance of conditions that heighten the probability of excess hostility. Armed with such knowledge, both coaches and athletes should then be better able to act in reasonable and useful ways when confronted with the frustrations and stresses of competitive athletics.

SUMMARY

This chapter has presented comprehensive material on the nature of human aggression, together with data from studies that have potential implications for competitive sport. It was not implied that all aggression is either bad or similar, but rather that the term *aggression* represents a multifaceted concept. The intentions of the aggressor, whether to commit injury for its own sake or to achieve an impersonal reward, are critical variables.

Various theories that attempt to explain human aggression were briefly surveyed. The social learning theory, whose leading proponent is Bandura, was believed to be the most valid. The model is a comprehensive one, encompassing as causative agents the long-term and immediate social setting, as well as the emotional and cognitive "set" of both potential aggressor and victim. The importance of "modeling effects" and of contingencies and reward schedules attached to aggressive acts are also stressed by Bandura.

Literature delineating the causes of human aggression was reviewed. Some pertained directly to sport, but most did not. However, many of the tasks employed involved physical skill, as well as exercise. For example, data from the work by Zillman, Ryan, and others were surveyed to illustrate the possible influences of physiologic arousal, produced by exercise, upon human hostility. It appears that the person's conscious evaluation of predisposing factors, the reasons for his or her level of activation, as well as the consequences of an aggressive act, combine in subtle ways to instigate, forestall, or altogether subdue subsequent hostility.

Literature, together with data emanating from studies of aggression in team sports, suggest that a number of variables may combine to heighten the probability of an aggressive act being committed. A list of these includes:

1. An unfit player.
2. A player in front of a hostile crowd.
3. A player on a losing team, in a closely contested game.
4. A team within the upper part of the standings playing one lower in the standings.
5. Competition between teams whose backgrounds are divergent in race, ethnic make-up, and/or political orientation.
6. A past background of hostility between the two racial-ethnic and/or political climates they represent.
7. The presence of an aggressive act by another that is either not punished or results in an advantage.

All these combine to make aggression quite probable. At this point, however, the actual weight that can be placed upon each of the above conditions and situations is unclear, if indeed the complexities of the world of sport *are* amenable to mathematical formulation at all.

In any case, even ignoring the moral implications, winning a game in many sports requires that excess aggression be held in check, and that well-thought-out instrumental aggression be expressed and directed in precise ways. Thus, the reduction of hostile aggression and the focusing of instrumental aggression is likely to come about when those concerned with sport (coaches, administrators, parents, and athletes) gain some understanding of the forces that heighten tension and hostility, and then take positive steps to eliminate potential problems before they burst forth into violence.[6]

QUESTIONS FOR DISCUSSION

1. Discuss the definitions and types of aggression presented in the chapter. Can you give examples of the ways the different types of aggression are exhibited in specific sports situations?
2. Is all aggression in sport bad? How may aggressive tendencies be reduced, or heightened?
3. What variables and conditions surrounding a team game are likely to heighten aggression? Which of these might the coach influence? Which are sometimes beyond his or her influence?

[6]The final chapter of Cratty BJ, Hanin YL: *The Athlete in the Sports Team* describes some operational ways in which violence may be reduced or eliminated in the international sports arena.

4. What kinds of child-rearing behaviors are likely to have molded an athlete to express overly hostile and aggressive behavior?

5. What theory of aggression is most acceptable to you? Why? Does the consideration of these theories aid in understanding the operations that may instigate or reduce aggression?

6. Discuss the findings of studies in which aggression was studied in youthful ice hockey players in Canada. Do you think these findings would also be found in other sports, and at other age levels? If so, why? If not, why not?

7. What implications, if any, do the studies in which aggressive models were reviewed have for aggression of youthful participants in contact sports?

8. What influence(s) may activation have on aggressive behavior? Can you diagram possible interactions between activation and hostile behaviors?

9. How do one's perceptions of an aggressor influence possible retaliation?

BIBLIOGRAPHY

ALLISON J, HUNT DE: Social desirability and the expression of aggression under varying conditions of frustration. *J Consult Psych* 23:6 (1959), 528–534.

ARDREY R: *The Territorial Imperative.* New York, Atheneum, 1966.

ARLOW JB: Perspectives on aggression in human adaptation. Panel discussion on the Role of Aggression on Human Adaptation by the American Psychoanalytic Association and American Association for the Advancement of Science, section on Psychology, Philadelphia, December 1971.

BANDURA A: *Aggression: A Social Learning Analysis.* Englewood Cliffs, New Jersey, Prentice-Hall, 1973.

———, ROSS D, ROSS SA: Imitation of film-mediated aggressive modes. *J Abnorm Soc Psychol* 66:1 (1963), 3–11.

———, Transmission of aggression through imitation of aggressive models. *J Abnorm Soc Psychol* 63 (1962), 575–582.

BANDURA A, WALTERS RG: *Adolescent Aggression.* New York, Ronald Press, 1959.

BARON RA: Aggression as a function of ambient temperature and prior anger arousal. *J Personal Soc Psychol* 21:2 (1972), 183–189.

———, Aggression as a function of audience presence and prior anger arousal. *J Exp Soc Psychol* 7 (1971), 515–523.

———, Exposure to an aggressive model and apparent probability of retaliation from the victim as determinants of adult aggressive behavior. *J Exp Soc Psychol* 7 (1971), 343–355.

———, Reducing the influence of an aggressive model: restraining effects of discrepant modeling cues. *J Person Soc Psychol* 20:2 (1971), 240–245.

———, BELL PA: Aggression and heat: the influence of ambient temperature, negative affect and a cooling drink on physical aggression. *J Person Soc Psychol* 33:3 (1976), 245–255.

BERKOWITZ L: *Aggression: A Social Psychological Analysis.* New York, McGraw-Hill, 1962.

———, Manifest hostility level and hostile behavior. *J Soc Psychol* 52 (1960), 165–171.

———, The concept of aggressive drive: some additional considerations. In Berkowitz L (ed): *Advances in Experimental Social Psychology.* New York, Academic Press, 2, 1965, 301–20.

———, RAWLINGS E: Effects of film violence on inhibitions against subsequent aggression. *J Abnorm Soc Psychol* 66 (1963), 405–410.

BROCK T, BUSS AH: Effects of justification for aggression and communication with the victim on postaggression dissonance. *J Abnorm Soc Psychol* 68:4 (1964), 403–12.

BUSS AH: Physical aggression in relation to different frustrations. *J Abnorm Soc Psychol* 67:1 (1963), 1–7.

BUTT DS: Aggression, neuroticism and competence, theoretical models for the study of sports motivation. *Int J Sport Psychol* 4:1 (1973), 3–15.

CHANEY OC: Involvement, realism and the perception of aggression in television programmes. *Hum Rel* 23:5, 373–381.

COLLIS ML: The Collis Scale of Athletic Aggression. Faculty of Education, University of Victoria, Victoria British Columbia, Canada.

CRATTY BJ: *Psychology in Contemporary Sport.* Chapter 9, "Aggression in Sport." Englewood Cliffs, New Jersey, Prentice-Hall, 1973.

DENGERINK HA, LEVENDUSKY PG: Effects of massive retaliation and balance of power on aggression. *J Exp Res Pers* 6 (1972), 230–236.

DOBB AN, KIRSCHENBAUM HM: The effects on arousal of frustration and aggressive films. *J Exp Soc Psychol* 9 (1973), 57–64.

———, WOOD LE: Catharsis and aggression: effects of annoyance and retaliation on aggressive behavior. *J Pers Soc Psychol* 22:2 (1972), 156–62.

DOLLARD J, DOBB LW, MILLER NE, MOWRER OH, SEARS RR: *Frustration and Aggression.* New Haven, Yale University Press, 1939.

EPSTEIN S, TAYLOR SP: Instigation to aggression as a function of degree of defeat and perceived aggressive intent of the opponent. *J Pers* 35 (1967), 265–70.

FESHBACK S: The cartharsis hypothesis and some consequences of interaction with aggressive and neutral play objects. *J Person* 24 (1956), 449–462.

———, The function of aggression and the regulation of aggressive drive. *Psychol Rev* 71:4, 257–272.

———, Aggression. In Mussen PH (ed): *Carmichael's Manual of Child Psychology.* II. New York, Wiley, 1970, 159–359.

FIGLER S: Aggressive response to frustration among athletes and non-athletes. *Int J Phys Educ* 15 (Fall 1978), 29–36.

FISHER G: Discriminating violence emanating from over-controlled versus under-controlled aggressivity. *Br J Soc Clin Psychol* 9 (1970), 54–59.

FISHMAN CG: Need for approval and the expression of aggression under varying conditions of frustration. *J Pers Soc Psychol* 2:6 (1965), 809–816.

FREUD S: *A General Introduction to Psycho-Analysis.* New York, Boni and Liveright, 1920.

———, *Why War?* In Strachey J (ed): *Collected Papers V.* London, Hogarth, 1950, 273–87.

GEEN RG, BERKOWITZ L: Some conditions facilitating the occurrence of aggression after the observation of violence. *J Pers* 35, 666–672.

GORDON JE, SMITH E: Children's aggression: parental attitudes and the effects of an affiliation-arousing story. *J Pers Soc Psychol* 1:6 (1965), 654–59.

GREENWELL J, DENGERINK HA: The role of perceived versus actual attack in human physical aggression. *J Pers Soc Psychol* 26:1 (1973), 66–71.

HICKS DJ: Imitation and retention of film-mediated aggressive peer and adult models. *J Pers Soc Psychol* 5:1 (1965), 97–100.

HOKANSON JE, GORDON JE: The expression and inhibition of hostility in imaginative and overt behavior. *J Abnorm Soc Psychol* 57 (1958), 327–333.

HOLMES DS: Effects of overt aggression on level of physiology arousal. *J Pers Soc Psychol* 4:2 (1966), 189–95.

HUSMAN BF: An analysis of aggression in boxers, wrestlers, and cross-country runners as measured by the Rosenzweig P-F Study, selected TAT pictures and a sentence completion test. Unpublished doctoral dissertation, University of Maryland, College Park, 1954.

JOHNSON RN: *Aggression in Man and Animals.* Philadelphia, Saunders, 1972.

JOHNSON WR, HUTTON DC: Effects of a combative sport upon personality dynamics as measured by a projective test. *RQ* 26 (1955), 49–54.

JULIAN JW, BISHOP DW, FIEDLER FE: Quasi-therapeutic effects of intergroup competition. *J Pers Soc Psychol* 3:3 (1966), 321–327.

KAUFMAN H, FESHBACK S: Displaced aggression and its modification through exposure to anti-aggressive communications. *J Abnorm Soc Psychol* 67:1 (1963), 79–83.

KAUSS D: Study of an American football team. Unpublished monograph, Perceptual-Motor Learning Laboratory, UCLA, Los Angeles, 1975.

KENNY DT: An experimental test of the catharsis theory of aggression. Unpublished Doctoral dissertation, University of Washington, University Microfilms, 1953.

KNOTT PD, LASATER L, SCHUMAN R: Aggression-guilt and conditionability. *J Pers* 42:2 (1974), 332–344.

LAYMAN EM: Aggression in relation to play and sports. In Kenyon G (ed): *Contemporary Sport Psychology.* Chicago, Athletic Institute, 1968.

LEFEBVRE LM, PASSER MW: The effects of game location and importance on aggression in team sport. *Int J Sport Psychol* 5:2 (1974).

LEYENS JP, PICUS S: Identification with the winner of a fight and name mediation, their differential effects upon subsequent aggressive behaviors. *Br J Soc Clin Psychol* V (1973), 374–377.

LIPETZ ME, OSSORIO PG: Authoritarianism, aggression and status. *J Pers Soc Psychol* 5:4 (1967), 468–472.

LORENZ K: *On Aggression.* New York, Harcourt Brace, Jovanovich, 1966.

MCCORD W, MCCORD J, HOWARD A: Familial correlates of aggression in non-delinquent male children. *J Abnorm Soc Psychol* 63 (1961), 493–503.

MCGUIRE JM: Aggression and sociometric status with preschool children. *Sociometry* (December 1973), 542–549.

MCMURTRY WR: Investigation and inquiry into violence in amateur hockey. Ministry of Community and Social Services, Ontario, Canada, 1974.

NELSON J, GELFAND DB, HARTMAN D: Children's aggression following competition and exposure to an aggressive mode. *Child Dev* 40:4 (December 1969), 1085–1097.

NOBLE G: Film-mediated aggressive and creative play. *Br J Soc Clin Psychol* 9 (1970), 1–7.

OGILVIE DM: Aggression and identification. *J Pers Soc Psychol* 1:2 (1965), 168–172.

PASTORE N: The role of arbitrariness in the frustration-aggression hypothesis, *J Abnorm Soc Psychol* 47 (1953), 728–731.

PETERSON R: Aggression as a function of expected retaliation and aggressive level of target and aggressor. Unpublished Ph.D. dissertation, University of Iowa, Iowa City, 1968.

PISANO R, TAYLOR SP: Reduction of physical aggression: the effects of four strategies. *J Pers Soc Psychol* 19:2 (1971), 237–242.

ROCHA RF, ROGERS RW: Effects of competition and reward on children's aggression. *J Pers Soc Psychol* 33:5 (1976), 588–593.

ROLAND A: Persuadability in young children as a function of aggressive motivation and aggression conflict. *J Abnorm Soc Psychol* 66:5 (1963), 454–461.

ROSEN S: An approach to the study of aggression. *J Soc Psychol* 46 (1957), 259–67.

RYAN ED: The cathartic effect of vigorous motor activity on aggressive behavior. *RQ* 41 (1970), 542–51.

SCHACHTER S: The assumption of identity and peripheralist-centralist controversies in motivation and emotion. In Arnold MB: *Feelings and Emotions.* New York, Academic, 1970.

———, The interaction of cognitive and physiological determinants of emotional state. In Berkowitz L (ed): *Advances in Experimental Social Psychology.* I. New York, Academic, 1964.

SCOTT JP: *Animal Behavior.* Chicago, University of Chicago Press, 1952.

———, Sport and aggression. In Kenyon G (ed): *Contemporary Sport Psychology.* Chicago, Athletic Institute, 1968.

SEJWACZ D, DION K: Effects of choice, and social undesirability on unprovoked aggression. Paper presented at the Midwestern Psychological Association Convention, May 1972, Cleveland, Ohio.

SHORTELL J, EPSTEIN S, TAYLOR S: Instigation to aggression as a function of degree of defeat and capacity for massive retaliation. *J Pers* 38:2 (1970), 189–95.

SHUNTICH RJ, TAYLOR SP: The effects of alcohol on human physical aggression. *J Exp Res Pers* 6, 34–38.

SILVERMAN WH: The effects of social contact, provocation, and sex of opponent upon instrumental aggression. *J Exp Res Pers* 5 (1971), 310–316.

SMITH MD: Hostile outbursts in sport. In Lowe B (ed): *Sport Sociology Bulletin* 2:1 (Spring 1973), 6–11.

SMITH MD: Parents', peers', and coaches' sanctions for assaultive behavior in hockey. Paper presented at the Congress: Sport in the Modern World, Munich, Germany, 1972.

TAYLOR SP: Aggressive behavior and physiological arousal as a function of provocation and tendency to inhibit aggression. *J Pers* 35 (1967), 297–310.

THIBAUT J, COULES J: The role of communication in the reduction of interpersonal hostility. *J Abnorm Soc Psychol* 47 (1952), 770–77.

THIBAUT J, REICKEN HW: Authoritarianism, status, and the communication of aggression. *Hum Rel* 8 (1955), 95–120.

VOLKAMER M: Zur Aggressivitat in konkurrenz-orientierten sozialen Systemen. *Sportswissenschaft* 1 (1971), 68–72.

WHEELER L, CAGGIULA AR: The contagion of aggression. *J Exp Soc Psychol* 2 (1966), 1–10.

WILKINS JL, SCHARFF WH, SCHLOTTMANN RS: Personality type, reports of violence, and aggressive behavior. *J Pers Soc Psychol* 30:2 (1975), 243–247.

WILLIAMS JM, HOEPNER BJ, MOODY D, OGILVIE BC: Personality traits of champion level female fencers. *Res Q* 41:3 (1970), 446–458.

ZILLMAN D, BRYANT J: The effect of residual excitation on the emotional response to provocation and delayed aggressive behavior. *J Pers Soc Psychol* (in Press).

ZILLMAN D, JOHNSON RD, DAY KD: Attribution of apparent arousal and proficiency of recovery from sympathetic activation affecting excitation transfer to aggressive behavior. Monograph, Department of Communications, University of Indiana, Bloomington, 1970.

————, JOHNSON RD, DAY KD: Provoked and unprovoked aggressiveness in athletes. Monograph, Department of Communications, University of Indiana, Bloomington, 1972.

————, KATCHER AH, MILAVSKY B: Excitation transfer from physical exercise to subsequent aggressive behavior. *J Exp Soc Psychol* 8 (1972), 247–59.

Audience Effects

An athlete never performs without an audience. At times, the presence of spectators is apparent to all. However, even a "solitary" workout may be accompanied by an unseen audience, a group of people residing psychologically and socially in the mind of the performer. This audience, the athlete knows, stands ready to judge his or her performance at some future time, harshly or with kindness and praise.

Social psychologists have long been interested in the audience effect, or social facilitation. The 1898 study by Triplett, frequently cited as a historical "first" in social psychology, reflected an interest in the audience's influence on physical performance. He investigated what he termed "dynamogenic factors" (the audience effect); and found that positive changes occurred in two physical tasks, bicycle riding and the winding of a reel, as people watched.

During the next decades, sporadic interest was shown in the social phenomena reviewed in the paragraphs that follow. However, before the 1930s the work was rather piecemeal and failed to reflect any theoretical rationale. By the 1960s, however, two theoretical viewpoints emerged to explain the effects of observers on performance. These concepts have begun to produce some order within disorder among those researching this interesting topic.

Dimensions of the Problem

There are numerous aspects to the study of social facilitation. Most subtopics have just begun to be explored in organized ways. Only infre-

quent interest has been accorded audience effects on athletic performance and motor skill. There are also studies, using both animal and
human subjects, that have dwelt on what is termed "co-action." This
effect, while similar to that of the audience, refers to the impetus given
performance when other individuals also perform in close proximity to
the individual or group being studied. Thus, team members exert co-
action effects on their teammates in games, while fans in the stands
represent the audience effect.

Numerous problems have been explored, or are important topics for
research. These include:

1. The audience may vary in size. One wonders how large an audience
   may be, for the addition of more members will fail to heighten arousal
   levels and thus cease to modify performance of a group or an individual.

2. The audience, through facial expressions, presence, and/or noise, exerts influence upon performers. It is difficult, however, to separate
   these effects in well-controlled studies, and in the real world of sport.
   Moreover, attempting to ascertain the athlete's interpretations and
   perceptions of the cries and noise an audience produces may be
   almost impossible, or at least difficult.

3. Audiences may be psychologically distant, or be made up of people
   who are well known and close to the performer. An audience may be
   made up of hostile enemies, whose judgments are either highly
   valued or of no consequence to the performer. The audience may
   reside somewhere in the midground between these two extremes,
   composed of some spectators about whom the athlete cares and some
   who are perceived as disinterested or bland. The effects of these
   various kind of onlookers has not been thoroughly researched.[1]

4. An audience may express varying degrees of disapproval or approval
   of the athlete's efforts. Moreover, the approval or disapproval shown
   may take the form of specific comments, or consist of general verbal
   and nonverbal communication.

5. Audience reaction may vary in time during the athletic performance.
   It may, according to the sociologic study of the boxing crowd by Furst
   (1972) and others, be rather intermittent, due to the cyclic nature of
   the sport witnessed. Other sports in which cycles predominate include wrestling, gymnastics, figure skating, and track and field. Moreover, so-called continuous team sports are also cyclic in the manner
   in which the crowd interacts and reacts to "peaks and valleys" in the
   performance.
      Thus, in sport the audience may periodically emit indices of ten-
   sion, identification, anxiety, and pleasure, interpolated by periods of
   reflection or relaxation. In many sports, the crowd tension gradually
   builds up, particularly if the competition remains close and a winner

[1]Although Dr. Victor Matsudo and his able colleagues in Brazil have begun to study
"psychological closeness" of audiences as influential of fitness scores obtained from youthful athletes.

is not known until the final minutes. In other contests, the audience may remain psychologically removed from the action, perhaps because of the one-sided nature of the contest or other factors that fail to arouse spectator interest.

6. The athletes' (or experimental subject's) performance may modify itself, depending on whether or not performers feel that the audience is evaluating them or not. Moreover, athletes may or may not feel that audience evaluation is either important, or based upon real competencies to assess them. Thus, perception of the audience's expertise may exert various effects on the quality and quantity of performance.

7. Several interactive effects within the sports world are just beginning to be noted by experimenters; (a) the influence of the contest on the audience, (b) the influence of the audience on the athlete or team, and (c) the rather circular and cyclic influences of the coach, athlete (and others), and audience on one another.

8. Several studies have reflected an interest in the "cross-sex" effect upon performance. There is some information that under certain conditions the sex of an onlooker, relative to the sex of the performer, may be critical in the modification of the latter's performance. Status differences in audience-performer relationships are also in need of study.

9. The personality of the performer may be critical in establishing the nature of the audience effects on performance. Important are such traits as anxiety and self-confidence.

10. The type of task is important to consider, including the complexity of the act, whether or not it is well learned, and how much force is required in its execution. Bird (1975), discovering no audience effects in tasks involving steadiness and eye-hand control, suggested that the nature of the act is critical to assess.

11. Learning to cope with an audience may exert significant influences on successive trials in a skill, or in a sport, under the duress of onlookers. Little has been done experimentally to study this kind of learning or accommodation effect, despite its probable importance in athletic competition.

12. Little has been done to determine whether learning to work in front of an audience is task specific, or whether it generalizes from task to task. That is, may an athlete, after learning to deal with the stresses of competition while being watched within a familiar sport, remain calm and effective when changing sports?

13. Clinicians and sport psychologists in several European countries have introduced audience stress into practice sessions in attempts to prepare the athlete for later confrontations with spectators. There seems a scarcity of studies, however, that attempt to verify the efficiency of this kind of "stress modeling."

Foot (1973), in an attempt to sort out the various terms relating to social facilitation, co-action, and the audience effect, formulated Figure 9-1.

Foot pointed out that:

1. The schema presented represents only a first attempt, prior to the formulation of a more detailed classification system and model.

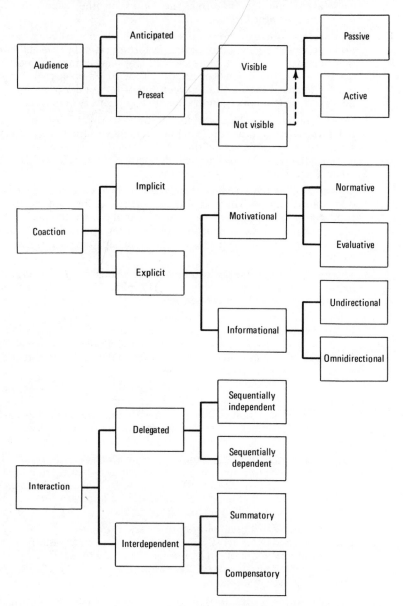

FIGURE 9-1. Proposal for the reclassification of group learning and performance. From Foot (1973), pp. 7–17.

2. The schema is meant to apply only to performance and learning in groups, including the acquisition of specific skills. Problem-solving tasks are excluded.

3. The diagram is based on the interchange of task-relevant cues rather than on the nature of the tasks themselves, in contrast to previous models.

Using this schema, Foot divides research into three main groups: (1) audience situations, (2) co-action, and (3) interaction. While the subdivisions to the right of the diagram, which describe the audience, are relatively clear-cut, those to the right of co-action and interaction need some clarification. For example, *implicit co-action* refers to those cases of co-action in which the interchange of cues has been minimized by the experimenter (or the situation). *Explicit co-action* implies that the interchange of certain social cues is possible. *Motivational cues* refer to achievements of group members and the standards they attain. *Normative* means accepted, or aspired, goals of individual attainment within the group. *Evaluative* suggests the provisions of social feedback, and the display of results actually attained by individuals.

Informational cues refer to information from others, which may in turn aid the performance or learning of individuals. This term, in other contexts, has also been referred to as vicarious, or imitative, learning. *Unidirectional information transmission* means that one or more members of the group are receiving information from one or more members of the group in a one-way fashion. *Omnidirectional information transmission* means learning or performance situations arranged so that each member can use and benefit from information provided by a number of co-workers, and can in turn ask questions and engage in two-way communication with others.

The interaction component of the schema thus involves task learning and performance, which requires dependence between group members. Team play in many sports is an obvious example. Situations in which players work directly with each other are more common in sport than is independent play. However, when performance is divided and delegated and specific functions assigned to various performers, this is termed *delegated performance.*

Sequentially independent task components implies that group members can execute their skills in any order, or at any time in relation to each other. An example would be the play of a golf team. When task components must be executed in a prescribed order, the term is *sequentially dependent* task performance.

An *interdependent task* suggests a completely interactive type of group functioning, as when individuals simultaneously apply themselves to the same task. Foot suggests that there are two types of interdependence in task performance: (1) *summatory,* in which group members' contributions are added together to produce a final outcome, and (2) *compensatory,* in which group members are constantly adjusting their performance so that the errors of others in the group are either corrected or reduced.

It is believed that Foot's classification system is the most comprehensive one to appear at this time. The often confusing and conflicting findings emanating from theoretical studies can often be explained with reference to his detailed breakdown. Unfortunately, the literature available, reviewed on the following pages, does not allow one to place studies in all the subclassifications formulated by Foot. Research by Bird and others indicates that co-action and audience effects are different when assessing performance fluctuations, while the tasks exploring some of the ideas presented by Foot are from the laboratory and often highly dissimilar from those seen in sport. Holding a stylus on a pursuit rotor bears little resemblance to an Olympic wrestling match, while rolling marbles up an incline into a "proper" hole is quite different from playing goalie on an ice hockey team.

Thus, the review that follows reveals only in general ways how the presence of an audience *may* cause performance fluctuations. It is hoped that some readers will have the desire and resources to further pursue some of the questions only touched upon by the available literature.

THEORIES OF SOCIAL FACILITATION

Two main theoretical positions have emerged to explain social facilitation. One might be termed "drive theory." Based on concepts involving arousal and activation, it has been advanced by Zajonc in a 1969 article. The second model has been proposed by Cottrell and his colleagues (1968). Their premise includes the observation that the mere presence of others is not the primary source of facilitative responses in motor tasks and endeavors. Rather, they suggest that "audience effects" are the results of social learning. Most important, they contend, are the evaluative effects of those observing the performance. These effects in turn produce what they term "evaluation apprehension" in the performer(s). This latter model postulates an intermediate variable, interpretation about social consequences, interposed between the mere presence of spectators and the measurable changes in arousal level and performance modifications.

Audience, Arousal, and Performance

Following a thorough review of the literature dealing with co-action and audience effects on both human and animal performance, Zajonc came to the following major conclusions: (1) Audience effects are particularly likely to improve simple motor responses. (2) Responses that are not well-learned are likely to be disrupted by the presence of an audience; conversely, well-learned tasks are likely to be enhanced in the presence of an audience.

In support of the initial premise is evidence from studies such as that by Travis (1925), who found that following a training period on pursuit rotor, significant audience effects were elicited. The pursuit rotor had been well-learned in this study, before an audience was added as a variable, and thus had become a simple task before the onset of social facilitation. Numerous other studies have produced similar findings, including that by Dashiell (1930), who found improvement in multiplication and word association tasks in the presence of others.

Studies carried out in the 1960s by Martens and others have produced data illustrating the possible validity of Zajonc's second major premise—that an audience does modify measures of arousal in experimental subjects. Martens' data also illustrate how an audience may tend to suppress progress during the initial stages of learning a motor skill, while facilitating learning in later stages. Martens and Landers (1969) also suggest that co-actors facilitated performance on a simple well-learned endurance task.

These data reflect much earlier work pairing reaction time with sound cues of varying intensities. Work of this nature, carried out during the early decades of the twentieth century, indicates that there is an optimum level of arousal necessary to perform best in a given task. This principle, named after some of the early workers in the field Yerkes-Dodson, has been modified in recent years, particularly when dealing with tasks that vary from simple to complex. Thus, in diagrammatic form, it can be seen that in more difficult tasks, a narrower range of activation-arousal is permitted to produce maximum performance, while in simple tasks the range of activation to produce maximum performance may be broader (Figure 9–2).

To summarize, Zajonc linked both the audience effect and co-action effects to certain tenets within the Hull-Spence Drive Theory. He hypothesized that the presence of an audience increases an individual drive level. In turn, during this heightened state of drive, a subject will respond to stimuli with those responses that are dominant (well-learned and simple). During early learning of a task, Zajonc assumes that raising

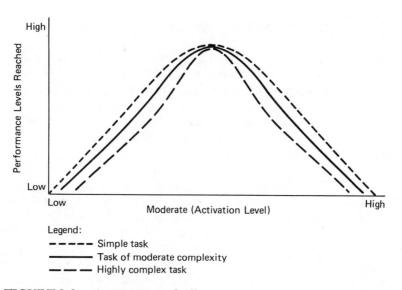

Legend:

– – – – – Simple task

————— Task of moderate complexity

— — — Highly complex task

FIGURE 9-2. Activation and effects upon optimum performance in tasks differing in complexity.

drive level elicits strong and competing incorrect response tendencies, which dominate the weaker, recently learned correct responses.

In the later stages of learning, during the performance of a well-learned task (or a task simple to execute), correct responses predominate when drive level is heightened. Thus, in front of an audience, performance on such tasks improves. Zajonc's major ideas are diagrammed in Figure 9-3.

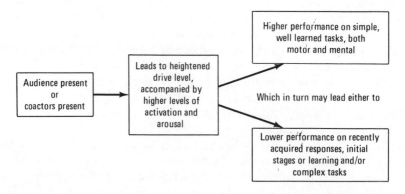

FIGURE 9-3. Zajonc's theory of social facilitation and co-action as related to performance and learning.

Drive and Social Experience

More recently, Cottrell has proposed a model to explain the audience effect. It involves not only the concept of drive level, but also social learning and the performer's perceptions of the possible or positive social outcomes derived from the audience's presence. Cottrell postulated that the evaluative tendencies and potentials of the audience as assessed by the performer, rather than the mere presence of onlookers, are critical molders of performance.

A study by Crabbe (1974) resulted in data consistent with Cottrell's hypotheses. The effects of social facilitation on the performance and learning of children of various ages was seemingly molded by the experiences the child had when performing in front of audiences. A balancing task was employed, in which the subjects attempted to stabilize a platform while standing on it.

An early study by Laird (1923) also demonstrated the influence of an audience's evaluation on performance. Using college-age students as subjects, a small audience of peers was used to "razz" them during the time they performed a physical task. This derogatory evaluation had measurably negative effects on performance. The emotional repercussions following the experiment were great. A number of the subjects threatened to terminate their membership in the fraternity from which both the subjects and the "razzers" had been obtained.

The arousal-activation effects of spectators verbally harassing performers was further confirmed in a study by Latane and Arrowood (1963). They found, as would be expected, that negative responses from audiences depressed scores on complex tasks, while facilitating performance on simple ones.

However, in a study by Kozar (1973), the data failed to illustrate any performance differences (in a balancing task) in front of supportive and nonsupportive audiences. This points to the need for further research on this problem, and on the numerous questions posed in the earlier parts of this chapter. Reference to Foot's model might be helpful in sorting out the reasons for dissimilar findings.

There are more data supporting Cottrell's contentions than going against them. Henchy and Glass (1968), as well as Cottrell (1968), obtained findings that support the importance of "evaluative potential" as an important molder of performance in front of onlookers. For example, in Cottrell's study one group of subjects learned a task alone, another group performed in the presence of an attentive audience (of two people), while a third group was in the presence of a two-person audience, both of whom were blindfolded and thus purportedly had "no evaluative potential." The subjects' performance differed little under the alone *vs.* the blindfolded conditions, thus confirming Cottrell's ideas.

Henchy and Glass reported similar findings. An audience of purported experts elicited significantly more dominant responses than did an audience whom the subjects were told were nonexperts. These data, as well as those from another investigation by Klinger (1969), demonstrated that the "potential for evaluation" seems more critical than the mere presence of an audience in molding human performance reflected in the raising of drive and arousal levels.[2]

In diagrammatic form, the model to explain social facilitation as proposed by Cottrell is seen in Figure 9–4. In essence, Cottrell interposes cognitive mediators and social learning experiences ("How is the audience feeling about me now? How have they felt about my performance in the past?") between the performer's view of onlookers and his or her performance changes.

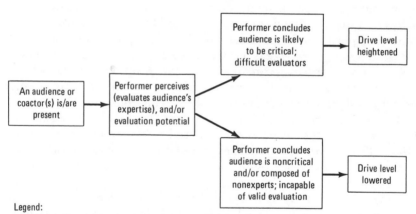

Legend:

1. If <u>Drive Level</u> is <u>lowered</u>, performance on simple well learned tasks is likely to be lowered; while performance on complex tasks, or those during initial stages of learning is likely to be helped.

2. If <u>Drive Level</u> is <u>heightened</u>, performance of simple tasks, well learned tasks is likely to be improved; while that on difficult tasks, and/or those in early stages of learning is likely to be impeded.

FIGURE 9-4.   The Cottrell model to explain social facilitation and co-action effects upon performance.

[2] At times, however, so-called nonevaluative blindfolded audiences may possess evaluative potential if all variables are not controlled. In the study by Haas and Roberts (1975), for example, both performers and blindfolded audience were exposed to sound cues reflecting quality of performance, and under these conditions the "nonevaluative audience" elicited performance effects. The study by Rajecki (1977) and others elicited no differences in performance between audiences, one of which was blindfolded and the other permitted to observe (using a maze task).

Athletes and Audiences

It is believed that Cottrell's model better explains how an athlete may be affected by audiences than do the postulates formulated by Zajonc. Several analyses of the psychodynamics of athletes' reactions to fans, obtained from interview data, confirm the way athletes think about what their audiences think. Moreover, the athletes' interpretations of the feelings and thoughts of their fans seem to influence performance. For example, clinical psychologists often find that under interview conditions, athletes express marked dislike for their fans. While the athletes realize that the presence of an audience may aid their performance, they also realize that: (1) the audience has not participated directly in the rigors of their training and (2) the fans are fickle, applauding them one day for good performance, and booing them the next for poor performance. Thus, athletes realize that despite their evaluative role, audiences participate vicariously primarily when the rewards of winning are apparent, withdrawing their support when losing seems possible.

Some athletes block off critical comments from fans, either during or following games, while others are quite sensitive to this kind of social evaluation. In the latter case, the athlete seems to be covertly saying, "I am discounting your superficial support and critical evaluations. I would rather maintain my own counsel, perhaps with the help of those whose evaluations I do value and trust, those of my coach and teammates. Thus, I will try hard, or relax, in ways dictated by my own feelings as based on the evaluations I make of others, not on the covert evaluations that are not always solicited." Thus, a strong case can be made for the importance of cognitive mediation when assessing the audience effect.

Co-action Effects in Sport

In the real world of sport, it is often difficult to separate audience effects from effects emanating from teammates' presence. Undoubtedly, co-action effects are quite strong in sport, as athletes labor with the help and under the scrutiny of their own co-workers on the team. In an effort to assess co-action effects, Obermeier and his colleagues (1977) conducted two field studies within "natural settings."

One study involved 65 dogs, who ran both with and without companions. Significant differences were found when the two conditions were compared. The authors suggest that this finding confirms Zajonc's hypothesis concerning drive level and its effect on well-learned responses, in this case running.

The second study by Obermeier's group employed 14 high school and college age subjects, running nine 400-meter dashes under the following conditions: (1) alone, (2) starting on the inside line (co-action), and (3) starting on the outside lane (co-action, but with less opportunity to observe competitors). Two hypotheses were suggested: (1) that running under co-acting conditions would be faster, and (2) that there would be differences in variability in 100-meter portions of the races between the groups starting from the inside and the outside lane because of the amount of visual information each condition permitted the runners about their co-actors.

The findings included: (1) subjects paced themselves more evenly when running; (2) 10 of the 1⁻ runners ran faster under co-acting conditions; (3) activation measures, including pulse rates and self-reports, did not differ among the groups.

The findings indicate less support for an activation hypothesis than for Cottrell's concepts of evaluation. The faster times elicited from the co-actors on the second and third 100 meters suggested that as they viewed their competition, and at times closed the "stagger" in the start, their thoughts may have urged them to better or at least to more variable performances than was true under the solitary running conditions. In general, it was found that the subjects preferred to run in the inside lane where they had more opportunity to assess and evaluate their opponents' abilities as they performed.

Additional studies of this nature, in the naturalistic settings provided by competitive sport, may further aid in the analysis of co-action as well as of audience effects on athletes in team and individual sports.

The Audience Effect on Children and Youth

Data from research in which the audience effect has been studied in younger children and youth confirms hypotheses from studies in which older subjects have been used. There is evidence from children and youth, however, that at times younger people may act differently in the presence of an audience than do older individuals. Further, these reactions may in turn translate into differences in performance.

The Polish researcher Missiuro (1964), for example, studied measures of activation, endurance, and muscular tension changes in young children as they performed in the presence of an audience. He concluded that children under the age of about 6 years generally became activated when exposed to an audience, but that this heightened arousal did not usually translate itself into improved performance, even in simple direct tasks. He concluded that it takes a level of maturity, reflected in middle childhood, before heightened drive levels due to the presence of spectators become useful in enhancing a child's performance.

Several researchers have explored the relationships between maturity and anxiety in youthful performers confronted with an audience. The interaction and influence of these two variables are often observed informally when observing a school play or musical performance. These same factors are also important when children perform physical tasks in the presence of others. Pavio (1964), for example, studied child-rearing antecedents of audience sensitivity. He concluded that mothers who ignored their children's success, and punished failure, produced children who later evidenced "audience anxiety."

Jones and Corbes (1968) also explored the effects of anxiety and the presence of peers on performance in children. They concluded that the presence of an audience, *not* anxiety, contributed most to the disruption of performance in a maze task.

Confirming the impression that the presence of others has marked effects on performance in preschool children are data from a study by Stevenson, Keen, and Knights (1963). They found that supportive statements from strangers had a more facilitating effect on the performance of a simple motor task than did similar comments coming from parents. This apparent reinforcing value of a stranger's comments, or even those of disliked peers, in contrast to effects from parents' comments can be explained with reference to several processes. (1) Parents who usually constantly reward or punish their children (verbally or physically) for both good and poor performance may begin after time to lose their reinforcing properties. (2) Because of their novelty and their apparently objective approach, strangers act as more powerful positive or negative reinforcers.

Thus, the coach of a youthful athletic team may, because of novelty, be a more potent reinforcer in the life of the child and may elicit better performance by heightening drive level in tasks well learned. At the same time, continued exposure to a coach whose comments are frequent, both negative and positive, may at times result in a lowering of the coach's potential to change performance, as may have been true earlier of the parents' comments.

Other data from studies of children and youth tend to confirm some of the propositions that relate audience effects to performance and learning. Crabbe (1974), for example, attempted to ascertain whether both second grade and preschool children were significantly changed during the early stages of learning a motor task. Both an easy and a difficult task were employed. His findings included the following:

1. The rate of learning for preschool subjects was greater in the "alone" condition than in front of an audience. However, the reverse was true among the second grade (7-year-old) subjects. He concluded that this finding supported Cottrell's suggestion that prior social evaluation experiences influence response tendencies. Had prior social experience

not been a critical variable, the performance and learning of the two age groups would have been similar or identical in front of an audience.

2. The *rate* of learning for preschool subjects was lower than for second-graders when both were being watched by others. Thus, in a sense Zajonc's theoretical position relative to drive level was partially supported. It is obvious that this type of investigation needs further expansion to include not only a greater variety of motor tasks, but children and youth of different ages.

Further investigations exploring variables important to the study of the audience effect in people of various ages are those by Clark and Fouts (1973) and Baldwin and Levin (1958). In the latter investigation, the effects of "public and private" success or failure on a repetitive motor task in children was studied.

Clark and Fouts also studied the possibility that the child's assessment of the evaluators influences performance in various ways. Their findings illustrate the importance of social evaluation to motor performance in children. It was discovered, for example, that the children performed *more poorly* on a simple pulling task in front of an experimenter with whom they had previously had positive experiences, than in front of an individual with whom they had had negative experiences. That is, the presence of individuals expected to evaluate someone negatively may heighten drive level, which in turn will improve performance on simple direct tasks.

The rather sparse data available make the formation of inferences more valid than the stating of solid principles. It may be fruitful to explore further the child-rearing antecedents of audience anxiety in children. Even in children, the evaluation of the social circumstances surrounding their performance, and of the potential evaluators themselves, may be more important than the mere presence of others as they perform.

Some of the studies cited indicate that higher drive levels are elicited when children perform in front of strangers, and even when exposed to people they dislike. Such effects seem likely to translate themselves into positive performance increments in both well-learned and simple direct tasks. Further studies of the conceptual influences on children's performances in front of onlookers would seem to be called for.

ANXIETY

Several investigators have explored the interaction of anxiety and the audience effect as people performed and learned motor skills. The diverse findings are probably due to the different and perhaps imprecise measures of anxiety employed and to differences in the tasks used.

Difficult to assess in such studies, and in the real world, are the influences of *learning* to perform in front of an audience, and coming to grips with anxiety in a performance situation.

Anxiety may influence drive level in complex ways. For example, in some studies, using both animals and humans as subjects, creating fear has been shown to lessen arousal. In other investigations, heightening anxiety has led to higher levels of arousal and activation. Indeed, several researchers have failed to find any significant differences in the physiologic responses denoting activation evidenced by subjects who obtained high and low scores on the anxiety scales.

It is possible that individuals may be discovered who possess specific anxieties about performing in front of an audience. Thus the relationship between "audience anxiety" to generally anxious states that may be "embedded in their personalities" can be studied. The nature of just how fear of audiences may be engendered in childhood also needs untangling experimentally, and via anecdotal data.

There have, however, been a handful of studies of some of these questions. For example, in work by Ganzer (1968) and Cox (1966), it was found that when learning a task, subjects scoring high on anxiety scales did not perform as well as did those scoring low on the same scales. Ganzer used Sarason's Test Anxiety Scale, while Cox employed the children's form of the Yale Test Anxiety Scale.

Some of the studies have involved rather subtle subproblems. For example, Wapner and Alpher (1952) found that an unseen audience seemed to represent a greater threat to individuals scoring high on anxiety scales than did an audience actually present. Paulus (1974), using expert gymnasts, found that when the subjects were warned that an audience was about to be present, it proved disruptive to performance. When groups of gymnasts were not aware that they were about to perform in front of a group, less disruption in performance occurred. Thus, a quality that might be termed "anxiety about a forthcoming audience" was seemingly "tapped." Studies involving the time between an athlete's being warned that an audience will be present and actual performance in front of onlookers may shed further light on this delayed effect.

It is not altogether clear just how audience effects and anxiety either combine or work independently when modifying performance and learning. For example, Martens (1968) found that once a task was learned, subjects scoring high in measures of anxiety performed significantly better than those scoring low. However, he also suggests that "anxiety is independent of the audience variable when performing a complex task."

It would also seem logical to assume that the larger the audience, the more anxiety would be engendered in a performer. However, Wankel (1977) found that the size of the audience did not affect anxiety. More studies of this relationship seem warranted.

At times, interpretation of the data is made difficult because of contrasting tasks. The findings derived from studies in which motor skills are employed do not always agree with those employing tasks that combine a motor and mental component. For example, Morris and his co-workers (1975) at Tennessee State University found that measures of both trait and state anxiety correlated neither negatively nor positively with measures of typing skill, in contrast to studies in which sports skills have been employed.

It thus appears that further work on the following problems are needed:

1. Changes in accommodation to audience anxiety, as a function of learning and as related to chronological age.
2. Relationships between measures of both state and trait anxiety and performance, with the former measures obtained over a time period and periodically prior to athletic performance.
3. Attempts to ascertain whether certain complexes of personality traits, or child-rearing backgrounds, in any way predict whether exposure to an audience with accompanying anxiety either raises or lowers activation levels in rather consistent ways in certain people.

CROSS-SEX EFFECTS

The sex of the observer vs. the sex of the performer has been studied in several pieces of work during the past several years. Stevenson, for example, in studies carried out in the 1960s, studied social facilitation as a function of this so-called cross-sex effect. His data revealed that the sex of an experimenter (audience) often influenced the rate of motor responses elicited from schoolchildren. In one investigation, larger increments in performance were elicted by female experimenters when voicing supportive statements than by male experimenters doing the same. This finding was interpreted by Stevenson as meaning that the "mother figure" has an important role in the upbringing of a child. The same kinds of results are found in studies using adult subjects.

Noer and Whittaker (1963) elicited the cross-sex effect in an indirect way. They suggested to female subjects that "girls do twice as well as boys in this task, but you didn't." A mirror star-tracing task was employed. The reverse suggestion was made to male subjects ("males do twice as well as females, but you didn't"). Cross-sex effects were found in the data reflecting covert intersex competition.

Further investigations in a variety of tasks, exploring such variables as personality traits and audience size, would seem helpful.

TRAINING EFFECTS

Vanek and Cratty (1970) described the way performance under audience conditions is trained for in the countries of Eastern Europe. Coaches in these countries at times use recordings of crowd reactions, as well as real crowds, during practice sessions to accustom athletes to the "confusions" of audiences. In this way it is hoped that some training effects, or modeling effects, will occur, and the performers will be aided when appearing before real audiences.

Thus, possible disruptions of complex performance will be trained for, as well as possible magnifications of simple task efforts. For example, weight lifters in these countries often train with records of competitive noises so that they will not be thrown off when lifting under competitive circumstances. Real crowds are sometimes brought in to verbally harass performers, in still another attempt to simulate the stresses of competitive conditions.

This writer is unaware, however, of experimental studies in which verification or negation of these training effects has been explored. The clinical observations available suggest that such modeling may take place in the following stages. The speed with which a coach may move from the first to other phases in the series depends upon his or her sensitivity to the athletes' speed of accommodation to the conditions.

1. An initial and prolonged period of time should be devoted to "overlearning" the skills and subskills involved in the sport, independent of onlookers. This stage should be prolonged in the case of difficult and complex tasks, and shortened if the tasks involve relatively simple and direct movements.

2. The next stage might include the introduction of crowd noises through recordings. The volume of this noise may be varied, and gradually increased until it approximates the levels to be encountered in competition. Likewise, the noise volume might be unexpectedly varied at times.

3. Next, silent spectators might be introduced during some practice sessions. Later, these spectators might emit positive encouragement, cheering, etc.

4. Finally, spectators might be "programmed" to verbally harass the athletes during practices. As the athletes become able to "take it," the vocalizations might become more and more pointed and personal in nature.

If the athlete's skills seem to break down under these progressive conditions, the mentor may have to "back up" to a less stressful level.

IMPLICATIONS FOR THE COACH

The coach may engage in several strategies to heighten the positive performance effects of the presence of an audience, while lessening the possible negative effects. For example, the coach should prepare athletes in advance for performance fluctuations they may experience in front of an audience. This preparation can consist of (1) merely informing them of the negative effects upon precise skills and positive effects upon simple direct acts, (2) importing audiences of varying sizes during practices so that habituation to the feelings of activation caused by an audience occurs, (3) subjecting them to first expected and then unexpected negative verbal appraisals from onlookers, and (4) holding conferences and discussions with the athletes about the possible anxieties engendered by various audiences, unseen and obvious, within the athlete's psychosocial "life space." During such discussion, athletes may be encouraged to look within themselves when setting preperformance standards and evaluating efforts following contests, rather than being unduly influenced by obvious or subtle appraisals from others.

It may be advisable at times, when an athlete evidences a great deal of anxiety about an audience, to gradually build up his or her tolerance to stress by gradually increasing the number of onlookers who are permitted to watch workouts and/or gradually changing the quantity of negative comments coming from contrived audiences.

Most helpful, before the various "games" suggested above are engaged in, is to search into the athlete's background and attempt to determine the causes of undue fear when performing in front of a group. This may be done with or without the help of a clinical psychologist. This type of background search may uncover the presence of one or both parents who continually set too-high performance standards, or an exceptional brother or sister with whom the athlete was continually compared and found lacking. In this way, coach and athlete can uncover the reasons for negative audience reactions instead of only being concerned with the obvious and immediate performance results.

Additionally, the athlete may need help in dealing with barely hidden negative feelings about the audience and fans. Many athletes, if not most, are not overly fond of the fans. While knowing that their presence is likely to help performance, most athletes harbor negative feelings about those who seem to trade on the blood, sweat, and tears they expend. At the same time, these negative feelings may arouse guilt in the athlete, which he or she may need to ventilate with the help of a psychological counselor and/or coach.

In addition to fan pressure, athletes are beset with social groups extraneous to the team itself, who are not present during competitions. These groups consist of parents, as well as other members of the community who try to "help." At times, these individuals contribute to the success of the team, they really care, and both the players and coaches appreciate their concern and interest. At other times, however, their presence may prove distracting and at times, if excessive, may harm individual and team efforts. It is usually not helpful, for example, if an unusual number of "hangers-on" are present during practices.

Thus, the coach should attempt to assess the motives and effects of these individuals, and to determine who may be a help to the total team effort and how much they should be around the team and its members. Additionally, however, it should be determined whose effects the coach may wish to neutralize, and finally, it should be ascertained which individuals should be removed from practices and locker rooms entirely.

SUMMARY

This chapter has pulled together information relating the effects of an audience on physical performance. Much of the data and findings can be best described as piecemeal, and few definitive answers are presently available. However, the model by Foot is believed to be a helpful starting point in attempting to sort out presently available data and trying to engage in further research.

Hopeful signs are the introduction of models by Zajonc and Cottrell, formulated to explain audience effects. The former suggests that the mere presence of an audience heightens drive level, which in turn seems to aid simple direct tasks, as well as well-learned ones. This same raising of drive, however, is believed to impede initial learning of a new task, as well as performance of a complex task.

Cottrell, on the other hand, proposes a "social evaluation" hypothesis, stating essentially that the degree to which the audience affects performance depends on the perceptions of the performer relative to the audience's evaluative potential. If the audience is judged to be critical and capable of adequate evaluations, the stress is likely to be greater than if the audience is either passive or absent. Much of the data supports this assumption.

Audiences are likely to activate a performer. However, at times, separating co-action effects (the effects of co-performers in the presence of the athlete) from the effects of fans is difficult. Field studies in which the audience effect has been studied in athletes are absent, as are investigations of whether or not an athlete in practice may be trained to accommodate to the stress of onlookers.

Maturation seems to focus energies and result in task improvement, after the age of about 6. Children and youths differ in the anxiety they exhibit performing in front of an audience, perhaps as a function of early child-rearing practices, which at this point have not been clearly defined.

Cross-sex effects on performance probably exist, but have not as yet been well researched. Further work is also needed to determine what predisposing personality traits, backgrounds of success and failure, and early childhood experiences contribute to or detract from performance as children, youth, and adults perform athletic skills in the presence of onlookers.

QUESTIONS FOR DISCUSSION

1. What is meant by the fact that an athlete never performs without an audience present?

2. What does the concept of "evaluative potential" mean, with regard to the audience effect? Can you give examples of audiences that evidence high *vs.* low evaluative potential?

3. What effects is the presence of an audience likely to have upon a simple physical act, upon a complex skill, upon a well-learned skill, upon a poorly learned skill?

4. What personality traits in the athlete are likely to influence his or her performance in front of an audience? What child-rearing practices are likely to later influence the way an athlete performs in front of a group?

5. Discuss the cross-sex effect, relative to influences upon physical performance.

6. What changes in the audience effect on motor performance are seen in children, youth, and adults of various ages?

7. Can accommodation to the audience effect be trained for? What attempts have been made to do that? What stages might be initiated within such "accommodation" programs?

8. What influence(s) does the audience seem to have on the learning of motor skills?

9. What are the differences between co-action effects and the audience effects on physical performance? May these effects always be separated

in the real world of sport? How are they separated in the experimental laboratory?

BIBLIOGRAPHY

ALLPORT FH: The influence of the group upon association and thought. *J Exp Psychol* 3 (1920), 159–182.

BALDWIN AL, LEVIN H: Effects of public and private success or failure on children's repetitive motor behavior. *Child Dev* 29:3 (September 1958), 165–170.

BEAM JC: Serial learning and conditioning under real-life stress. *J Abnorm Soc Psychol* 51 (1955), 543–551.

BENTON AA: Reactions to demands to win from an opposite sex opponent. *J Pers* 41:2 (1973), 430–436.

BERRY JE, MARTIN B: GSR reactivity as a function of anxiety, instructions and sex. *J Abnorm Soc Psychol* 54 (1957), 9–12.

BIRD AM: Effects of social facilitation upon females' performance of two psychomotor tasks. *Res Q* 44:3 (1973), 322–330.

——— Cross sex-effects of subject and audience during motor performance. *Res Q* 46:3 (1975), 379–384.

BURWITZ L, NEWELL KM: The effects of the mere presence of coactors on learning a motor skill. *J Mot Behav* 4 (1972), 99–102.

CARMET DW, LATCHFORD M: Rate of simple motor responding as a function of coaction, sex of the participants, and the presence or absence of the experimenter. *Psychonomic Sci* 20 (1970), 253–54.

CLARK NJ, FOUTS GT: Effects of positive, neutral and negative experiences with an audience on social facilitation in children. *Percept Mot Skills* 37 (1973), 1008–1010.

COTTRELL NB: Performance in the presence of other human beings: mere presence, audience, and affiliation effects. In Simmal, Hoppe, Milton (eds): *Social Facilitation and Imitative Behavior.* Boston, Allyn & Bacon, 1968, 91–110.

COTTRELL N, RITTLE R, WACK D: The presence of an audience and list types (competitional and non-competitional) as joint determinants of performance in paired-associates learning. *J Pers* 35 (1967), 425–434.

COTTRELL NB, WACK RH, SEKERAK GJ, RITTLE RH: Social facilitation of dominant responses by the presence of an audience and the mere presence of others. *J Pers Soc Psychol* 9 (1968), 245–50.

COX FN: Some relationships between test anxiety, presence or absence of male persons, and boys' performance on a repetitive motor task. *J Exp Child Psychol* 6, 1–12.

CRABBE JM: Social facilitation effects on children during early stages of motor learning. Paper presented at the March 1974 meeting of the American Association of Physical Education, Health, and Recreation.

CRATTY BJ: "Social motives." In *Movement Behavior and Motor Learning.* 3rd ed. Philadelphia, Lea and Febiger, 1974, Chap. 14.

———, "Spectators and fans." In *Psychology in Contemporary Sport.* Englewood Cliffs, New Jersey, Prentice-Hall, 1973, Chap. 14.

———, "The audience." In *Social Dimensions of Physical Activity.* Englewood Cliffs, New Jersey, Prentice-Hall, 1967, Chap. 7.

DASHIELL JF: An experimental analysis of some group effects. *J Abnorm Soc Psychol* 25 (1930), 190–199.

FOOT HC: Group learning and performance: a reclassification. *Br J Soc Clin Psychol* 12 (1973), 7–17.

———, LEE TR: Social feedback in the learning of a motor skill. *Br J Soc Psychol* (1971), 309–319.

FURST RT: The boxer and his audience: an empirical assessment. Paper presented at the 2nd Annual International Congress of Sports, German Olympic Committee, Munich, 1972.

GANZER VJ: Effects of audience presence and test anxiety on learning and retention in a serial learning situation. *J Pers Soc Psychol* 8 (1968), 194–199.

GATES G: The effect of an audience upon performance. *J Abnorm Soc Psychol* 18 (1924), 334–44.

GILL DL, MARTENS R: The informational and motivational influence of social reinforcement and motor performance. *J Mot Behav* 7:3 (September 1975), 171–182.

HAAS J, ROBERT GC: Effect of evaluative others upon learning and performance of a complex motor task. *J Mot Behav* 7:2 (June 1975), 81–90.

HARRISON J, MACKINNON PCB: Physiological role of the adrenal medulla in the palmar anihidrotic response to stress. *J Appl Physiol* 21, (1966), 88–92.

HENCHY T, GLASS DC: Evaluation apprehension and social facilitation of dominant and subordinate responses. *J Pers Soc Psychol* 10 (1968), 446–54.

HULL C: *A Behavior System, An Introduction to Behavior Theory Concerning the Individual Organism.* New Haven, Yale University Press, 1952.

JONES JC, CORBES CJ: Effects of anxiety and presence or absence of peers upon performance and levels of aspiration. *Psychology in the School* 2:5 (April 1968), 175–77.

KLINGER E: Feedback effects and social facilitation of vigilance performance: mere coaction versus potential evaluation. *Psychonomic Sci* 14 (1969), 161–62.

KOZAR B: The effects of a supportive and non-supportive audience upon learning a gross motor skill. *Int J Sports Psychol* 4 (1973), 27–38.

LAIRD DA: Changes in motor control and individual variations under the influence of "razzing." *J Exp Psychol* 6 (1923), 233–246.

LANDERS DM: Observational learning of a motor skill: temporal spacing of demonstrations and audience presence. *J Mot Behav* 7:4 (December 1975), 281–288.

LANDERS DM, LANDERS DM: Teacher versus peer models: effects of models' presence and performance level on motor behavior. *J Mot Behav* 5:3 (September 1973), 129–140.

LATANE B, ARROWOOD J: Emotional Arousal and Task Performance. *J Appl Psychol* 47 (1963), 324–327.

MARTENS R: Effect of an audience on learning and performance of a complex motor skill. *J Pers Soc Psychol* 12 (1969), 252–260.

———, *Social Psychology and Physical Activity.* New York, Harper & Row, 1975.

———, LANDERS DM: Coaction effects on a muscular endurance task. *R Q* 40 (1969), 733–37.

———, LANDERS DM: Evaluation potential as a determinant of coaction effects. *J Exp Soc Psychol* 8 (1972), 347–59.

———, Palmar sweating and the presence of an audience. *J Exp Soc Psychol* 5 (1969), 371–374.

MISSIURO W: The development of reflex activity in children. In Jokl E, Simon E (eds): *International Research in Sport and Physical Education.* Springfield, Illinois, C. Thomas, 1964.

MORRIS LW, SMITH LR, ANDREWS ES, MORRIS NC: The relationship of emotionality and worry components of anxiety to motor skills performance. *J Mot Behav* 7:2 (June 1975), 121–130.

NOER D, WHITTAKER J: Effects of masculine-feminine ego involvement on the acquisition of a mirror-tracing skill. *J Psychol* 56 (1963), 15–17.

OBERMEIER GE, LANDERS DM, ESTER MA: Social facilitation of speed events: the coaction effect in racing dogs and trackmen. In Landers DM, Christina RW (eds): *Psychology of Motor Behavior and Sport,* Champaign, Illinois, Human Kinetics Publishers, 1977.

PAULUS PB, JUDD BB, BERNSTEIN IH: Social facilitation and sports. In Landers DM, Christina RW (eds): *Psychology of Motor Behavior and Sport.* Champaign, Illinois, Human Kinetics Publishers, 1977.

———, CORNELIUS WL: An analysis of gymnastic performance under conditions of practice and spectator observation. *Res Q* 45:1 (1974), 56–63.

PAVIO A: Childrearing antecedents of audience sensitivity. *Child Dev* 35 (1964), 397–416.

RAJECKI DW, ICKES W, CORCORAN C, LENERZ K: Social facilitation of humans' performance: mere presence of others. *J Soc Psychol* 102 (1977), 297–310.

RAPHELSON AC: The relationships among imaginative, direct verbal and physiological measures of anxiety in an achievement situation. *J Abnorm Soc Psychol* 54 (1975), 13–18.

ROBERTS GC, MARTENS R: Social reinforcement and complex motor performance. *Res Q* 41:2 (1970), 175–181.

SCHACHTER S: *The Psychology of Affiliation.* Stanford, California, Stanford University Press, 1959.

SINGER RN: Effects of spectators on athletes' and non-athletes' performance on a gross motor task. *R Q* 36 (1965), 473–82.

SORCE J, FOUTS G: Level of motivation in social facilitation of a simple task. *Percept Mot Skills* 37 (1973), 567–572.

SPENCE JT, SPENCE KW: The motivational components of manifest anxiety, drive and drive stimuli. In Spielberger CD (ed): *Anxiety and Behavior.* New York, Academic, 1966, 291–326.

SPENCE KW: *Behavior Theory and Conditioning.* New Haven, Yale University Press, 1956, 262.

STEVENSON HW: Social reinforcement with children as a function of chronological age, sex of experimenter, and sex of subjects. *J Abnorm Soc Psychol* 63 (1961), 147–154.

STEVENSON HW, ALLEN S; Adult performance as a function of sex of experimenter and sex of subject. J Abnorm Soc Psychol 68 (1964), 214–16.

STEVENSON HW, KEEN R, KNIGHTS RM: Parents and strangers as reinforcing agents for children's performance. *J Abnorm Soc Psychol* 67:2 (1963), 183–86.

SUTARMAN A, THOMPSON ML: A new technique for enumerating active sweat glands in man. *J Physiol* 117 (1952), 510.

TRAVIS LE: The effect of a small audience upon eye-hand coordination. *J Abnorm Soc Psychol* 20 (1925), 142–46.

TRIPLETT N: The dynamogenic factors in pacemaking and competition. *Am J Psychol* 9 (1898), 507–33.

VANEK M, CRATTY BJ: *Psychology and the Superior Athlete.* New York, Macmillan, 1970.

WANKEL LM: Audience size and trait anxiety effects upon state anxiety and motor performance. *Res Q* 48:1 (1977), 181–186.

WANKEL LM: The effects of social reinforcement and audience presence upon the motor performance of boys with different levels of initial ability. *J Mot Behav* 7:3 (September 1975), 207–216.

ZAJONC RB, HEINGARTNER A, HERMAN E: Social enhancement and impairment of performance in the cockroach. *J Pers Soc Psychol* 13 (1969), 83–92.

10

Theories of Motor Learning: Social-Psychologic Implications

Introduction

Models formulated to explain skill acquisition, prior to the late 1960s, were often simplistic speculations rather than penetrating and thorough theoretical statements. Some of these first models borrowed their ideas from learning theories that had been used to explain verbal, perceptual, and/or cognitive learning, rather than focusing on motor learning.

By the end of the 1960s and the beginning of the 1970s, however, more vigorous theoretical attempts emerged in the writings of several scholars, reflecting an interest in just how humans "put together" complex skills. Adams' (1971) closed loop theory was followed by a more expansive statement by Schmidt (1975). Although Schmidt admits borrowing concepts from Bartlett (1923) and others, it is believed that his model is one of the more viable conceptual frameworks in contemporary writings on this subject.

Borrowing ideas from theories about perceptual learning, and concepts first espoused by the Russian biomechanist-neurologist Nicholas Bernstein (1967), Schmidt's model contains several underlying principles:

1. The individual cannot store the multitide of specific motor responses it is possible to reproduce. Rather, the "motor memory" contains a smaller number of generalized "schemas."
2. When a "motor problem" confronts an individual, the general classifi-

216

cation of movement (schema) that seems to be required is first called up, then a specific response is molded to the demands of the task.

3. Skill learning takes place as the performer reduces differences between actual performance at a given time and the "model of movement" that represents an ideal response to the situation.

Schmidt's model is continually undergoing examination by experimenters, and thus the serious scholar should consult his writing and the work it has inspired for a more thorough look at the concepts. However, some of its main tenets are employed in the following discussion, because the ideas of schema theory have important social-psychologic implications for coaches attempting to impart skills to athletes.

This chapter will examine Schmidt's theory with respect to its social-psychologic implications. Bernstein, Adams, and Schmidt have placed varying degrees of emphasis on kinesthetic feedback, as well as conceptual evaluations of skill acquisition formulated by the *learner*. However, in the world of athletics there are usually at least two sets of perceptions and ideas which interact, and sometimes clash, within any situation: those of the athlete-performer and those of the instructor-coach.

For example, the learner "selects" from a general throwing schema the one type of throw that may be best in a given situation. At the same time, the observing coach speculates about the appropriateness of the athlete's selection. While the athlete executes the throw, and at the completion of the act, he or she evaluates the quality of the movement, using sensory information and perhaps observations of the result of the movement (how far away it landed). The observing coach at the same time forms ideas as to the quality of the action.

Further intellectual and perceptual activities in which both coach and athlete may participate include: (1) assessing the need for further practice, (2) ascertaining the discrepancy between some idealized model(s) and the actual performance, and (3) deciding how good both the form and performance exhibited really were. A final decision both must make is when enough practice has occurred and a satisfactory skill level has been attained.

The interactions between such speculations and perceptual judgments formulated by coach and athlete need not be complicated and should not cause problems. *If* their perceptions of form, effort, and results are identical, few problems should occur. Assuming this to be true, communication is a simple matter. Both coach and athlete have identical goals in mind, perceive each approximation of the skill practiced the same, and agree when learning has taken place. Unfortunately, however, this kind of congruence does not always occur.

The example assumes that only two individuals are involved, when actually more than one coach is often present, while the perceptions of fellow athletes, parents, and interested fans may further cloud the picture as an athlete attempts to acquire skill.

The discussion that follows attempts, through examples, to clarify some of the issues of interpersonal communication problems that may arise when both a coach and an athlete try to agree on such concepts as "skill," "correct," "incorrect," "learning," and "ideal model." It is the intent of the material in this chapter to (1) heighten the reader's sensitivity to the types of interpersonal problems that may arise as skill is acquired under the direction of another and (2) to aid in the reduction of these problems with appropriate preventive measures both before and during the time learning takes place.

Formulation of the "Ideal Model": Initial Considerations

Early in the interactions between coach and athlete, there should be a great effort made to agree on what final result is expected. The results of the effort should be clear to the athlete as well as to the mentor. This type of initial goal setting has several dimensions, including:

1. What each considers the ideal *result* of the performance trials.
2. What both consider to be the ideal method of execution, the best form to use for the hoped-for result.
3. The variations in form and results that seem tolerable to both coach and athlete.

Obvious ways such agreements may be reached include viewing films, perhaps with the help of an expert biomechanist. Frequent conversations between coach and athlete during the initial stages of learning also help. An expert performer, used as a demonstrator, is often useful. The congruence of these agreements will in turn influence the quality of further interactions between coach and athlete, and the performance quality the latter will reach.

During these early discussions, the response demands of the sport, which may range from very precise in pistol shooting to less rigorous accuracy in team handball, should be considered. Moreover, individual differences in background of the athlete, in his or her physique and cardiovascular qualities, should be discussed and taken into consideration.

Gentile's (1972) interesting ideas outlining the possible reactions of a performer to various outcomes seem appropriate to consider at this point. Her observations of an athlete's reactions are expanded in the latter part of the discussion to include reactions of both coach and athlete.

Gentile cites four possible interpretations an *individual* may make after completing a skill, taking into consideration both the method of execution (form) and the results of the effort.

1. If the expected goal or result is accomplished, and the execution "felt correct," the conclusion is that "all is well."
2. If the form feels correct to the athlete, yet the result is not as expected, the appraisal is "Something is wrong here!"
3. If the form is not felt to be correct, yet the results obtained are satisfactory, the reaction is "surprise!"
4. If the act is believed executed incorrectly, and the results are also inappropriate, the appraisal is likely to be "Everything went wrong!"

Extending Gentile's ideas within a social context involving both coach and athlete, the possible appraisals, assessments, and confusions multiply considerably and could include the following.

1. Both the coach and athlete agree about the high quality of performance (form) and about the results obtained. Their collective appraisal is likely to be "All is good, we agree, performance is as expected." Coach and athlete are likely to be pleased with each other.
2. Coach and athlete may both perceive execution as faulty, and yet both may believe that performance results are acceptable. This could result in the appraisal "We are both surprised!" or maybe "We both need to redefine just what good form consists of." Or perhaps the athlete begins to question whether the coach is aware of what good form really is.
3. Both coach and athlete perceive form as faulty, and results are less than hoped for. Their possible appraisal: "We are in agreement, something is wrong; let's work together to correct the problem."
4. Both might believe the execution of the task is good, but that results are less than expected. Their possible reactions could include "We must find out what is wrong with our collective ideas about "good form" or perhaps "We have expected performance results that are too high at this point in the training regime."

The examples enumerate situations in which both coach and athlete are in agreement, about form as well as outcomes. However, this agreement does not always exist. Thus, the following examples indicate appraisals when coach and athlete are *not* in agreement.

1. The athlete perceives that the execution was correct, while the coach does not. Both believe that the outcome was acceptable. Possible reactions from the athlete might include "The coach is not competent to teach me correct form . . . or to judge my execution." The coach may be both surprised and confused.
2. The coach may believe both execution and outcome are unacceptable, while the athlete views both effort and outcome as appropriate. Possible appraisals include frustration on the part of the athlete: "The coach

cannot judge me or the task requirements correctly." The coach may feel "The athlete does not believe me. He is difficult to coach."

3. Both may agree about appropriate form and execution; while the athlete may view the results as less than acceptable, the coach may be happy with the results. The athlete may then feel that "The coach does not set high enough standards for me," while the coach may internally verbalize, "The athlete is unrealistic in his goal setting, at this time in his practice regime."

Variations are almost infinite and depend on the degree to which athlete and coach communicate following the execution of the skill, and on the degree of their agreement and disagreements about both execution and results. The main point is, however, that disagreements about form, execution, progress, and variation present immediate and important communication problems. These "wounds" may become increasingly "infected" as their association continues, and as the stress of competition heightens. Thus, steps should be taken as early as possible to come to grips with possible differences in perceptions of what is happening. The remediation of these differences impinges directly upon the quality of performance manifested by both individuals and teams.

Discrepancy and Discrepancy Reduction Between Model and Execution

Schmidt (1975), Bernstein (1967), as well as others[1] have employed the concept of discrepancy reduction when explaining skill acquisition. This concept suggests that skilled learning takes place in stages, marked by a gradual reduction in the difference between some model of attainment and the quality of successive trials by the performer. It is assumed that learning takes place as the skill is executed exactly (or nearly like) the hypothetical "perfect model."

This process of discrepancy reduction has several problem dimensions, including:

1. The ideal model may encompass an ideal level of effort, or of activation, which may or may not be approachable by the athlete or perceived accurately by the coach.
2. The speed with which the model is approached, in a given number of practice sessions or trials, may or may not be agreed upon by both coach and athlete.
3. The variation in the degree to which the athlete approaches the model in day-by-day performances may not be acceptable to the coach. Thus,

[1]See Cratty BJ: *Movement Behavior and Motor Learning*, 2nd ed., 1975, p. 329.

the speed with which the skill is acquired may not be satisfactory to both coach and athlete.

Given these three problem components of discrepancy reduction, the following communication problems may arise.

1. From a positive standpoint, if both athlete and coach are satisfied with the athlete's speed in reducing discrepancies between an ideal model and actual performance, the likely appraisal of both will be "All is well, we are comfortable with the progress."

2. If the athlete believes he or she is exerting appropriate effort, and the coach does not, the likely reaction by the athlete is "I have a slave-driving coach who harbors unrealistic expectations about my performance capacities," while the coach may feel that "I have a lazy athlete on my hands, who does not work up to capacity."

3. The coach may be unhappy with the speed with which the athlete is reducing differences between an ideal model and his actual performance. The athlete, on the other hand, may be satisfied with the progress made. The likely results and feelings are: (a) The coach may feel that the athlete is not learning fast enough, while (b) the athlete may feel that the coach is not sensitive enough to the problems encountered as he tries to acquire the skill, and of his limitations and special needs.

4. The coach may not be satisfied with the daily (trial by trial) reduction in discrepancies and in the variations of skill around some hypothetical learning curve. The athlete, on the other hand, may not understand, or be overly concerned with, daily performance fluctuations in training. The likely outcomes are that: (a) The coach may feel that the athlete is "inconsistent, despite my best coaching efforts." The athlete may feel that (b) "The coach does not understand my daily moods, temporary fatigue, and other things that impinge upon my performance, including personal problems and boredom during practice sessions that at times are uninteresting."

There are obviously innumerable other possibilities relating to the assessment of skill improvement and variations in performance, which may cause problems between coach and athlete.

Toleration and Understanding of Performance Variations

It is believed that incongruities between the perceptions of the coach and the athlete about performance variations represent one of the most serious communication problems, one that can strain the interpersonal relationships between coaches and athletes.

Contemporary biomechanists are well aware that a skill, if measured precisely, is never performed in exactly the same way from trial to trial. Tasks ranging from those on the athletic field to those found in the factory have been measured. Minute variations in velocities, forces, and or spatial configurations occur from trial to trial, in what is apparently the same skill and in one which has been purportedly well learned.

It is also obvious that various skills (diamond cutting and ditch digging come to mind) contain differences in the precision of the responses required. In American football, a field goal kicked from the center of the field requires extremely accurate placement of the foot to the ball, coupled with high velocities, while football coaches seldom care how a defensive lineman in the same game reaches and "sacks" the quarterback.

Athletes are not alike in their perceptions of the precision with which they are able to and/or prefer to execute various movements. Coaches also differ in their preferences for, and ability to judge, the precision of various skills they are teaching.

Psychologists have identified people who seem to have various preceptual preferences. Most of the work has been done using visual stimuli. Among the types studied are those they name "levelers," who are not overly concerned about slight differences between stimuli to which they are exposed. They tend to "ignore" slight differences perceptually. On the other hand, "sharpeners" are very concerned with, and can accurately detect, slight differences in stimuli of various kinds.

It is highly probable that both sharpeners and levelers exist in the athletic community among both coaches and athletes. Thus, it may be expected that a sharpener-coach may be paired with a leveler-athlete. Conflicts in this situation may be expected, as they attempt to interact and communicate about the precision with which a skill is performed and learned.

The reverse pairing could also occur. The overly precise athlete may be taught by a coach who pays less attention to performance details. In such cases, the chances of interpersonal conflicts during the learning of skills are obvious.

Of particular importance is the degree to which the athlete and coach may agree upon the response variation permissible in a given sport situation. The coach may tolerate individual differences when an athlete executes a jump shot in basketball, and take into consideration differences in technique, body build, and the like. On the other hand, the coach may be rigid in his expectations of what constitutes "correct form." Somehow, the two must find a common meeting ground.

Toleration of individual differences may be predicated on either false or correct assumptions a coach may make about the biomechanical principles inherent in many sports skills. In most skills there are imperative principles, which if violated will lead to less than optimum performance, if not accidents and injuries. Aside from these principles, however, there are often wide variations, which may match a player's unique neurologic and physical make-up and contribute to performance. A player who is made to suddenly change his form when exposed to a new coach who finds his or her performance characteristics "odd" may evidence obvious decrements in performance.

It may also be possible that an athlete has been successful while using biomechanically unsound techniques. This athlete may have spent so much time practicing and conditioning that form imperfections have been overcome and compensated for.Thus, the problem for the coach is first to obtain as sound a knowledge as possible of what is biomechanically sound and correct, and then to permit whatever individual variations seem sensible and appropriate. Radically changing an older athlete's form may be less advisable, even if violating principles of physics, than changing that of a younger athlete.

Availability of Schemas and Subskills

Another problem when teaching skill involves the perceptions of the coach and athlete about the athlete's previous experience. Or to use the jargon of a schema theorist, "Just what schemas have been stored within the response mechanisms of the learner?" The coach should ascertain what subskills have been exercised within general schemas, as well as what general patterns of skills may be familiar to a younger or older athlete. This problem arises when coaches confront athletes for the first practices together.

The coach should attempt to answer the following questions:

1. Has this athlete (team) had experience resulting in a general acquaintance with the skill family (schema) to be taught?

2. Has the team (athlete) been exposed to the particular subskills before? To what degree must I introduce new skills, or maintain and improve skills already acquired?

3. To what degree might the athlete (team) transfer the performance of another skill (within the same general skill family) to the skill being taught? To what degree might the coach point out similarities and differences between some related, previously learned skill, and the present skill? To what degree might principles from an apparently unrelated skill be applied to the present situation?

Often initial attempts to introduce a skill are blunted if satisfactory answers to these questions are not obtained. Finding answers is likely to enhance skill acquisition, particularly if the answers are mutually arrived at by coach and athlete.

When Has Learning Taken Place?

A final group of problems, with which the coach and athlete must deal in tandem, concerns three major questions.

1. When has learning been achieved? When has a skill become so refined that there is little or no discrepancy between the ideal model and the skill as performed?
2. How much overlearning should be engaged in to firmly implant the skill within the "memory" motor of the athlete? When is retention assured? Will re-performance of the skill under the stress of competition result in any significant and harmful variations? Will the stress of competition enhance the quality of the skill?
3. How much practice constitutes too much exposure to the task? How can I prevent boredom, with accompanying skill decrements during long seasons and practice sessions?

The answer to the first question depends on the degree of concordance initially achieved between coach and athlete about what model they are attempting to approximate. If this initial agreement is "fuzzy," it is likely that the termination of training will bring problems, and interpersonal conflicts will arise or be heightened.

Further, the coach should be aware that while practice tends to perfect skill, and some overlearning may be productive, too much practice can often lead to "staleness." Thus, as a training regime is drawing to a close, the coach and athlete should have learned to communicate well enough that the latter can tell the former when enough is enough. Most important, during the final practice sessions coach and athlete should be together concerning their mutual perceptions of the final quality of performance.

IMPLICATIONS FOR THE COACH

The concepts dealt with in the previous paragraphs hold numerous implications for coaches attempting to improve their teaching skills. For example, most of the information available emphasizes the importance of good and clear interpersonal communication between coach and athlete. Not only should the coach engender an emotional environment that encourages the athlete to air opinions about the acquisition of a skill or the progress of physical conditioning, but the athlete should also be encouraged to communicate feelings about what is happening.

Initially, it seems imperative that both the athlete and coach agree as to what are reasonable goals, and what skill acquisition consists of.

This kind of agreement may not always come about by merely exchanging words; rather the two (or more) should attempt to acquire films, not only of an ideal model but also of the athlete's initial attempts at mastery. During this period, both general and specific initial subskills in the possession of the athlete should be discussed, relative to their "distance" from the ideal model.

As learning and/or conditioning progresses, the coach should be highly sensitive to anger and other signs of interpersonal discord. If this occurs, the coach should attempt to ascertain whether the two are in agreement concerning the goals and subgoals as well as whether or not the personal dissonance is due to reasons other than agreement on goals about conditioning and skill acquisition.

During this learning period, both athlete and coach may need to meet and readjust performance standards and objectives relative to improved physical conditioning. Indeed, the subtle interactions between the acquisition of physical capacities and skill acquisition should be carefully discussed, perhaps with the help of a physiologist and biomechanicist. That is, the precise performance of many athletic skills depends not only on the refinement of a neuromotor program, but also on supporting subsystems consisting of variables that contribute to muscular strength and cardiovascular power. Thus, the athlete whose skills are apparently not improving as rapidly as the coach may like may either be failing to learn quickly or may be delayed in the exhibition of skill because of a lag in the overall conditioning program. The pole vaulter's form may not be superb because of the need for a minor adjustment in take-off, swing, or push-off, *or* because of a lack of muscular power in the upper body, or of running speed prior to the take-off.

Also, as skill acquisition and training progress the coach should remain tolerant of individual differences in the athlete's performance. These differences may not have been apparent during the initial stages of skill acquisition, and may begin to surface as training and conditioning are engaged in. In the performance of many athletic feats, there is more than one way to get the job done. The athlete may exhibit purported form anomalies, which may appear both biomechanically incorrect and aesthetically displeasing. At the same time, the athlete may be engaging in what for him or her *is* appropriate form, due to unique neuromotor and/or structural make-up and possibly to compensation for subtle neuromotor problems. When these apparent skill problems are encountered coaches should not exhibit "knee-jerk" correction reactions. Rather, thought should be given to *why* the athlete is performing in a given manner, and when correction is given it should be carried out in language that is easily understood, based on objective data with which both athlete and coach agree and couched in terms that are not emotionally loaded.[2]

During the final stages of skill acquisition, several compromises between athlete and coach may also need to be discussed. At the moment of a given contest, the athlete's skill level, while not perfect, may be adequate. The dates of important competitions do not always coincide with the complete and perfect acquisition of skill and/or the achievement of perfect muscular and cardiovascular conditioning. Thus, just prior to critical contests, the athlete should be made to feel at least adequate, not deficient in skill. While both athlete and coach may be aware of the differences between ideal model and actual performance, there is little need for the coach to emphasize and exaggerate the differences and thus overstress the athlete.

During these final stages, therefore, the coach should be content if the athlete has approximated some ideal model both coach and athlete formulated previously. Both athlete and coach should at this point come to grips not only with the lack of perfectibility of human neuromotor performance but also with the less than perfect way coaches often perceive skill models desired and exhibited by their charges.

SUMMARY

The preceding paragraphs have attempted to delineate the nature of problems that may arise between coach and athlete within a context provided by contemporary schema theories of motor learning. There have been few attempts to suggest easy solutions for these problems. However, it is believed that an important initial first step in the solution of interpersonal conflicts between coach and athlete is to define the nature of possible discord.

A thread that has been woven into this chapter is the problems of human communication. Most of the problems discussed may be avoided, or dealt with expeditiously, if the two parties communicate clearly and often concerning expectations, goals, and their perceptions of what they believe is happening at a given moment. If both people involved really listen and try to understand the viewpoint of the other at frequent intervals, many interpersonal conflicts between coach and

[2]Careful case-study analysis of the acquisition of skill has revealed that for the best results the correction of only one skill component should be attempted at a given time. Thus, the coach, if too anxious to correct everything at once, may in truth be blunting rather than enhancing skill acquisition of an athlete.

athlete would not occur at all. However, this ideal is seldom achieved in love, work, play, or sport.

From an operational standpoint, improved skill acquisition can be achieved if some of the following measures are taken.

1. Early in the development program, the coach and athlete, perhaps aided by other experts, should attempt to formulate an acceptable model of attainment. This initial step may be aided by films, demonstrators, and/or a videotape.

2. Early in the relationship, both coach and athlete should formulate a calendar of training, which represents a reasonable time in which acceptable levels of skill or skills can be expected to be acquired.

3. If the athlete (or team) is relatively inexperienced or immature, a thorough analysis of past experience in sport in general, and in the sport being undertaken, should take place. This should be done in order to find out "where the athlete comes from," and thus where performance can be taken in a given period of time. To express it more academically, the attempt should be made to determine what schemas are in the possession of the athlete and what subskills reside within those schemas.

4. At frequent intervals, determined in advance, coach and athlete should come together and try to formulate an agreement about how fast skill acquisition is really taking place. They should try to relate prior judgments about how fast they both thought it should take place to how rapidly learning is really occurring. If delays in learning are occurring, the possible reasons should be discussed, as should questions about whether or not the two agree upon the "closeness of fit" between the immediate performance and the ideal model.

5. An attempt may be made by behavioral scientists (sport psychologists) interested in the progress of the athlete to match personality types of athletes to those of coaches with more precision than the chance associations that now occur. This kind of matching might, for example, pair the perceptually flexible (leveler) coach with an athlete who also tends to be a leveler. Likewise, the coach and athlete who are more precise and rigid in their judgments of skill attainment might be placed into a compatible dyad.

6. Perhaps most important, the coach should seek in every way to become thoroughly familiar with the skills he or she is coaching. The confidence of the athlete, as well as potential communication problems, hinge on the expertise of the coach.

QUESTIONS FOR DISCUSSION

1. What main premises are made by those advancing modern theories of motor learning?

2. What does the concept of "discrepancy" mean within the theories presented?

3. What may be accomplished early in the association between an athlete and a coach to reduce the social-psychologic problems they may later encounter as one attempts to teach skills to the other?

4. Give an example of how the coach and athlete may be at odds when attempting to initially determine just what schemas are available to the latter?

5. How might problems relative to speed of reduction of discrepancies arise during the interactions of the coach-athlete dyad?

6. What about differences in variability of performance, as related to an exact mode, when coach and athlete interact?

7. What problems in transfer of skill may arise between coach and athlete when they are attempting to apply training drills to game situations?

8. What problems may occur when an athlete and coach differ about whether or not a skill has been acquired? How might such differences be resolved, at the time and through earlier interactions?

9. How might differences in the perception of effort expended hamper communication between coach and athlete?

BIBLIOGRAPHY

ADAMS JA: A closed-loop theory of motor learning. *J Mot Behav* 3 (1971), 111–150.

BARTLETT FC: *Remembering.* Cambridge, England, Cambridge University Press, 1923.

BERNSTEIN N: *The Coordination and Regulation of Movements.* London, Pergamon, 1967.

CRATTY BJ: Schema with correction and motor learning. *The Physical Educator* (March 1963), 23–24.

EDMONS EN, MUELLER MR: The role of schemata in perceptual learning. *Psychonomic Sci* 6 (1966), 377–78.

GENTILE AN: A working model of skill acquisition with applications to teaching. *Quest* 17 (1972), 3–23.

NEWELL KM CHEW RA: Recall and recognition in motor learning. *J Mot Behav* 6 (1974), 81–86.

SCHMIDT A: A schema theory of discrete motor skill learning. *Psychol Rev* 82:4 (July 1975).

11

Leadership

An important quality of a team, as well as groups engaged in most endeavors, is the nature of the leadership available. At times, team leaders are given titles—coach, trainer, and captain are examples. At other times, leaders simply emerge. Subtle delegation and acceptance of authority occurs after a group has had a life of even short duration. Some are designated leaders, while others are relegated to follower roles. Thus, on a team there may not only be more than one leader but more than one type of leader.

During the 1950s, researchers devoted a great deal of effort to understanding the nature of leadership in small and large groups. Most of this effort was expended attempting to discover motivation and productive leadership behaviors within business and commerce, but at times sports teams, combat units, and individuals in educational settings were subjects for experimental work.

Among the questions these researchers explored are the following:

1. What traits, if any, can be isolated as typical of "good leaders"?
2. What situational factors influence leadership behavior?
3. What aspects of group dynamics mold leadership behavior and result in the emergence, or demoting, of leaders in work and play groups?
4. What developmental characteristics in children's play groups have implications for the immediate as well as long-term assumption of leadership?
5. Is leadership situational in nature, or can people be identified who are "natural" leaders in a variety of situations?

6. Can leadership be taught or improved? Can teaching about group dyamics, communication, and qualities possessed by leaders enhance and improve certain leadership behaviors?

7. What child-rearing experiences, placement in the birth order of the family, and similar early social variables influence the tendency later in life to seek or reject positions of leadership?

Specific questions related to leadership in sport have only been touched upon by the available literature. Among the practical questions arising are:

1. What qualities are athletes looking for in their designated team leaders?

2. What personal qualities are disliked by athletes in their leaders, coaches, and trainers?

3. How do leaders emerge on teams? Is the possession of athletic ability important? What about qualities possessed by team captains involving interpersonal relationships?

4. How much of the leadership of a sports team should come from team members, and how much from the coach? Are formal or informal "field leaders" or "floor leaders" imperative to the success of a team?

5. How might team captains be chosen? When during the season? By whom? For what reasons?

6. Should team captains be given formal training for their roles? If so, what form might this training take?

7. What qualities are important in coaches, and how do specific personal qualities of coaches interact with specific needs and psychologic tendencies of athletes?

These and related questions are invariably raised in both obvious and subtle ways during the course of a competitive season. Formulating sound answers is not an easy task. However, it is hoped that some of the material that follows makes tentative inroads into these queries.

Developmental Dimensions of Leadership Behavior

It is possible to identify a number of situations in infancy and early childhood that may be precursors of the later assumption or rejection of leadership functions. The young infant, for example, may be exposed to an authoritarian model within the family. Whether or not this model (mother, father, brother, sister, etc.) is a member of the infant's own sex, and whether or not he or she is successful, seems to make a difference in the assumption of ascendant behavior by the child.

The writings and research of Toman (1961) and others on the birth order of children suggest that the leadership and followership roles children assume when interacting with their siblings reflect in future behaviors and tendencies to lead. The first-born, for example, is more likely to gravitate toward leadership roles later in life because of early experiences in being a leader of brothers and sisters.

Shortly after the child's exposure to the family, and to the accompanying norms, sanctions, and punishments it contains, he or she enters the play group. Thus, a second and important group of modifiers of later ascendant behavior impinges on the child as he or she forms groups in the sandbox and athletic field.

Children may, for example, be accepted or rejected by their earliest play companions. Children may possess psychologic attributes and/or physical skills that enable them either to be given or to seize leadership roles in childhood games, during their third, fourth and fifth years of life.

Parten (1933A), for example, has suggested a continuum on which one may consider the degree of leadership or followership exhibited by children at play. This ranges from a dominant role to a more passive-following type of behavior. The scale is depicted in Table 11–1.

Based on systematic observations, Parten felt that leadership in children's playgrounds emerges in either of two ways: (1) via diplomacy, reflected in a child who artfully and by indirect suggestions controls a number of children, and (2) via more forceful bullying behavior, reflected in a child who applies physical and or psychologic force to oppress a group he or she has chosen to dominate.

Other studies conducted earlier in the century have indicated that there may be sex differences in the way leadership is acquired in children's play groups. The boys were shown to achieve leadership through the exhibition of physical prowess. The girls tended to gain status by engaging in persuasive verbal behaviors. With the changing sex roles currently occurring in the United States, this kind of finding may no longer be a valid one, however.

Many situations in a child's subculture contain opportunities to exhibit physical competencies. It is thus not surprising that data from numerous studies indicate that to some degree the possession of ade-

TABLE 11–1.

Following-passive	Interactive		Dominant-leader
Child follows another's directions	Follows others but at his or her own volition	An intermediate position following and leading	Tends to direct group most of the time

←——————————————————————————→

quate to superior motor abilities facilitates the acquisition of both social status and opportunities to lead.

Typical findings reflecting this contention are presented in a paper delivered at the National Convention for Health, Physical Education and Recreation in 1972. Obtaining responses from 170 boys and girls (ages 11 to 19 years), Broekhoff found that both boys and girls agreed in ratings of peer friendships ("a good person to do homework with") and in their perceptions of the physical ability of their classmates. Additionally, relationships between social status and physical performance measures including softball throwing, pushups, pullups, and broad-jumping, were positive and high. These relationships were slightly higher when the data from the boys were analyzed than when the girls' scores were compared. Broekhoff summarized by explaining that "physical fitness, power and agility are positive factors for acquiring social status, especially for the boys in the eyes of the girls."

In a study carried out during a soccer-football season, encompassing six teams of children (ages 7 to 15 years), Cratty and Passer (1975) found that children rated highest in competence by their peers were the most likely to be chosen leaders. Findings of innumerable studies attest to the circularity of such variables as popularity, physical prowess, and leadership potential among children and youth. Figure 11-1 reflects these interacting effects.[1]

To summarize, children, like people in a variety of situations, who perceive themselves as competent not only tend to achieve social status but to seek situations in which to exhibit and exercise their abilities. Often, these situations in children's play groups involve the assumption of leadership roles.

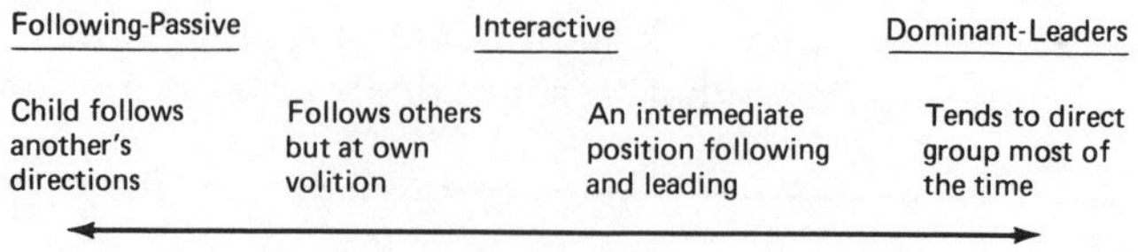

Following-Passive	Interactive		Dominant-Leaders
Child follows another's directions	Follows others but at own volition	An intermediate position following and leading	Tends to direct group most of the time

$$\longleftarrow \hspace{4cm} \longrightarrow$$

FIGURE 11-1.

[1]The reverse of this cycle is also operative when children, early in life, realize that they are physically inadequate. This in turn may produce feelings of failure, inadequacy, and other feelings that both encourage them to avoid play situations and, if they need to obtain leadership, to do so in situations other than those requiring physical prowess.

This kind of circular, self-fulfilling prophecy becomes operative rather early in life. A child enters such a cycle and continually tests his or her prowess in order to obtain social rewards and opportunities for status and leadership. At some point, theoretically, a "topping off" place is reached, when the child reaches a level of competition in which his or her competencies are obvious compared to those possessed by others. At this point, the child or youth may compensate in other areas of expertise, may suffer feelings of anxiety and defeat, or may make some other adjustments as his or her physical prowess is no longer valued at increasingly higher levels of competitive sport. One healthy compensation is to adjust goals and learn to enjoy sport for recreational reasons, instead of attempting to always be the best.

Definitions of Leadership

Innumerable definitions of leadership have been proposed. For the most part, these reflect the theoretical orientations of those formulating them. Fiedler (1971), perhaps jokingly, pointed out that there are almost as many theories of leadership as there are psychologists working in the field.

Freud, for example, likened a leader to a father figure from whom group members derive succor, warmth, and emotional rewards. The father figure–leader may be surrounded by jealousy, competition for attention, and similar interpersonal behaviors, which may render a group or dyad less than effective when performing a task.

Some definitions of leadership focus upon process. Stodgill (1968), for example, pointed out that "leadership is the process of influencing group activities toward goal setting and group achievement." Dubin (1951) writes that "leadership is the exercise of authority and the making of decisions," also reflecting a process orientation.

Other scholars have viewed the leader as an individual possessing various personality traits. Cattell (1951), for example, states that the "leader is the person who creates the most change in group performance." Cowley (1928) writes that the "leader is one who succeeds in getting others to follow him." Homans (1950) said that "the leader is the man who comes closest to realizing the norms the group values highest, this conformity gives him high rank, which attracts people, and implies the right to assume control of the group."

Thus, Homans implies that leadership includes control, sensitivity to the group's feelings, and values, as well as knowledge of the rank and status achieved by members within the hierarchy. From Homans's standpoint, therefore, a leader is someone proficient at understanding and manipulating human relations, as well as one who is aware of group norms and values.

Some writers have differentiated between emerging leaders and formal leaders. The former are people who derive status and leadership right from the group itself, while the latter have the title bestowed by higher authorities. This difference will be alluded to in other sections of this chapter, and of course may be seen in many teams.

There seems general agreement among scholars that leadership implies some kind of power relationship. That leader (A) exerts some kind of authority over a person (B) and C/D, or others. Thus, leadership implies that someone is willing to follow and at the same time to confer power and status on another.

It is beyond the scope of this text to thoroughly review the vast amount of literature dealing with theories and views of leadership. Basically, however, the theoreticians have had two primary concerns: (1) To find out who become leaders; this search is reflected in hundreds of studies of leadership traits. (2) To determine how one becomes an *effective* leader. This problem has been dealt with in research exploring "leadership styles," as related to group performance and group make-up.

Personality Attributes of Leaders and Coaches

A great deal of effort has been expended attempting to isolate personality traits "typical" of leaders. In an important early paper on this subject, Stodgill found small to moderate positive correlations among leadership status, intelligence, height, weight, rated personal adjustment, social poise, and dominance. For the most part, however, these correlations are relatively low and not very predictive of leadership potential. Mann (1965) found these same nonpredictive correlations. However, he did find, as have others since, that a leader's abilities and traits seemed related to the specific goals the group was attempting to achieve. Thus, within scientific groups, on sports teams, and in other work groups, traits seem rather closely related to the group's perceptions of the task at hand and the degree to which an individual may help them to achieve success in the task. A team captain, for example, has been found to be more often chosen because of an apparent ability to help the group win contests than because of any specific personality traits.

The coach as a leader. Relatively predictable conditions surround a large percentage of sports competitions, which seem to reflect in the familiar "coaching stereotype." Athletic contests are visible, involve stress, and require vigorous training beforehand. Thus, a rather rigid role is often assigned to the coach—one who drives for excellence and conditioning, and who otherwise presents a tough and relatively inflexible front to both the team and its followers.[2]

Hendry's review (1972) of studies focusing on the coaching stereotype seems to reflect the way data from personality trait studies carried out with coaches (and physical education teachers) reflect the rather rigid role assigned to them by popular belief. Hendry has described studies whose data indicate that coaches, as well as "physical educationalists," seem to be rather dominant, are able to express aggression easily, and are not interested in the dependency needs of others. They prove to be inflexible in many ways. The portrayal of the "authoritarian coach" also contains data indicating that coaches are rather conservative in many ways, and willingly accept authority from others perceived as higher than they are, including God, church, and national leaders.

However, as Hendry (1968) found, some of the apparently secure bombastic behavior seen in coaches may be undergirded by feelings of insecurity and anxiety. Thus, it is unclear whether the apparent behavior seen in coaches is a reflection of true personality, a type of compensation, or some attempt to act out a role society has assigned to them.

Two papers, one by Hendry (1968) and another by Hendry and Whiting (1968) suggested that this type of coaching stereotype tends to perpetuate a closed conceptual (and behavioral) system. An admired coaching figure serves as a model for athletes, who tend to imitate him or her when they become coaches. This kind of circularity, reflecting modeling effects, is depicted in Figure 11–2.

Although this type of closed conceptual system is taken by many to illustrate the rather dogmatic and, by inference, negative personality complex ingrained in coaches, careful studies carried out in the 1970s question this common assumption. In one of the better designed studies of coaches' personality traits, Longmuir (1972) found that "coaches are not more dogmatic than others in a wide variety of other occupations." He further concluded that whether or not the coach was perceived as dogmatic was largely dependent upon the rigidity of those making the judgments, i.e., athletes.

Andrud (1970) also found that coaches in his sample, consisting of 19 coaches enrolled in a football clinic, were about average in scores reflecting restraint, friendliness, and thoughtfulness. At the same time, as is typical of such studies, it was found that the coaches were highly ascendant and possessed the drive to succeed.

[2]According to the work of Williams and Youssef (1972), coaches in turn assign stereotypic roles to the athletes in their charge also!

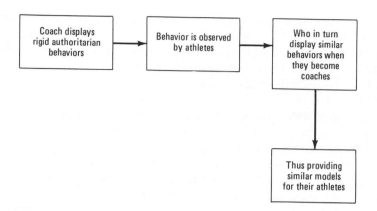

FIGURE 11-2.

Using 150 coaches as subjects, Sage (1972) published data indicating that the football and basketball mentors surveyed were no different in the degree to which they tended to exploit situations, and people, and in general evidenced traits resembling Machiavelli.

Although this brief review reveals contradictory findings, it is apparent that although coaches tend to resemble the common stereotypes in traits that reflect energy and ascendance, they are not always inhuman, insensitive people. Indeed, there is increasing evidence that the more successful coaches at higher levels may be more people-oriented than many would imagine.[3]

While there are obvious advantages to being an energetic but human coach, the rigid authoritarian mentor may produce some positive outcomes in competitive situations. Teams under stress, if relatively inexperienced, may be more comfortable with a strong leader, and an authoritarian personality may relate better to athletes who possess similar traits.

However, an authoritarian coach may be impeded in the sensitivity and flexibility he or she can exhibit when attempting to understand and handle interpersonal problems that arise on the team. Finally, this type of rigidity may prevent the coach from examining and using new and potentially helpful practices indicated by research in the biologic or behavioral sciences.

[3]A more comprehensive review of coaching personalities can be found in Ball DW, Loy JW: *Sport and the Social Order,* Menlo Park, California, Addison-Wesley, 1975, in Chapter 9, "An Occupational Analysis of the College Coach," by George Sage, pp. 391–456.

For example, Loy (1968) examined the possible relationships between selected personality traits and the tendencies of coaches to be either "early" or "late" innovators of new practices in swimming. The sports innovation studied was a form of interval training.

Loy found that the more sociable, flexible, intelligent, and self-sufficient female coaches tended to adopt the practice earlier than did those who did not possess these qualities to the same degree. Overall, the more than 100 male and female coaches from whom data were collected, and who were labeled "early innovators," were found to be more creative, cosmopolitan, and higher in professional and educational status than those who did not quickly adopt the new and helpful practice. These data thus suggest that extreme rigidity and inflexibility in the behavior of at least some coaches may serve as an impediment to the adoption of new coaching practices.

A most promising research program was initiated by Smith, Smoll, and Curtis (1979). They first developed an instrument to systematically classify coaching behaviors in what they termed "natural settings." The tools, first published in 1977, contain 12 behavioral categories, in which observers may place various "bits" of coaching behaviors reflecting the degree to which the coach either (1) positively or negatively reinforces an athlete, (2) offers technical help, (3) corrects mistakes, and (4) evidences spontaneous behaviors, apparently not triggered by any incident during play.

The findings from a 1978 study in which this instrument was employed suggest that a short-term training program lasting 2 hours, to which coaches were exposed and which aimed to improve the quality of their behaviors, did exert a significant change in the way they later coached their teams. In this initial study, 18 coaches took part in a "workshop for change."

The training program consisted of techniques involving not only written and verbal presentations of appropriate behavioral guidelines, but also self-monitoring techniques. The coaches were asked to keep a record of their own behaviors as they perceived them. In addition to the changes in coaching behaviors recorded as the result of this workshop, it was found that these changes were most apparent to children who evidenced low scores on a test of self-esteem.

The training program in a 1979 study also contained the techniques listed above. In addition, the coaches were admonished not only to immediately reward appropriate game behavior, but also to accompany corrections by immediately pointing out how the situation could have been handled correctly by the player. Rather than use sarcasm, it was pointed out, the coach should employ good instructional techniques, accompanied by encouragement, and thus establish his or her "role as a teacher." In this second study, the behaviors of 16 coaches in the control group were not as effective as the behaviors of 18 who had participated in the training session. Those who had been exposed to the attempts to change behavior not only evidenced positive changes, but obtained positive and significant shifts upward on measures of self-esteem administered to the children exposed to the coaches who took the training.

It therefore appears that coaches may behave in a variety of ways, reflecting a rather broad range of personality traits. Certain traits, however, may be accompanied by the tendency to act in rather rigid ways with people and to reflect rigidity when new practices are available for adoption.

Most promising, however, is the presence of an objective tool through which behaviors of coaches can be classified and studied. Equally encouraging are the increased presence of studies in natural settings, which indicate that not only may coaching behaviors be changed in positive ways, but that these changes reflect how they are perceived by the children they coach, as well as being reflected in shifts upward in the self-esteem of the children.

LEADERSHIP AND THE TASK SITUATION

One of the more elaborate models for the study of leadership was advanced by Fiedler (1967). His theory is based on several major assumptions:

1. The trait-oriented theory of leadership is not encompassing enough to include the complexities of interactions between leaders, subordinates, situations, and ultimate effectiveness.

2. Leadership effectiveness is largely situational. Critical in the determination of effectiveness are such variables as whether or not the leader is task-oriented or concentrates upon affiliative needs and motives.

3. Important are social factors that delineate the rigidity of the structure within the task situation.

Fiedler also believes that whether or not the leader exerts "fate control" over his subordinates is important. Fate control means that the leader can manipulate the subordinates in rather absolute ways. The leader's knowledge of the task, as compared to the subordinate's, as well as the emotional control he or she may exert as leader, is also important. Secondary factors include whether or not the members like the leader, the similarity of the group's attitudes, and whether or not the leader has some control over *his* superior.

Fiedler thus postulates what he terms an "interactional approach" to the study of leadership.[3] A critical measure he employs to assess "leadership style" is a questionnaire purporting to assess how individuals view their "least preferred co-workers" and their "most preferred co-workers." The scale is used to determine whether the respondent-leader views both least preferred and most preferred co-workers as friendly or unfriendly, cooperative or uncooperative, etc. It is assumed that if individuals view those who contribute little to the total effort as generally not very worthwhile and not possessing desirable personality traits their orientation is toward performance not social affiliation. The reverse is true if the respondent views those contributing little to the effort as perhaps very desirable individuals. That is, the latter respondent tends to judge people *not* on the basis of their performance contribution if they are "people oriented."

The self-esteem of task-oriented individuals, according to Fiedler, is closely related to whether or not they perceive themselves as doing a good job; although such individuals may attempt to enhance interpersonal relationships in groups they lead, they do so in order to accomplish their primary objective to be successful in the task.

Thus Fiedler, unlike earlier theoreticians, suggested that leadership effectiveness is dependent upon the *interaction* between the relative rigidity or structure of the social context in which the power is exerted and the degree to which the leader is task-or people-oriented. Data obtained by Fiedler based on this model suggest that the highly task-oriented leader is effective within two basic situations: (1) when the task structure is very loose and/or unfavorable, and (2) when the task structure is very rigid and favorable. A leader who is oriented toward human values is most effective when the structure of the situation is intermediate in favorableness, not too loosely or too tightly organized. Thus, the overall implication is that *both* task-motivated as well as human-relationship-oriented individuals may be effective leaders, provided they are placed in, or match, the correct situations.

Some of Fiedler's early data were obtained from basketball teams, in the early 1950s. These studies focused on both leadership behaviors and the value orientations of individual team members. Although extensive work has not been done with teams, the following generalizations may prove valid when further studies are carried out within Fiedler's framework.

1. In informal recreational teams, and/or those composed of inexperienced relatively immature members in which the relationships be-

[3]A similar model was advanced in the late 1950s by Tannenbaum and Schmidt, who suggested that the degree of group-centered *vs.* boss-centered leadership desirable is a function of forces in the leader, in the situation, and in the group itself.

tween leaders and followers are rather clear-cut, the leader who is
task-oriented may be effective in helping the group to be successful.

2. When there is, or has been, a large amount of leadership-member
   ambiguity and dissonance, a strong task-oriented leader may also
   prove effective. This type of leadership-effectiveness relationship is
   sometimes seen when a new coach comes into a situation that was
   highly disorganized and contained poor athlete-coach relationships.

3. Conceivably, a task-centered leader will also prove effective for highly
   structured teams, which perform in situations where excellence is
   expected and in front of spectators who impose a great deal of pressure
   and stress.

4. On the other hand, when the structure is moderate and associations
   between coach and athletes have been relatively good, and prolonged,
   a human-relations-oriented leader may make the most helpful contribution to team success.

In a study by Cratty and Sage, discussed in Chapter 1, the task-
specific nature of leadership was revealed. Using a large maze task,
experimenters found that groups who came to perform, and who had
already selected leaders on the basis of social attributes (fraternity
pledge classes), did not perform as well or hold as productive intertrial
discussions as did groups whose membership did not include prese-
lected leaders. The latter groups selected their leaders by first finding
out who had performed best on the task at hand, and then these individuals led discussions on how to accomplish the task with increasing efficiency in subsequent trials.

The implications for a task-specific approach for the selection of
leadership in athletics seem obvious. Care should be taken to select
team leaders whose interpersonal skills and values help that team to
accomplish the task of winning. In studies of high school basketball
teams, it has been found that captains of the more successful ones were,
for the most part, those who were perceived as best able to help the
team win, rather than individuals who were simply well-liked. Data
from other investigations indicate that in groups who value performance, partner choices for games will usually include those whom the
others perceive as performing well, independent of friendships.

In groups that value human relationships, friendship choices are the
rule when members form cooperating dyads to compete against others.
Thus, although it seems that winning is the sole criterion for leadership
effectiveness, this may *not* be the goal of all teams formed to engage
in sport. It is obvious that many recreational teams *do value* close
human relationships and affiliative needs more than they do winning.
In groups of this nature, therefore, leaders with good social skills and
a value orientation that involves good human relationships are obviously desirable.

The search continues, however, for important variables that produce leadership success. Eagly, for example, suggests that Fiedler's concept of leadership style is only a minor determinant of success. Eagly argues that sex differences exist in the forces that influence leadership effectiveness. In male groups, leaders who are highly oriented toward interpersonal success can reduce members' tensions and hostilities and thus ensure group success, a possibility not accounted for in Fiedler's model.

Skinnerian learning theory is also reflected in hypotheses and models explaining leadership behaviors. Marak (1964), for example, points out that as the result of his study, a viable reinforcement model emerged, which explains leadership. He was able to modify and magnify leadership behaviors in individuals by offering them rewards for behaviors reflecting ascendance over the course of a meeting with others.

These few examples do not exhaust the numerous attempts to determine the qualities that determine leadership effectiveness. The lists of personal traits that purportedly enhance leadership effectiveness are numerous and include one by Beer and his colleagues (1959) which contains such qualities as self-acceptance, need achievement, and interpersonal skills. Enumerations of leader traits by Carter (1950) and others contains such qualities as the ability to propose action, to argue and disagree, to carry out action, as well as the tendency to express feelings of anger, friendliness, and the like.

Although the 30 years of research dealing with leadership has produced few viable models, and has raised more questions than answers, it does appear that leadership is a multidimensional concept, largely tied into what one is willing to accept as effectiveness (task performance or forming close human relationships). It is usually found that leadership is largely task-specific. The likelihood of a leader in one situation emerging as an effective leader in a dissimilar one is not as great as many casual observers might believe.

The coach as a leader. The interactions of players and coach in leadership situations in which the latter is primarily in control are often volatile and picturesque, to say the least. Not only is a certain role often expected of the coach-leader by the players, but the reverse is also often true. For example, Kauss (1975) found that coaches in a university football setting tended to view the newly recruited sophomores as largely "professional potential," as they had recruited them with these phrases and promises. However, as the athletes matured on the team, fewer were perceived in that way as their university playing days were nearing an end.

A study carried out with 17 English soccer-football teams produced data that relate directly to the topic of leadership in coaching. Cooper and Payne (1973), from the University of Aston in Birmingham, England, went about determining which of three psychologic orientations in both players and coaches (including assistants) were most predictive of group success. The orientations studied were assessed through a questionnaire, and consisted of the following.[4]

1. *Self-orientation:* This orientation reflects an individual who desires direct personal rewards, regardless of the effects on others working with him. This person may be a dominating, introspective, and socially insensitive individual.

2. *Interaction orientation.* This reflects a mind-set of an individual who is concerned about forming and maintaining harmonious and happy relationships, at least in superficial ways. If these needs interfere with performance, the individual often finds it difficult to contribute to the task at hand, or to be of real help to others.

3. *Task orientation.* A person who is task-oriented is concerned primarily with completing the job, solving the problem, working persistently, and doing the best job possible. Despite a seemingly selfish orientation, this person usually works well within a group, perceiving that contributing to the group effort will contribute to overall success in the task.

Cooper and Payne's findings are useful and provocative, and include the following.

1. The more successful teams had significantly more players who were high on self-orientation and lower in interaction and task orientations. Athletes who were most successful, and competed in national and international contests, were highest within this apparently selfish type of orientation.

2. In general, the staffs (coaches, etc.) were lower in self-orientation than were the player groups surveyed, while the defense players were lower in self-orientation than were the forwards, which is as expected.

Reflecting on this second finding, the authors of the study were uncertain whether former players who become coaches become less selfish, or whether players who were originally less selfish enter the coaching ranks.

Lefebvre and Cunningham (1974) delved into the ways coaches interacted with players following success and failure. The coaches' perceptions of the effort and ability expended by players was examined in this study dealing with soccer-football players and coaches. Using principles found in attribution theory (see Chapter V), it was found that: (1) Both the head and assistant coaches agreed on the players who succeeded because of effort, while they often disagreed as to those who

---

[4]A chapter devoted to value orientations is also found in Cratty BJ, Hanin YL: *The Athlete in the Sports Team* Love Publishing Co., Denver, Colorado, 1980.

were successful because of ability. (2) After success (winning), players of high ability received fewer communications from coaches, and the coaches also seemed to dwell less on the superior athletes' ability and effort after failure.

Cunningham and Lefebvre concluded that it is critical that coaches create an appropriate psychologic climate for players, providing them with appropriate input to increase their feelings of competence as a season progresses. However, they also warn, the great variability of players' talents and motivations, and also differences between what players *believe* helps them do well and what actually contributes to their success, requires that the coach be cautious when communicating his feelings to them following winning and losing contests.

Further research welding attribution theory to coaching and athletic behaviors and interactions should be fruitful. Work of this nature should provide helpful insights into the often complicated communications, relationships, and hostilities between coach and athlete. A further look at the importance of the interpersonal perceptions of athlete and coach is found in this chapter.

SPATIAL RELATIONSHIPS ON SPORTS TEAMS AND LEADERSHIP

An interesting body of literature has grown up during the years, which indicates that where individuals are placed, or locate themselves, may influence the assumption and bestowing of leadership. Someone who is sitting at the end of a conference table often facilitates communication in subtle ways, making that person a leader simply because of where he or she is located relative to the group.

Additionally, the individual's position in a communication chain or network seems to influence how he or she acts as a leader or follower. For example, the person in a network through which all or most communications inevitably flow may be expected to exert greater power than an individual on the periphery of the network. This type of variable as influential of interpersonal relationships has been summarized by Tubbs and Moss (1974).

The tendencies of position and location to influence leadership have also been studied within athletic teams. In studies by Grusky and Loy and their colleagues, it was found that in some teams certain "central" positions enhance the chances of those occupying them to achieve leadership roles. For example, Grusky (1963) found that individuals who had occupied the more central positions on an American baseball team (infielders and catchers-pitchers) were more likely to later become field managers or coaches. Loy and Sage (1968), surveying high school baseball teams, obtained similar findings. Pitchers and catchers, occupying these rather central positions on the team, were more likely to be selected as "valuable" by their teammates. Thus, they suggested that Grusky's idea was a helpful starting point when attempting to understand team leadership and interactions.

However, Loy and Sage did not find that personality traits were correlated to the positions held. Unlike Grusky, they found that "low interactors" on the periphery of teams did not evidence more psychologic aloofness or independent behaviors, in contrast to those central to the team. They suggested that skill level may be a more influential variable when contrasting "centrality" to personality traits and needs for leadership than are social-psychologic variables and team position played.

Interpersonal Perceptions of Coach and Athlete

There has been a plethora of studies dealing with how leaders and followers perceive each other. Typical is a 1954 effort by Halpin, using a Leader Behavior Description Questionnaire, from which responses were obtained that purportedly reflect how combat crews in airplanes felt about their leaders.

Other similar work includes studies in which university presidents were assessed by their faculty, business leaders by their subordinates, and leaders in government by their constituents. However, until recently, little work had been carried out in which athletes were asked to evaluate qualities in their coaches which they thought helpful and harmful to their performance. At this point, the available data seem to (1) reflect directions in which further research might be helpful and (2) offer helpful guidelines that may aid coaches to become more effective in their jobs.

Snyder (1972B), for example, found that both high school basketball coaches and their players perceive the coach as a "significant other" in the lives of players. The coach was perceived as an important advisor about future educational and occupational plans. Moderate correlations were obtained by Snyder between the advice given by coaches and the actual directions of the athletes' future educational strivings.

The coach, according to Snyder, does not act in a random manner when advising players. Further analysis of his data revealed that the coach's attention is not evenly applied, as responses from 300 players revealed that the players perceived the coach spending significantly more time with "star players" than with the less adroit on the teams.

Snyder conjectured that the coach is "likely to have a considerable ego involvement in the athletic and academic success of his more visible players." Data from studies of communication patterns on sports teams, carried out in the Soviet Union also reveal this tendency for coaches to selectively attend to the more capable players.

Information from a most interesting survey of feelings expressed by athletes about coaches also reflects this tendency of some coaches not to "travel" up and down the team's status hierarchy when dispensing their social attention. Percival (1971) published data indicating that athletes prefer coaches who are willing to relate to all members of the team, rather than mentors who seem to bestow their attentions primarily on the better players.

Although Percival's results are presented in a lighthearted manner, the outcome of this poll of 382 athletes in Canada has serious implications for coach-athlete relationships. For example, it was found that athletes in individual sports tended to be more critical of their coaches than were athletes in team sports. Percival felt that this might have been caused by the tendency of team sport athletes to relate their problems at times to their teammates, whereas in an individual sport, the athlete must usually relate only to the coach. Overall, only 24 percent of the athletes surveyed gave their coaches a generally positive rating, while 66 percent afforded their mentors a negative evaluation.

Percival's survey also compared the athletes' ratings of coaches with the coaches' ratings of themselves. The most marked discrepancy occurred in the area of "personality." Of the coaches, 72 percent scored themselves as possessing a positive "coaching personality," whereas only 32 percent of the athletes gave the same positive rating.

The coaches were rated higher in their knowledge of the sport, with 52 percent of the athletes indicating that they thought the coaching was of good technical quality. Percival also employed anecdotal data in an effort to construct what he termed "coaching types" of a negative and of a positive nature. Included among the more positive types of coaches were:

1. *The supporter.* A coach of this type is described as always on the athlete's side, giving emotional support when the action is tough and admonishing for mistakes when appropriate, but in judicious ways and at appropriate times. A coach of this type usually counters a loss by offers of positive encouragement for better future performances.

2. *The shrink.* The shrink is perceived by players as well-equipped to activate players to optimum levels before important competitions and able to deal with defeat as well as victory. The shrink understands athletes' feelings prior to, during, and following athletic competition, and offers helpful counseling at all these times.

3. *The tourist.* This is the coach who can relate to all team members,

substitutes as well as stars. He is one who spreads himself or herself socially and technically, and who tours the team, giving everyone relatively equal attention.

4. *Mr. Cool.* This coaching type is exemplified by an individual who remains unruffled under stress of competition, while remaining able to make "cool" decisions. He portrays positive attitudes under stress, and is a model of self-control for his athletes. Mr. Cool administers helpful criticism to athletes in private, and can settle down players when they become too excited.

More numerous were Percival's categories of "negative coaching types," only a few of which will be listed here.

1. *The insulter.* By far the most disliked coaching type is the coach who dispenses sarcasm in large amounts.

2. *The shouter.* The athletes perceive this coach as basing his success on the decibel rating he is likely to achieve while yelling at team members.

3. *Hitler.* Perhaps self-explanatory!

4. *The scientist.* The scientist is a coach who becomes so engrossed in the "latest findings" that he double-thinks himself into defeat, or so confuses his athletes that they do not know what to do in practices, training, and games.

5. *General Custer.* This coach "goes down" with an antiquated idea or strategy, refusing to change his mind in the face of athletic disasters.

6. *Shakey.* This nervous mentor may smoke two cigarettes at once during a contest, transmitting his nervousness to his players. Shakey is closely related to what Percival named the "choker," a coach who may remain cool during practice but who goes into shock when the contest starts.

7. *The hero.* This coach is constantly concerned about everyone knowing that he or she is indeed the coach. The coach who plays this role is always highly visible, constantly congratulating winners, while perhaps ignoring losers, with whom he finds it difficult to identify.

Although Percival's survey and characterizations would seem to add fuel to the fires of disgruntled athletes everywhere, it should be remembered that the stresses inherent in athletics may often engender hostilities in the athlete. Further, at times this anger may be directed toward the coach and his characteristics, and may be hostility which the athlete actually feels toward himself, his opponents, or the situation. Thus, the coach may at times serve as a convenient "whipping boy". Thus, rather than reflexively retaliating when a player's anger shows, the coach might pause to reflect as to whether he is truly deserving of the athlete's wrath or is a convenient and potentially useful safety valve for the athlete's aggressions, which might otherwise be directed inward, or toward officials, opponents, fans, or friends.

In a considerably more sophisticated study, Carron and Bennett (1977) examined factors that contribute to effective interpersonal interactions between coaches and athletes. A sample of 54 pairs of athletes and their coaches was used. Following a survey of the coaches at their university, 36 of the athlete pairs were designated as compatible by the coaches, and 18 were believed to be incompatible.

The primary rationale underlying the study was that to effectively study coach-athlete compatibility one must study the needs and involvement of athlete *and* coach, rather than concentrating on the coach's personality traits and behaviors. In order to assess possible differences between the coach-athlete pairs previously designated as compatible and incompatible, an assessment tool, published by Schultz (1967), was employed.

Schultz's measurement device makes two major assumptions.

1. Interpersonal needs are expressed within three main behavioral areas: needs for control of others, needs for affection and love, and needs that involve inclusion of others.

2. An accurate assessment of behavioral interactions, based on these three classifications, involves looking at other individuals' needs to *express* or *receive* behaviors reflecting each type of need when with one or more others.

Finally Schultz, as well as Carron and Bennett, makes the assumption that compatibility of two people (in this case coach and athlete) is dependent on an equilibrium achieved between them, based upon reciprocal needs of the three types described.

For example, an athlete who needs to receive affection is not likely to be compatible with a coach whose needs involve not expressing affection. An authoritarian coach would not be compatible with an athlete who does not need to receive control. And finally an athlete who needs to feel included will not get along with a coach who cannot give the athlete such a feeling.

The results offered highly important insights into how both the compatible and incompatible coach-athlete dyads seemed to mutually behave toward one another. In line with the hypotheses, it was found that both coach's and athlete's need patterns were important to consider. For example, in compatible dyads the coaches needed to be able to exchange control functions with the athletes, to share decision-making behaviors. The affection dimension was also important in compatible dyads; the athlete-coach pairs who seemed to get along best consisted of one who liked to receive affection and another who was not reluctant to express affection.

Most important was the inclusion dimension of the scales administered to both coach and athlete. In incompatible dyads, the athletes were usually characterized by their coaches as reflecting a marked need to exclude their mentors psychologically from what was going on. The athlete was thus perceived by the coach as having a low tendency to initiate inclusive behavior; while at other times the coach was also perceived as having a low tendency to initiate inclusive behavior.

Carron and Bennett are careful not to assign causal attributes to the relationships. They speculate that (1) behavioral incompatibility may have been caused by failure of athlete and/or coach to initiate inclusive behavior or (2) failure to initiate inclusive behavior could have caused incompatibility. However, on a descriptive level, the data are highly provocative. A further limitation to their study is the fact that the dyads judged compatible had been together longer (2.68 seasons) than had the incompatible coach-athlete pairs (1.85 seasons). Thus, further studies seem warranted, using Schultz's instrument, in which a temporal dimension is added. That is, it would be highly useful to determine just how compatible and incompatible coach-athlete pairs develop over time, during a season or two, or three. In any case, it is hoped that this investigation is the first of a series of similar ones exploring and shedding light on a critical problem area in sport.

IMPLICATIONS FOR THE COACH

There are many implications for effective coaching behavior and the promotion of leadership among team members, contained not only in this chapter but throughout the text. Essentially, an understanding of the preceding material may aid the coach (1) to modify certain situations to optimize individual and group performance, (2) to better prepare for circumstances and situations involving social interactions over which he or she has little control, and (3) to forestall and redirect potential social-psychologic problems that may arise as athletes and coaches come in conflict under the stress of competition.

Specifically, the coach may engage in three types of behavior when dealing with the social-psychologic climate permeating his or her team. These are: (1) exhibiting behaviors intended to promote some kind of positive interpersonal interactions, (2) exhibiting behaviors designed to modify the structure of the group (selecting a team captain, for example), and (3) instigating procedures intended to assess the social-psychologic forces and variables impinging upon the athletes and situation. This final function usually calls for the assistance of a psychologist or social psychologist, both when formulating the evaluation program and when interpreting the data.

One of the more promising types of research, notably that by Smith and Smoll, offers an important way for coaches to become better acquainted with themselves. The behavioral assessment tool they use can provide the coach with invaluable help in the years ahead. It is often difficult if not impossible for individuals to accurately perceive what behaviors (both quality and quantity) they are emitting without such an assessment device.

Other research cited in the chapter is also of critical importance when formulating implications for coaching behaviors. The work by Carron and Bennett shifts emphasis on studying the personality and behavior of the coach to the study of the coach-athlete dyad. The data from this study and others cited suggest helpful guidelines for the formation of supportive and positive coach-athlete relationships. Offering the athlete some control over training procedures, for example, enhances the emotional "vibrations," as does the degree to which the coach is able to express some affection toward the athlete. Data from these studies should be consulted with care by the coach in today's society.

Studies from several countries, including the Soviet Union and Canada, attest to the importance of spreading one's attention to all members of the team. The coach who concentrates only on star performers when lavishing praise, support, and technical help is assessed and rejected by the less able members of a team. And it is often the efforts of those who support the star that contribute most directly to overall success. Thus, coaches who concentrate primarily on players they see as contributing most to the team success are likely to be less than effective with the total team membership.

The coach should also take special care when selecting leaders among the team members. Indeed, this is usually an operation assigned to both coach and athletes.

As it is traditional on many American sports teams to democratically elect team captains, the team leader is the one who receives the votes of his teammates. However, the coach may in various ways modify the way this kind of leadership is obtained and exerted. Just when and how the captain is elected is in the hands of the coach, as are decisions about how many captains may be selected and the nature of their duties.

Counseling the team prior to the season election may aid the members to choose wisely. It is usually desirable to elect an individual well qualified to lead them in *game or competitive situations,* rather than an individual who may possess outstanding *social skills* outside the team practices and games.

Additionally, the coach may suggest that more than one captain be chosen. This common practice permits more than one person to exhibit leadership behavior, but as the season progresses, it may encourage a "real" leader to emerge. At the beginning of the season, a captain may be elected for each game or competition, or periodically throughout the season. In this way, leadership traits and potentials may be utilized to best advantage, as conditions during the season may fluctuate.

It is usually important to announce in advance just what decisions are alloted to the elected captain and which are the sole purview of the coach and coaching staff. This kind of explanation of division of power usually prevents difficulties further up the line.

It is also believed desirable that either the coach or a professional behavioral scientist attached to the team give *the elected captain(s) formal instruction* in leadership skills. Regular conferences with the team captain(s) could include information concerning the facilitation of interpersonal communication, the use of subtle leadership, and personal counseling skills. This last subject could include which problems might be best dealt with by the team captain and which are best left to the coach or to a trained mental health counselor.

Although these formal conferences may be scheduled at regular intervals throughout the sports season, the coach should take pains to be readily available to the team captain(s) at all times. Often, athletes have pressing problems they feel most comfortable airing to their captain-peers, rather than to the more stern authority figures represented by the coaches. Thus, the team leadership may profit from formally scheduled leadership skills conferences as well as from informal contacts resulting from an "open door" policy maintained by the coach.

Finally, the power of the coach to give both praise and punishment makes his or her position unique within the social-psychologic matrix of the team. He makes many decisions about rewards and punishments, rewards as subtle as changes in facial expression when a skill is performed well, to punishments as severe and obvious as dropping an athlete from the team.

Among such rewards and punishments, which have a strong impact on athletes, are:

1. How often should an athlete be rewarded by a word, a gesture, or promotion on the team roster?
2. In what form will a given athlete "feel" a reward or punishment most vividly?
3. What real changes can be expected from an athlete with a given type of reward or punishment?
4. What "things" will the athletes really perceive as rewards and punishments? Are these the same "things" the coach perceives as rewarding or punishing?
5. How can the coach best disseminate rewards and admonitions; e.g., to athletes in groups, or in individual conferences?

The answers to these questions are not simple. However, they are critical to the functioning of the team, or to its malfunctioning.

All athletes are not *really* rewarded by the same kinds of perks and behaviors. A constantly negative coach, or one who continually smiles his rewards upon the heads of his players, can both lose effectiveness, in contrast to the coach who *selectively and discriminatingly* extends praise, rewards, and admonitions.

SUMMARY

Studies focusing on leadership behaviors and processes both within and without a sports setting have been reviewed. The information these studies contain leads to some tentative conclusions.

1. Developmental studies indicate that various parameters of leadership behavior emerge upon surveying behavior in children's play groups composed of those in the third, fourth, and fifth years of life.

2. Personality trait studies of leadership, on sports teams or in other work groups, reveal little about what might be termed general leadership.

3. For the most part, leadership effectiveness must be defined in terms of what one means by effective (i.e., winning contests or promoting close human relationships).

4. In general, leadership is situationally determined. A leader of a team may not find himself or herself in leadership roles in other situations.

5. Leaders are generally viewed by group members as those most able to aid in the accomplishment of group goals. Thus, team captains, in most studies, are selected by their teammates as those who help the team to win, independent of physical prowess.

6. Studies of the personality of coaches often contain conflicting findings. The apparent authoritarian role of the coach is not always reflected in personality traits indicating that the coach is rigid psychologically.

7. Psychologically inflexible coaches may be less likely to adopt new practices than coaches who are more flexible in nature.

8. Position on a sports team often bestows leadership potential, with those in central roles on the team more likely to assume current and future leadership than those on the periphery.

9. Athletes when polled like coaches who refrain from sarcasm, relate to low- as well as high-status members of the team, and prepare themselves psychologically and technically to take charge of the team and its members.

10. Compatibility between a coach and an athlete is dependent upon the degree to which their needs are complementary. The needs studied

recently include those reflecting control, psychologic inclusion, and affection.

QUESTIONS FOR DISCUSSION

1. What are some definitions of leadership? What types of leadership are found on sports teams? How is this leadership decided on?
2. How might leadership behavior be enhanced?
3. Is leadership specific to a given type of task? Or might an individual exert leadership in various situations in effective ways?
4. What qualities are looked for in leaders on teams? How might these qualities be enhanced by the player himself or herself, and/or by the coach?
5. What early experiences in a child's life might influence him or her to either seek or avoid leadership roles?
6. What behaviors may a coach engage in to enhance his or her leadership qualities in the eyes of the team?
7. What kinds of overt behaviors are likely to detract from the acceptance by the team of a coach's leadership efforts.
8. Discuss Fiedler's model of leadership behavior. Can you apply this model to specific types of sports situations, relative to optimizing leadership potential?
9. Discuss the differences in effects upon a team of a coach who is task-centered vs. one who may be people-centered? Can one say with certainty which kind of orientation is best? If so, why? If no, why not?
10. Under what conditions is an authoritarian coaching personality helpful to an athletic team?
11. Discuss the implications of the study by Carron and Bennett reviewed in this chapter.

BIBLIOGRAPHY

ALBAUTH GR: The influence of resentment as identified in college basketball coaches. *75th Proceedings of the National College Physical Education Association for Men,* 1972.

ANDRUD WE: The personality of high school, college and professional football coaches, as measured by the Guilford-Zimmerman Tempermament Survey. Master's thesis, University of North Dakota, 1970.

BASS BM: *The Orientation Inventory.* Palo Alto, California, Consulting Psychologists Press, 1962.

BEER M, BUCKHOUT R, HOROWITZ MW, LEVY, S: Some perceived properties of the difference between leaders and non-leaders. *J Psychol* 47 (1959), 49–56.

BORG WR, TUPES E, CARP A: Relationships between physical proficiency and measures of leadership and personality. *Personnel Psychol* 12 (1959), 113–116.

BROEKHOFF J: Relationships between social status and physical measurements of boys and girls, from the 4th through the 6th grade. Paper at the National AAHPER convention, Houston, Texas, 1972.

CARRON AV, BENNETT BB: Compatibility in the coach-athlete dyad. *Res Q* 48:4 (1977), 671–679.

CARTER FL, HAYTHORN W, HOWELL M: A Further investigation of the criteria of leadership. *J Abnorm Soc Psychol* 45 (1950), 350–358.

CARTER FL, NIXON M: An investigation of the relationship between four criteria of leadership ability for three different tasks. *J Psychol* 27: (1949), 245–261.

CATTELL RB: New concepts for measuring leadership in terms of group synality. *Hum Rel* 4 (1951), 161–184.

CLARKE HH, CLARKE DH: Social status and mental health of boys as related to their maturity, structural and strength characteristics. *Res Q* 34 (1961), 288–298.

COOPER R, PAYNE R: Personality orientations and performance in soccer teams; leaders' and subordinates' orientations related to team success. Unpublished study, University of Aston, Birmingham, England, 1973.

COWLEY WH: Three distinctions in the study of leaders. *J Abnorm Soc Psychol* 23 (1928), 144–157.

——, *Social Dimensions of Physical Activity.* Chapter 5, "Leadership Status and Physical Activity." Englewood Cliffs, New Jersey, Prentice-Hall, 1967, 44-58.

CRATTY BJ, PASSER M: Psychological effects of participation in youth soccer. Unpublished study, Perceptual-Motor Learning Laboratory, UCLA, 1975.

——, *Psychology in Contemporary Sport.* Englewood Cliffs, New Jersey, Prentice-Hall, 1973. Chapter 13, "Leadership in Sport."

——, SAGE JN: The effects of primary and secondary group interaction upon improvement in a complex movement task. *RQ*, 35, Part 1 (October 1964), 164–175.

DUBIN R: *Human Relations in Administration, the Sociology of Organization.* Englewood Cliffs, New Jersey, Prentice-Hall, 1951.

FEINBERG MR: Relations of background experiences to social acceptance. *J. Abnorm Soc Psychol* 48 (1953), 206–214.

FIEDLER FE: *A Theory of Leadership Effectiveness.* New York, McGraw-Hill, 1967.

———, Assumed similarity measures as predictors of team effectiveness. *J Abnorm Soc Psychol* 49 (1954), 381–88.

———, *Leadership.* New York, General Learning, 1971.

GRUSKY O: The effects of formal structure on managerial recruitment: a study of baseball organization. *Sociometry* 26 (1963), 345–350.

HALPIN AW: The leadership behavior and combat performance of airplane commanders. *J Abnorm Soc Psychol* 49 (1954), 19–24.

HENDRY LB, WHITING HTA: Social and psychological trends in national caliber junior swimmers. *J. Sports Med Phys Fit* 8 (1968), 198–203.

———, Assessment of personality traits on the coach swimmer relationship and preliminary examination of the father-figure stereotype. *RQ* 39 (1968), 543–551.

———, Chapter 3, "The Coaching Stereotype.", in Whiting HTA (ed), *Readings in Sport Psychology,* Henry Kimpton Publishers, London, 1972.

HOMANS GC: *The Human Group.* New York, Harcourt Brace, 1950.

KAUSS R: Analysis of an American football team. Unpublished study, Perceptual-Motor Learning Laboratory, University of California, Los Angeles, 1975.

LEFEBVRE LM, CUNNINGHAM JD: Achievement, attributions for performance, and attraction: a social-psychological study of a college soccer team. Unpublished study, University of California, Los Angeles, January 1974.

LONGMUIR GE: Perceived and actual dogmatism in high school athletes, and coaches: relationships and some consequences. Doctoral dissertation, University of New Mexico, 1972.

LOY JW JR: Sociopsychological attributes associated with the early adoption of a sport innovation. *J Psychol* 70 (1968), 141–147.

———, Where the action is? a consideration of centrality in sports situations. RH Wilberg (ed): *Proceedings* 2nd Canadian Psychomotor Learning and Sports Psychology Symposium. University of Windsor, Ontario, October 1970.

———, Sage JN: The effects of formal structure on organizational leadership: an investigation of inter-scholastic baseball teams. In Kenyon GS (ed): *Proceedings* 2nd International Congress of Sport Psychology, Washington D.C., Contemporary Psychology of Sport. Athletic Institute, 1968.

MANN RD: Toward an understanding of the leadership role in formal organizations. In Dubin R, Homans, Mann, Miller (eds): *Leadership and Productivity.* New York, Chandler, 1965, 68–103.

MARAK GE: The evolution of leadership structure. *Sociometry* 27 (1964), 174–182.

NELSON DO: Leadership in sports. *RQ* 37:2 (1968), 268–75.

PARTEN M: Leadership among pre-school children. *J Abnorm Soc Psychol* 27 (1933), 430–440.

——Social play among pre-school children. *J Abnorm Soc Psychol* 28 (1933), 136–147.

PERCIVAL L (ed): The coach from the athlete's viewpoint. *Proceedings, Art and Science of Coaching Symposium.* Toronto, Canada, Fitness Institute, 1971.

POLANSKY N, LIPPITT R, REDL F: An investigation of behavioral contagion in groups. *Human Rel* 3 (1950), 319–348

RUSHALL BS: Behaviour control in swimming. *Aust J Sports Med* 4:6 (April 1972).

——Pettinger J: An evaluation of the effect of various reinforcers used as motivators in swimming. *RQ* 40 (1969), 540–545.

SAGE GH: Machievellianism among college and high school coaches. 75th *Proceedings of the National College Physical Education Association for Men,* 1972.

——Value orientations of college coaches compared to male college students and businessmen. 75th *Proceedings of the National Physical Education Association for Men,* 1972.

——An occupational analysis of the college coach. Chapter 9. In Ball DW, Loy JW (eds): *Sport and the Social Order: Contributions to the Sociology of Sport.* Menlo Park, California, Addison-Wesley, 1975.

SAGE J, LOY JW, INGHAM AG: The effects of formal structure on organizational leadership: an investigation of collegiate baseball teams. Paper presented at the Research Section of the 1970 AAHPER conference, Seattle, Washington, March 1970.

SCHULTZ WC: *The Interpersonal Underworld,* 5th ed. Palo Alto, California, Science and Behavior Books, 1966.

——*The FIRO Scales.* Palo Alto, California, Consulting Psychologists Press, 1967.

SMITH RE, SMOLL FL, CURTIS B: Coach effectiveness training: a cognitive-behavioral approach to enhancing relationship skills in youth sport coaches, *J Sport Psychol* 1 (1979), 53–58.

———, SMOLL FL, HUNT E: A system for the behavioral assessment of coaches. *Res Q* 48:2 (1977), 401–407.

SNYDER EE: Athletes' careers: the role of the coach in the athlete's future educational attainment. Paper presented at the Scientific Congress in conjunction with the 20th Olympics, Munich, Germany, August 1972.

———, High school athletes and the coaches, educational plans and advice. *Sociol Educ* 45 (Summer 1972), 313–325.

SORRENTINO RM: An extension of the theory of achievement motivation to the study of emergent leadership. Ph.D. dissertation, State University of New York, Buffalo, 1971.

STOGDILL R: Personal factors associated with leadership: a survey of the literature. *J Psychol* 70 (1968), 141–147.

TANNENBAUM R, SCHMIDT WH: How to choose a leadership pattern. *Harvard Business Review* 36:2 (March–April 1958), 96.

TOMAN W: *The Family Constellation.* New York, Springer, 1961.

TUBBS S, MOSS S: *Human Communication: An Interpersonal Perspective.* New York, Random House, 1974.

WEINER B, FRIEZE L, KUKLA A, REED L, REST S, ROSENBAUM RM: *Perceiving the Causes of Success and Failure.* New York, General Learning Press, 1972.

WILLIAMS LR, YOUSSEF ZI: Consistency of football coaches in stereotyping the personality of each position's player. *Int J Sport Psychol* 3:1 (1972), 3–11.

12

Stress and the Athletic Team

Teams inevitably come under stress during the competitive season. At times, this stress gradually builds up over the course of succeeding contests. Unlike other work groups, however, in athletic teams there is often a periodicity to stress. The intermittent nature of the strain is due to the cycles in the competitive season, usually marked by periodic confrontations. Additionally, one may place stresses in sport in subdivisions marked by periods of preparation for contests, stress during the competitions themselves, and stress after the completion of a contest or following the entire competitive season.

The concept of stress has physiologic as well as social and psychologic connotations. Among some of the more important questions raised by those interested in the nature of group stress are the following.

1. Is the influence of stress on group performance debilitating or facilitating of performance?

2. What is the influence of stress on interpersonal relationships among team members? between athletes and coaches?

3. Is stress contagious? What are the interpersonal influences of one or more individuals on the team who evidence stress, on other athletes and on the coach?

4. What influences does a tranquil coach, in contrast to a nervous one, have on the team?

5. What might be learned about group stress in work teams involved in expeditions, sea-lab experiences, military work, and the like, which may be applied to the sports team? In what ways do these groups differ from athletic teams with regard to stress reactions?

6. How might one take into consideration research concepts dealing with group stress when planning productive practice sessions for athletic teams?

7. How are such qualities as group cohesion, leadership and followership behaviors, "affective tone," and interpersonal communication modified under stress?

Definitive answers to these and other questions are not always spelled out by the available literature. The pages that follow, however, will attempt to derive some tentative conclusions. It is hoped that readers will come to a better understanding of the psychodynamics of group stress in sport, and thus influence more effective behavior on the part of both coach and athlete.

A Theory of Stress

The term and concept, stress, was popularized in the literature by an endocrinologist, Hans Selye, in a series of scientific papers beginning in 1936, and resulted in texts published in the 1950s and 1960s. Selye, while a young Viennese medical student, began to recognize basic indices of "stressed organisms," independent of the problems that seemed to plague them.

Selye first used the word *stress,* borrowed from physics, to describe the *results* of some kind of traumatic impingement on the organism. In more recent writings, he suggests that he should have used the term to designate the event or trauma affecting the organism, and the word "strain" to denote what happens to the organism or individual.

Following an address to the American Psychological Association, the word *stress* began to achieve popularity in the behavioral sciences. The concept of the stressed organism spread through many branches of the behavioral sciences, including psychiatry, psychology, and social psychology. The term began to replace words denoting psychologic and physiologic conditions formerly named anxiety, emotional distress, conflict, ego-threat, frustration, lack of security, tension, arousal, and the like.

The word *stress* also gained popularity because it tended to unify mind-body relationships. Selye's concepts provided the impetus to research in which physiologic measures were contrasted to psychologic assessments. The nature of modern society, containing the problems it does, has also provided the term *stress* with an aura helpful to many. Innumerable programs, devices, and cults have emerged to purportedly reduce the stress of modern living.

It is difficult to summarize Selye's rich ideas in a few paragraphs, as his work extends over decades and has resulted in hundreds of publications.[1] In the following pages, however, some of his main concepts are reviewed.

Selye describes the way stress is manifested in the body within what he calls a "general adaptation syndrome." This syndrome, he contends, is reflected in both time and space (within specific bodily organs). The temporal components of the syndrome he divides into subperiods: (1) An initial "alarm stage," during which the body first encounters the stressor; this includes a shock period when resistance may be temporarily lowered and a countershock phase when defensive mechanisms become active. (2) A stage of resistance, which is marked by maximum adaptation by the organism to the impingement, if the bodily and psychosocial resources are present. (3) If the stress is too persistent or powerful, a "stage of exhaustion" may be reached, during which adaptive mechanisms break down.

According to Selye, one should seek to impose, or accept from the environment, optimum stress levels, which in turn result in continued and helpful adaptation by the individual. In this way, he suggests, the individual becomes increasingly able to "handle" stress. He warns, however, that too much stress sustained over a period of time may result in a state of exhaustion that is chronic, and may be signaled by breakdowns of the psychologic and physiologic mechanisms that maintain the person's integrity.

The spatial components of the general adaptation syndrome include adrenocortical changes, modifications of muscle tone, heart rate, blood content, and gastrointestinal functions. These bodily functions, if kept within reasonable bounds, do not evidence breakdown under stress. But if the organism is overstressed, this may be reflected in such maladaptive changes as gastrointestinal ulceration, adrenocortical enlargement and hyperactivity, pathologic heart conditions, and strains to muscles, tendons and joints.

Selye extended his theory in the 1950s to include a broad range of stressors, in addition to disease and physical trauma. These included learning, loving and other psychologic and social "events" and situations. Such encounters should not be avoided, Selye suggests, but sought in optimum amounts. The avoidance of stress, he contends, produces an organism which is unadaptable and is likely to break down under miminal disrupting conditions.

Extensions of Selye's model into the real world of sport are not difficult. For example, when one exercises, it may be considered stress.

[1]See Selye (1950, 1952) and summaries by Cofer (1964) as well as by Appley and Trumbull (1967).

Thus, optimum physical fitness of groups and individuals fits well within the theory.

The psychologic and social stresses encountered by athletic teams and applied by society, fans, coaches, and teammates represent an important type of stress for an athlete. These stresses, if "brought down" too hard upon the "head" of a sports team, may result in varying amounts of social disintegration of the team organism under competitive conditions.

Thus, the coach as well as team members should (1) seek to achieve helpful adaptations to exercise and to social-psychologic stresses, (2) seek to apply stresses themselves in optimum amounts to achieve this adaptation, and (3) avoid overstress in all forms.

Definitions

Selye infers that stress is a kind of nonspecific response superimposed upon various specific manifestations of an "insulting agent" impinging upon the organism. He further points out that a variety of responses may be forthcoming from an individual under stress. And while these responses from the same individual may not vary too much over time, and from situation to situation, there are marked interindividual differences in stress reactions. This finding makes the measurement of stress a rather perilous undertaking.[2]

Others have extended and modified Selye's concepts and ideas. Appley and Trumbull (1967), for example, state that psychologic stress is elicited by conditions that approach the "upper thresholds of tolerability" and produce states of anxiety tension and upset. Stress produces behavior that deviates momentarily, or over time, from the normal. They cite behavior reflecting the presence of psychologic stress as including muscular tremors, stuttering, performance shifts, increased reaction time, erratic performance rates, malcoordination, and fatigue.

Appley and Trumbull further suggest that the concepts of anxiety and stress are closely similar psychologic states. Spielberger (1971), and others, suggest that anxiety and stress are related in the following ways.

1. Generalized trait anxiety implies a rather constant and persistently high level of fear or foreboding. Thus, if a relatively high level of general (or trait) anxiety is present, it is likely to lower the individual's threshold of dealing with stressful events.
2. State anxiety has been defined as a short-term reaction to a specific

[2]See Cratty BJ, the chapter on "Stress, Anxiety and Tension" in *Movement Behavior and Motor Learning,* Lea and Febiger, Philadelphia, 1973, for a more thorough discussion of definitions of stress, anxiety, and tension, as well as for a review of ways of assessing each of these conditions.

condition or situation. Thus, it is almost inseparable from what Selye and others would term stress, or situational stress.

3. Muscular tension may or may not be a manifestation of some kind of internalized emotional state, including anxiety. Patterns of muscular tension change are unique to an individual under stress, yet are different from person to person.

4. Individuals under states of constant stress may begin to manifest symptoms reflecting heightened levels of baseline or "trait" anxiety.

As will be seen, there is relatively little evidence of whether or not groups function under stress in the same manner as do individuals. However, some significant inroads into this rather treacherous problem area have been made, and are surveyed below.

Groups Under Stress: An Overview

During and following World War II, numerous clinical and experimental studies were published dealing with symptoms and outcomes of groups under stress. Typical of the early works of this type are those by Gordon et al (*The Split Level Trap,*) and Menninger (*Psychiatry in a Troubled World*). Grinker and Spiegel described wartime stress in *Men under Stress,* while Kardiner and Spiegle also focused on the soldier in *War Stress and Neurotic Illness.*

Among the findings, from these and other works, that have potential relevance to the team are the following.

1. Most of the time, men and women under stressful conditions are more fearful of failing to live up to social expectations than of incurring physical harm. That is, people are more prone to "failure anxiety" than "harm anxiety" when confrronted with difficult conditions.

2. Prior to and following confrontations with stressful circumstances, many groups and individuals evidence higher levels of stress and anxiety than when actually participating in the situation itself. That is, anticipation of a potentially stressful situation, or preperformance anxiety, and reflecting back upon difficult conditions, may tend to magnify stress more than actually facing and dealing with feelings experienced during actual performance.

Stress on sports teams may be cyclic. Further, in sport, stress may vary considerably according to whether a team feels pressure to continue their success, to achieve success gradually as the season progresses, or to avoid being last in the standings as the season ends. A team who as the season progresses finds itself in the middle of the standings may experience decreasing levels of stress as the season nears a close. They need not strive for the championship, nor must they avoid being last. Figure 12-1 presents a hypothetical model depicting how teams at

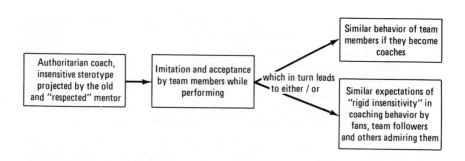

FIGURE 12-1.   Stress in sport, as a function of team standing and of time during the season.

various levels in the standings may incur stress as the season progresses. The conscious or unconscious knowledge of how to avoid stress (by being mediocre) may tend to blunt the efforts of sports teams more often than is realized.

There are also indications from psychologic data obtained from the America SeaLab Program and Antarctic expeditions that when placed

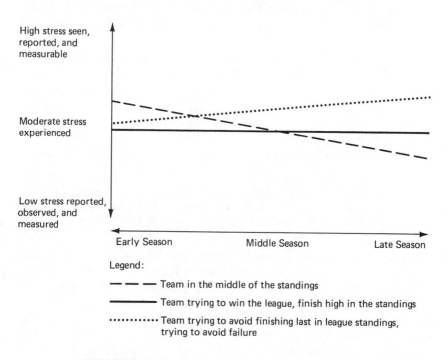

FIGURE 12-2.   Stress and cognitive mediators.

under stress, group members tend to keep interpersonal conflict to a minimum. They often subordinate their real feelings when they perceive conflict situations about to arise. Additionally, these and other findings indicate that groups generally become more cohesive under moderate stress, and remain so unless stress levels become intolerable; at this point, the group tends to disintegrate as a social and performing unit. This principle conceivably applies to sports teams during a season, as they encounter various amounts of social approval, interpersonal tension within the team, and censure for their successes and failures.

Thus, as with individuals, there seems to be an optimum amount of stress tolerable by a group, which if accommodated to may make the group more psychologically healthy but if exceeded may lead to its demise.

The literature also suggests that the degree of stress both individuals and groups perceive and experience in a situation may not be directly related to objective reality. Rather, there seem to be various "cognitive mediators" operative, reflected in interpretive processes that intervene between the real event and the stress reactions experienced. This hypothesis is depicted schematically in Figure 12-2.

Stress Is Contagious

Several sources of data indicate that stress is socially contagious. If an individual is adjacent to, or interacting with, another who is under stress, it is likely that both will evidence indices of upset. For example, Caudill (1958), an anthropologist reviewing research which indicates that individuals in close proximity often evidence similar physiologic reactions if one or the other becomes unsettled, suggests that stress may *only* be considered within a social context. Watson and Kanter found that changes in heart rate and blood pressure of both a patient and his psychoanalyst were similar when the patient begins to describe stressful life situations.

Some research of this nature has focused upon sport. An early study by Hill (1956), found that when stress reactions of two rowing crews from Harvard were compared, using an eosinophile count, the more successful of the two crews evidenced less interindividual variability in this measure of excitability than did the less successful rowing group. In another study with Harvard crews, Renold (1951) also found that, although individual differences existed in stress measured in the blood, characteristic patterns of stress were seen when the physiologic make-up of the crew, the coxswain, and the coach were evaluated during competition. In 1958, Caudill suggested that studies of this nature be extended to teams in which the roles were dissimilar, in contrast to the relatively similar tasks required in rowing teams. Extensive work of this nature in team sports other than rowing is not prevalent in the literature at this point.

There have been at least four studies, carried out with coaches, depicting their reactions as they viewed their own teams in competitions. Burris Husman published data in 1969 that reflected marked heart rate changes in coaches of both swimmers and basketball players. Their heart rates rose markedly, up to 114 beats per minute, during critical times in contests when their teams performed. During less critical parts of the competitions, when winning or losing was already decided, or during practice sessions, these same stress reactions were not marked.

More recent work by Alleson (1971) and his colleagues, as well as by Corbin and his associates (1970), extends these findings. For example, in the study by Alleson, telemetered heart rate measures were obtained from coaches who were responsible either for the offensive or defensive teams in American football. They found that there were significant differences in the heart rates of the coaches, depending on whether or not the subgroups they coached were actually participating.

This same study found that stress reactions, as measured in heart rate changes, varied depending on whether or not the game was closely contested. Thus, recognition of defeat significantly lowered heart rate, as did satisfaction with obvious victory. During critical points in the competitions, the heart rates of the coaches at times reached 74 to 80 percent of their maximum, and from 200 to over 275 percent over their resting heart rate. Thus, the hearts of these coaches seemed at times to be literally bursting from their chests under the emotional stresses of merely *watching competition.* As a result of these data, as well as similar findings by Corbin, Alleson and his co-workers formulated the following recommendations:

1. Coaches should have an annual medical evaluation of their cardiovascular systems to prevent trauma due to emotional stresses encountered in their occupation.

2. In order to prevent cardiovascular "incidents," coaches should participate in regular exercise programs to enhance their ability to deal with the stresses inherent in coaching.

Alleson further recommended that measures of anxiety might be correlated to the stress indices obtained from coaches in order to formulate a more comprehensive picture of what was going on.

The type of behavioral contagion seen in these studies between a coach and his team undoubtedly occurs when substitutes observe competition, and when players co-act in athletic contests. However, at this point, I am unaware of extensive work in which interpersonal indices of stress among players have been analyzed using telemetry.

However, coaches should be aware of the degree to which substitutes may be over- or underactivated (stressed) prior to entering a contest. During competition, the degree to which participants evidence stress should also be a constant concern to mentors, and judicious substitutions made when warranted.

Group Personality and Reactions to Stress

If, as has been described in Chapter I, there *is* such a phenomenon as group personality, it is possible that some collection of personality traits makes some groups more susceptible to stress reactions than others. Literature relating group traits (possessed collectively by members) to stress tolerance is not extensive, however.

Lazarus, in a summary of studies conducted before 1965, points to several "cognitive and personality" factors, which may underlie a group's ability to react to threat and to cope well with potentially stressful situations. Included in such cognitive judgments are those about the nature of the threat, the degree of harm anticipated, and most important the resources the group feels they may possess with which to overcome the anticipated threat.

Gunderson (1973) and his associates, who studied the adjustment of people to the stress of "wintering over" in Antarctica, concluded that criteria falling into three categories were critical when evaluating a group's tolerance for stress: (1) the degree to which the group was task-oriented, (2) the emotional abilities of the individuals, and (3) their social compatibility. Whether data gathered from this type of isolated group, working through weeks of darkness in isolated circumstances, can be applied to athletic teams, however, is problematical.

Birth Order and Stress Tolerance

A number of researchers have explored how birth order potentially influences (1) the percentage of people who select stressful undertakings and (2) individuals' apparent tolerance for stress. The personality qualities that have been examined include self-reliance, fear, feelings of well-being, affiliation needs, and willingness to face stress individually or in groups.

These studies, carried out with such groups as fighter pilots, as well as children in stressful situations produced in laboratories in general point out that personality patterns seen in first-borns include higher need achievement, greater dependency on parents as models, lower self-esteem, and the need for greater support in stressful situations than is true among second- and third-borns.

Thus, the implication is that (all things being equal, which they seldom are!) first-borns are less likely to hold up in stressful situations than are those born later in the family. First-borns may need to face stress using group support. The way these data are reflected in the selection of athletes into individual and team sports, and into those involving contact and possible physical harm, has been discussed in Chapter II.

Stress Modeling

A case could be made for the fact that *all* training experiences to which athletes are subjected involve preparing them to meet the stresses of competition. However, from time to time coaches in various parts of the world in a variety of sports have taken special pains to expose athletes to unusual stresses of a social and psychologic nature in an effort to prepare them to compete well. An example of this was when audiences were introduced to team practices to help athletes accommodate to the social stresses of observers.

Isolation stress has also been used by coaches in Eastern Europe and in other parts of the world. This involves placing a potential international competitor in a situation that requires self-coaching for a period of time. This type of stress is imposed when it is believed that a top athlete may be shifted to a team situation and coach who may be unfamiliar with his or her unique characteristics just before encountering international competition. Therefore, an effort is made to "stress" the athlete socially, and to model stresses he may later encounter within a training regime that lacks a familiar mentor. In this way, it is hoped that breaking away from an accustomed coach may prove less traumatic than would otherwise be true.

Various tactical stresses are often applied to teams. The two-minute drill in American football is one example. In this situation, last-minute opportunities to score are enhanced by practicing a rushed situation in practice. Basketball teams often practice under conditions that replicate "a few seconds left, and a close game," so that they become able to handle similar stresses in competition. Track and field athletes, particularly distance and middle distance runners, are often placed under tactical stresses by their coaches. These and other examples remain interesting and potentially useful, but at the same lack scientific verification in the absence of supporting data.

More needed than evidence of just how this type of stress modeling may or may not be effective are studies that illuminate how team stress may be reduced. The investigation by Stoudenmire, in which relaxation training involving muscular tension reduction lowered measures of anxiety, would seem to be a helpful starting point.

SUMMARY

Stress has many dimensions, only some of which were discussed on these pages. Focus was primarily on how stress affects and is dealt with by groups, primarily sports teams. According to Hans Selye, who has popularized the term, evidence of stress ranges from physiologic and biochemical to social and psychologic measures that a potential threat is being dealt with.

Based on the available clinical and experimental evidence, the following generalizations seem valid.

1. People evidence different patterns of muscular tension and physiologic accommodation when faced with stressful situations. However, a single individual tends to evidence relatively the same pattern under stress on successive occasions.

2. Creation of conditions, during the practices of athletic teams,which replicate social and psychologic irritants of competition, is a technique often used by coaches to prepare teams for optimum performance under stress.

3. Such obvious and subtle variables as the personality traits of group members and the birth order of important central figures in a group may determine how the group reacts to stress.

4. With the imposition of moderate stress levels, groups will tend to "pull together" and become more cohesive. However, if stress levels are heightened, a group's performance may suffer, until the entire team effort may disintegrate.

5. Stress is socially contagious. The stress levels in coaches are influenced by critical points in the competitions they oversee, while individuals in close proximity when working on productive sports teams have registered relatively similar stress indices, based on biochemical analyses of their blood.

6. An important variable influencing how individuals and groups deal with stress is their interpretations of the nature of the threat, and the resources they possess to meet and defeat the intrusion on their harmony.

QUESTIONS FOR DISCUSSION

1. Discuss the concept of stress in relation to the idea of anxiety? Are the two terms and ideas similar or different? How?

2. What factors contribute to group stress? Is group stress on a team always harmful?

3. What is situational anxiety? How does this differ, if at all, from stress?

4. Discuss Selye's model for stress in relation to conditioning a swimming team or long-distance runner?

5. How can group stress be reduced?

6. What are the roles of cognitive mediators in the control and under-standing of both individual and group stress?

7. How might the coach exploit the fact that stress is usually "catching" from one individual to another? How might this contagion be harmful in a given team situation? Be specific, give examples.

8. How does group stress manifest itself, relative to intensity, prior to, during, and following competition? How might a coach deal with the varying degrees of stress that may be experienced by an individual and/or a team?

9. How might a given player reduce or heighten group stress? What are the likely attributes of such an individual?

10. How does team success and failure influence group stress during a prolonged season?

BIBLIOGRAPHY

ALLESON PHE, OLSEN DC, FISHER AG, BRYCE G: The effects of stress situation in football games on the heart rates of football coaches. Unpublished study, Human Performance Laboratory, Brigham Young University, Provo, Utah.

APPLEY MH: Neuroendocrine aspects of stress. In Flaherty, BE (ed): *Psycho-physiological Aspects of Space Flight.* New York, Columbia, 1961 139–157.

———, TRUMBULL R: *Psychological Stress.* New York, Appleton-Century-Crofts, 1967.

BASOWITZ H, PERSKY H, KORCHIN SJ, GRANKER RR: *Anxiety and Stress, an Interdisciplinary Study of a Life Situation.* New York, McGraw-Hill, 1955.

CATTELL RB, WISPE LC: The dimensions of syntality in small groups. *Hum Rel J of Soc Psych* 28 (1948), 57–78.

CAUDILL W: Effects of social and cultural system in reactions to stress. New York, Social Sciences Research Council, June 1958.

COFER CN, APPLEY MH: *Motivation and Theory.* New York, Wiley, 1964.

CORBIN CB: Effects of vicarious sports participation on heart rates of subjects varying in levels of anxiety and age. Unpublished study, Kansas State University, 1972.

———, TOLSON H, FLETCHER R, CUNNINGHAM C: Heart rate variations during a basketball game. *Coach and Athlete* (October 1970), 18–22.

CRATTY BJ: Chapter 15, "Stress, Anxiety, and Tension." In *Movement*

Behavior and Motor Learning, 3rd ed. Philadelphia, Lea and Febiger, 1974.

———. *Psychology in Contemporary Sport.* Chapter 7, "The Coach, His Personality and Emotions." Englewood Cliffs, New Jersey, Prentice-Hall, 1973.

FENZ WD, EPSTEIN S: Gradients of physiological arousal in parachutists as a function of an approaching jump. *Psychosom Med* 29:1 (1967), 33–51.

FRENCH JR Jr: The disruption and cohesion of groups. *J Abnorm Soc Psychol* 36 (1941), 361–377.

GAZES PC, SOVELL F, HUNSICKER JW: Dellastatious, continuous radio-electrocardiographic monitoring of football and basketball coaches during games. *Am Heart J* 78 (1969), 509–512.

GRINKER RR, SPIEGEL J: *Men Under Stress.* Philadelphia, Blakiston, 1945, 344.

GUNDERSON, EKE, NELSON PD, ORVICK JM: Personal history correlates of military performance at a large Antarctic station. San Diego, California, U.S. Navy Medical Neuropsychiatric Research Unit, Unit Report No. 64-22, August, 280–286 (1973).

HANSEN DL: Cardiac response to participation in little league baseball competition as determined by telemetry. *R Q* 38 (1967) 384–88.

HARMON J: Emotional reactions of college athletes. *R Q* 23 (December 1952), 391–397.

HILL SR: Studies on adrenocortical and psychological response to stress in man. *Arch Intern Med* 97 (1956), 269–298.

JOHNSON WR: A study of emotion revealed in two types of athletic contests. *R Q* 20 (1949), 72–79.

LATANE B, ECKMAN J, JOY V: Shared stress and interpersonal attraction. *J Exp Soc Psychol* 1 (1966), 80–94.

LAZARUS RS: Chapter 6, "Cognitive and Personality Factors Underlying Threat and Coping." In *Psychological Stress,* New York, Appleton-Century-Crofts, 1967.

MICHAEL ED: Stress adaptation through exercise. *R Q* (1957), 50–54.

MORRIS HH, STOCKHOLM A: A baseball pitcher's heart rate during actual competition. *R Q* 40 (1969), 645–649.

RADLOFF R, HELMREICH R: *Groups Under Stress.* New York, Appleton-Century-Crofts, 1968.

RENOLD A, et al: Reaction of the adrenal cortex to physical and emotional stress in college oarsmen. *N Engl J Med* 45 (1951), 754–757.

SELYE H: Unmasking of faces of stress. *Med Tribune* (October 1961), 4–10.

———. Perspectives in stress research. *Perspect Biol Med* 2, 403–416.

———. *The Physiology and Pathology of Exposure to Stress.* Montreal, Acta Inc., 1950.

———. Stress and Disease. *Science* 122 (1955), 625–631.

———. *The Stress of Life.* New York, McGraw-Hill, 1956.

SPIELBERGER CD, GORSUCH RL, LUSHENE RE: *The State-Trait Anxiety Inventory.* Palo Alto, California, Consulting Psychologists Press, 1970.

———. Trait-state anxiety and motor behavior. *J Mot Behav* 3:3 (September 1971), 265–279.

STOCKHOLM A, MORRIS HH: A baseball pitcher's heart rate during actual competition. *R Q* 40 (1969), 645–649.

STOUDENMIRE J: Effects of muscle relaxation training on state and trait anxiety in introverts and extroverts. *J Pers Soc Psychol* 24:2 (1972), 273–275.

VANEK M, CRATTY BJ: Chapter 8, "Model Training." In *Psychology and the Superior Athlete.* New York, Macmillan, 1970.

WELFORD AT: Stress and achievement. *Aust J Psychol* 17 (1965), 1–11.

13

Implications for the Athlete

One of the primary themes permeating most of these chapters has been the supposition that much of the time athletes talk to themselves, form judgments, and otherwise deal intellectually with the meanings and consequences of their physical efforts. Thus, in some circumstances they take important and central roles in their own training—athletes often coach themselves.

While self-coaching in obvious ways may be seen more in mature athletes, this kind of egocentric concern probably occurs more often within the minds of the less mature than many coaches realize. In the early 1960s, I knew a young athlete about the age of 12 who traveled from gymnasium to gymnasium in the Los Angeles area seeking advice and what coaching he could. He later represented the United States in two Olympic Games.

Not only do individual sport athletes often deal with their own technical problems, but members of teams, in ways both obvious and sometimes unknown to their coach, plan their own strategies and training regimes.

While coaches vary in the degree of self-determination they encourage in "their" athletes, all but the most naive realize that self-coaching is a common phenomenon among performing members of the athletic community.

If one accepts these assumptions as valid, it is important at this point to discuss how some of the preceding material can be used by the athlete to improve both mental-emotional outlook on sport and actual physical capabilities.

It has been the intent of the writer to aid athletes as well as coaches. It was hoped that the work in the previous chapters illuminated various social and psychologic factors that may both positively and negatively influence them as athletes and as people. With these objectives in mind, the following implications were formulated.

The material in this chapter has been divided into three sections: (1) a discussion of the athlete's relationships with his teammates and competitors, (2) the athlete's associations with his coach, and (3) the athlete's feelings about the fans and others in the sports community.

TEAMMATES AND COMPETITORS

The athlete on a team or in an individual sport experiences social relationships that are usually rather complicated. The athlete, for example, must both compete and cooperate with teammates at various times, and in different ways, in the course of the season. The athlete must usually compete with others on the team for the privilege of playing, while at the same time cooperating with the same individuals to defeat a common opponent. Therefore, in some ways, the athlete's feelings about teammates and their feelings about him or her resemble the emotions engendered when competing with members of another team.

Competition with others often takes elusive forms. For example, a world class athlete in sports producing exact performance measures (swimming, track and field) competes not only with people present at a given competition, but with *all* the other top performers in the world. These athletes know that the results of a day's efforts will be published and scrutinized by coaches and athletes in many countries.[1]

For years, social psychologists and others have studied the intricate feelings and social machinations of people in competitive work groups. Several persistent themes from this work are of potential importance to the competing athlete.

For example, individuals attempting to achieve at high levels in business and other fields of endeavor, including sport, may experience a number of rather disquieting emotions coming from family, friends, and others. The competing industrialists or athletes may feel that people do not like them very much, and as they achieve more and more,

[1] I know of one coach of Olympic athletes who, with the cooperation of his collegiate team, carefully fatigued the athletes just before collegiate meets, during the year prior to the Olympics. Their potentially best marks were thus not posted in these meets, which left their foreign competitors unaware of their potential. When these athletes finally reached the Olympics at the end of that year, they posted superlative marks, surprising their competitors from other countries.

these negative feelings from others tend to become magnified. Success is often accompanied by some degree of social rejection by former friends within an organization. This may be particularly true when one must inevitably "push someone aside" in order to reach the relatively fewer positions at the "top."

Not long ago, I counseled a tennis player ranked at about the middle of the 500 players in the world. In recent matches, he informed me, he had felt that he had met competitors who were ranked well above him internationally and could easily have defeated them. Instead, he began to shake and to experience other signs of anxiety, which resulted in his losing the matches.

Further conversation revealed that he had many attributes that made him a valued social companion on the tennis circuit. He was well liked, and from a prominent family. Further, he valued the acceptance he had been receiving from other players, including many who were of world prominence.

As the interview progressed, it appeared that he was both sending and receiving social vibrations that are common in various competitive arenas where a relatively large number of people are competing for a small number of prominent positions at the top. He evidenced what has been termed "success phobia."

Essentially, the cycle of feelings in an athletic context goes like this:

Athlete: "I like to be liked."
Others: "We like you as long as you do not achieve too much, or take places we would like to have in the status hierarchy."
Athlete: "But I would also like to do well, to achieve!"
Others: "Fine, we would like you to do well also, as long as it does not interfere with *our* climb to success. As long as your efforts enhance our chances for success, we will leave you alone, or support you."
Athlete: "Ahh, I find I *do* have ability, I *am* getting better, I *can* achieve. I think I will!"
Others: "Watch out! Not too fast! Do not step on our toes or threaten us, or we won't like you so much, or may take a hearty dislike to you!"
Athlete: "Why are others feeling this way? Why do my former friends seem cold? What is happening?"

It was these latter disquieting feelings that the tennis player had begun to experience. At this point, both he and other competitive athletes in similar situations have choices. The choices are largely dependent on the strength of the athlete's needs to achieve in contrast to his needs for social acceptance.

For example, athletes may exercise their fullest capacities and win, and then deal as best they can with the hostilities of those they have prevented from winning, or who are jealous of their success. About half of all competing athletes lose, more in swimming and track meets!

Further, successful athletes may reject former friends in turn. They may accept the inevitable, that to succeed will engender negative feelings from others. They may glory in the "heady wine of success" while ignoring the barbs of their competitors. Data indicating that world class athletes tend to become more and more introverted may reflect their tendency to pull into a social shell, away from the jealousies of others, as they achieve more and more personal success. However, the decision to reject the feelings of others may not occur without an internal emotional struggle, as was the case of the tennis player under discussion. Moreover, this rejection from others may engender anxiety and regrets.

On the other hand, the athlete may "back down," consciously or unconsciously, from the social pressures. He or she may judiciously lose at times when he could actually win. In this way, friendships are saved, and the competitor remains well-liked. Performance potential has been compromised for the fulfillment of social needs for acceptance. This type of compromise may be engaged in both by individuals and by teams.[2]

There are, of course, other compromises, given the conditions described. Athletes may somehow manage to be "pretty good," and rank among the five or ten best in their country, or in the world. In this way, athletes may achieve some athletic prominence which they may value, and at the same time remain accepted within a community of athletes whose friendships they also value.

This mid-ground decision may be felt by some to be a "cop-out." For in truth the athlete is blunting his or her performance in ways that may be later regretted, and produce anxieties similar to those experienced with the loss of friends.

Thus, in summary, the athlete who begins to feel cut off from former friends with increasing success is not alone. Knowing in advance that social rejection by some usually accompanies high levels of achievement may encourage some athletes to go on, to achieve, despite the subtle and obvious social pressures applied to them, encouraging them to be almost as good as they might have been.

Other feelings from one's teammates may not be as ominous. Work groups, including athletic teams, tend to like one another more and more as they experience success together. Indeed, those who are simply

[2]There were rumors that the first International Congress of Sport Psychology was called together in Rome, in 1965, because the organizers were attempting to determine why an apparently superior national soccer team lost to an inferior competitor in a recently completed competition.

present in a success-laden environment usually have warm friendship spread liberally over their heads, even if they have had no direct role in the group's achievement. The locker room attendant and other stadium help are often honored by winning teams, despite their relatively small role in the team success.

Furthermore, as a successful season progresses, teammates begin to like one another more and more, and this in turn makes them want to be together in contexts other than those involving athletics. Social contacts are instigated after practice.

But here also there are some hidden boulders in the rushing rivers of success. Teammates who have formerly only seen each other on the practice field make friends with the families of their teammates. As a result, there may be a reluctance to criticize the performance of those with whom they are performing. Players who have formed close social contacts may modify their team play in ways related to friendship patterns. They may tend to make their close friends on the team "look good" by passing to them frequently, prior to scores. They may spend brief rest periods during practice talking about subjects related not to athletics, but to their social interests.

Thus again, there may occur a trade-off between needs for affiliation and performance success. Moreover, this incongruence in needs may grow more pronounced as the season progresses. Toward the end of some seasons, the "social noise" between close friends on the team may interfere with team play and clear communications. The best efforts of the coach to maintain harmony and to teach skills may be clouded. The team may win fewer games than they had counted upon. If friendships had not become so intense, more victories might have been achieved.

It has thus been suggested that team success may work in subtle ways against future success. The chain of internalized thoughts may proceed somewhat as follows:

Beginning
of the
   Season: "We don't know how good we are. Let's work hard and see what we can do!"

             "We are winning, we are good! We like each other because of the success we are feeling together! Let's have a beer together after practice! Can your wife and kids come over to the house sometime?"

Middle of
the
   Season: "George and Bill and their kids are nice people. I don't want them to lose their positions to newer players, and want them to look good in practice and games. I will pass to them more often, so they can score."

"What seems to be going wrong? We don't seem to be winning so
much, although the talent was here at the beginning of the season!
There is some dissension on the team. The coach becomes angry
when we do not always pay attention to his lectures before practices.
He is concerned about the effort we expend in these last games."

Countering these possible negative social events and feelings is not
always easy. At the same time, becoming aware of potential problems
is a positive first step in their resolution.

There are numerous other facets of the social relationships between
teammates, which have not been discussed. The communication problems that may arise between players of different backgrounds can prove
important in team and individual sports.[3] Differences in age and experience can lead to similar problems. Individuals select athletics as a means
of expression for many reasons. Tolerance for individual differences in
athletes is not only an important requisite for coaching effectiveness,
but also for becoming a "socially lubricating" member of a team.

THE ATHLETE AND THE COACH

The athlete and the coach may harbor various feelings about each
other. To some degree, these feelings depend on the athlete's need to
be controlled, his or her acceptance of authority, and the degree of
authority the coach needs to exert. The athlete's beliefs about the
coach's competencies are also important, for if the athlete believes that
the coach knows the sport, a minimum number of personality conflicts
are likely to occur.

A few years ago, I spoke all day to a world association of coaches.
Midway through the afternoon, an American coach arose and said, "I
don't see why athletes come to me. Most do not like me, and I do not
see why they do it." The man speaking was one of the more prominent
coaches of the Olympic sport represented at the meeting.

I pointed out that an athlete was not going to him to be liked, or to
like him, but to gain expertise in the sport. The athlete wanted to be
coached by one of the best in the country. Thus, the athletes with whom
he was not getting along really did not care about forming warm social
relationships; they simply wanted to perform well. They knew that in
many ways the coach could enhance their performances.

[3]See the chapter and examples of communication on sports teams in Cratty BJ, Hanin
YL, *The Athlete in the Sports Team* Love Publishing Company, Denver, Colorado, 1980.

If an athlete perceives the technical skills of the coach to be superior, I pointed out, social friction is not only likely to be at a minimum, but any problem that does occur can be minimized by both parties. There is little doubt that both social compatibility and mutual respect between athlete and coach because of the technical skill of the latter are important. High technical ability on the part of the coach may cause an athlete to negate or overlook possible social problems, whereas lack of adequate knowledge of the sport may magnify social friction between coach and athlete. The athlete may focus his or her hostility on personal mannerisms of the mentor, whereas in truth the performer is unhappy over the quality of the expert help being offered and the teaching that is taking place.

It is highly desirable, however, for a coach to possess adequate to good social skills, including real feelings for his or her athletes, *in addition* to technical knowledge of the sport. More and more at higher levels of coaching expertise, the coach who has both technical skills and an understanding of human relationships is emerging in many individual and team sports.

It *is* possible, however, that the coach and athlete may not like each other. That probability is only slightly less likely in a team sport than in an individual sport. The level of interpersonal hostility may ebb and surge at various times during a season, and even during a single important contest—human relationships are stressed under stress.

The athlete should recognize that he or she may not like the coach for sound and viable reasons. These might include incompetence, insipid personality, unethical behaviors, or other obvious deficiencies. However, it should *also* be realized that the coach is often a recipient of hostilities and frustrations engendered by the nature of athletic competition itself, which may be independent of the coach's best efforts and personality characteristics. The frustrations of competition are often not absorbed by the exercise inherent in the sport itself. Thus, the coach may be an unwilling, and unknowing, scapegoat for feelings of inadequacy and frustration the athlete himself may harbor. The coach may serve as a handy whipping boy for aggressions and frustrations the athlete may actually feel toward the situation, competitors, or self. Self-hate can easily be transferred into apparent dislike of the coach.

The athlete should therefore realize that negative feelings about the coach may be triggered by personal inadequacies and needs to transfer the responsibility of losing to someone else. While the coach may possess some undesirable qualities, his or her very presence, accompanied by frustrating conditions, may prompt an athlete to bestow unpleasant feelings on an undeserving head.

Another interesting type of problem may arise because of the growing need of some athletes, particularly at the national and international levels, to coach themselves. Sometimes, this problem surfaces because the athlete has reached levels of expertise that have exceeded the abilities of a coach with whom he or she has started. Sometimes the athlete, wishing to work alone, can do so reasonably well. At times, the athlete wants to find a coach with more knowledge, and may not wish to "hurt" his original mentor.

I spoke a few years ago to an international competitor in track and field. He was experiencing guilt pangs about leaving a long-time coach who had started him in his event. He had begun to realize, however, that this coach simply did not possess the skills needed to help him at the level at which he was presently competing (the Olympics). At the same time, the athlete was experiencing guilt about leaving his former sponsor and friend. After discussion, however, it became clear to him that a break in the relationship was probably best, and that his performance would not suffer but would conceivably improve under another coach.

Breaking off with a former coach may produce guilt feelings, revolving around the belief that the athlete may be "letting down" a former friend and mentor. Also, because of the ending of what might have been a supportive emotional relationship, the athlete may feel uncomfortable. However, changing one's coach may not be a negative act, but a very positive one.[3] If an expert is *not* constantly available at high levels of competition, the athlete may produce more in individual sports if he or she constantly "shops" for expert advice from more than one mentor.

Some athletes about to enter international competition experience feelings of isolation when taken from a familiar coach and surroundings to less familiar training sites manned by new coaches. In some countries, athletes about to undergo such changes are placed in contrived "isolation situations." They may work for a period of time on their own, with little or no supervision. In this way, they may accommodate to feelings of isolation when changes in their practice and coaching regime occur prior to international competition.

While athletes in the Eastern block countries are usually afforded psychological support for the management of pre- and postcompetitive stresses, this kind of help is often lacking for athletes in other parts of the world. For example, American competitors must usually manage their own anxieties and fears before, during, and after contests.

[3]Several case studies cited in Cratty BJ, Hanin YL *The Athlete in the Sports Team*, deal with this changing of coaching phenomena in athletics.

In the chapter that follows, the coach is extended guidelines for what is termed "selective association" prior to competitions, as a means of adjusting anxiety levels of athletes. However, the coach often has numerous athletes and details to attend to before and during competitions. Thus, athletes must often manage their own fears and problems.

Thus, the athlete must first decide whether the activations felt are greater or less than optimum, or whether they are desirable and lend themselves to the production of superior performance. If it is decided that too much activation is present, athletes may decide to: (1) seek a quiet place and talk themselves into a more tranquil frame of mind, perhaps negating the importance of the contest mentally, or (2) carefully select the company they associate with before a contest. If too activated, the athlete may select a more tranquil fellow athlete or assistant coach to be with, while if not excited enough, the athlete may search for a more stimulating companion.

If an athlete feels at some optimum level of activation prior to a contest, he or she may prefer to remain alone rather than to spend time with someone who may undesirably raise or lower the level of activation.

This principle may be extended to opponents. Athletes in some contact sports perform best when they can somehow engender anger at their opponents. While perhaps this is not an altogether mentally healthy practice, this type of athlete may prefer not to associate with an opponent prior to a contest, because of the possibility of finding out that the competitor is really a nice person after all.

Postgame associations with opponents is not a frequent occurrence in American sports. This kind of unfortunate isolation is not practiced by the more enlightened and gregarious English, whose soccer and rubgy matches are almost always followed by a postgame party. A postgame rugby party, like any social function involving former opponents following a highly competitive contest, may provide important social lessons, and such practices should probably be initiated in the United States.

In summary, the coach's behaviors and personality are seldom a neutral experience in the life of a youth who feels their impact. Few adults are *unable* to recall the *exact content* of phrases reflecting praise or disdain emanating from coaches they encountered during their formative years. Thus, athletes should attempt to get in touch with their real feelings about the nature of their relationship with their coach. They should assess whether or not the vivid association is having a negative or positive effect on their personality and their future emotional and athletic development. The athlete *should not* hesitate to seek out a positively oriented mentor, and should reject and leave a potentially destructive coach. The privilege of athletic participation is not worth the sacrifice of emotional health.

THE ATHLETE AND THE FANS

In Chapter VIII, we saw that often the athlete does not like the fans. This should not be construed to mean that fan reaction, both immediate and long-term, is not an important facilitator of the athlete's effort. Fans really care but often for selfish purposes. They may seem to athletes to be "riding on the backs" of those whose perspiration during practices is the real contributor to athletic excellence. Most athletes are aware that fans are taking vicarious pleasure from their efforts, and must come to terms with this reality when performing in the presence of highly interested observers.

Fans are fickle. It is obvious to all but the most naive that those cheering one day may be booing on another, while even within minutes accolades may quickly change to derision. Whether or not an athlete makes others aware of his or her dislike of the fans is another question which every athlete has to work out. For the most part, it is prudent to keep such feelings "under wraps."

At the same time, athletes should be aware of possible changes in their performance in front of the fans. Simple forceful acts are performed with more dispatch, while complex or newly learned ones may suffer under the spotlight of observation. The athlete should seek every opportunity to learn well, indeed to overlearn, complex skills that need to be performed later under fan pressures. Practicing important skills in front of others during practice sessions might help.

Furthermore, the type of audience may exert an important influence on the performance of a team, as was pointed out in Chapter VII. A hostile "away" crowd may engender undue aggression, which may translate itself into sloppy and/or highly penalized play. Thus, athletes in team sports may have to be careful of fouling excessively when not in front of a friendly group of fans.

Unseen audiences also plague and support an athlete, both in competition and in training. Parents, friends, and peers have obvious influences on the athlete's effort and emotions, and even on their tendencies to express undue aggression in competition. These groups, when their influences are negative, may have to be controlled or circumvented by both the coach and the athlete. There are times when the athlete may have to help the coach keep various members of this audience under control. Athletes of all ages may have to help their parents to understand their possible negative influences on athletic performance, by attending practices and otherwise offering advice and "making noise" during competitions. Athletes may have to help their own parents understand that there are other things to life than athletics.

There are often people at practice sessions and who roam locker rooms who are not peers, parents, or the usual fans. They may be classified as "superfans," extremely zealous hangers-on whose motives for association with the sports scene may vary widely. At times, these individuals may prove disruptive to the athlete's performance and attention. If this kind of pressure is present, it should be called to the attention of the coach, and the athlete should be protected. Exclusion of such people from practices and locker rooms is often a positive measure.

IMPLICATIONS FOR THE COACH

Helping the athlete and the total team deal with stress and the accompanying fears inherent in athletic competition is among the most important functions a coach possesses. Closely associated with the management of fear is the appearance of hostility in various forms, aggression a player may direct against himself or herself, teammates, and/or coach. Thus, the perceptive coach must many times consider the interactions between the emotions of fear and hostility.

Excess fear may also produce a weakening lethargy, in an athlete or an entire team. Steps taken by the coach to reduce or eliminate fear and anxiety are worthwhile.

Encouraging athletes to set reasonable goals is one way the coach can help them deal with the fear of losing in forthcoming competitions. If the demands made on the athlete (many times by himself!) are too great or unreasonable, the fear of losing can be pronounced. Thus, the coach who sets reasonable, attainable goals can aid the athlete to reduce excess precompetition anxiety.

Helping the athlete feel worthwhile as a person, independent of athletic prowess, is another way the coach can help athletes to handle fear. If the coach makes the athlete really feel that the mentor cares about him or her as an individual, and not only about point production, the fear of losing may not be as pronounced.

In some small (and large) towns in the United States, less mature athletes may find themselves surrounded by peers, parents, coaches, and other adults whose apparent feelings about them hinge almost entirely on their athletic successes and failures, and who may seem to stand ready to let young athletes know that they are relatively worthless if they lose or do not expend effort on the athletic field. These individuals, highly identified with the community's team, in truth are fearful of tarnishing their *own* self-concept if the team loses, and they transfer this disquieting feeling to hapless young athletes.

The coach can and should act as a buffer against such negative social forces. The coach should aid athletes to feel that at least the coach cares about them as people, whether their efforts are winning or losing ones. With this kind of secure base, better individual and team performance is often the result.

Another way to help the athlete deal with anxiety is to aid the performer to place these community, state, or national pressures in the proper context. It should be made clear to athletes that if a team loses in a regional, state, or national competition, it is *not* the end of the world, and that they should be proud of the effort it has taken to reach a position where attention is directed toward their efforts. Further, the coach may point out, the rest of the world (state or nation) may not care about the outcome of a competition, and may not even know that their particular athletic organization exists.

The athletes, at this point, might be encouraged to win for selfish reasons, their own self-respect and the feeling that athletic accomplishment is good in and of itself. Asking more effort from athletes because of pressures from social groups surrounding them may have more negative than positive effects.

Fear and anxiety are "catching." Thus, the coach should be sensitive to the transmission not only of fear from teammates, but also of unsettled feelings radiating from the coach or coaching staff. Coaches are constantly being scrutinized by those over whom they exert authority. Athletes, particularly before important competitions, look for (and sometimes satirize) mannerisms which give clues that their coaches are afraid. And while team members may often joke about the nervous twitchings of coaches, their presence does little to place athletes at ease before or during difficult competitions. The coach should not be reluctant to take advantage of the services of a team psychologist, in an effort to reduce these outward manifestations of nervousness.

The judicious use of data described at the completion of this chapter is also helpful in the reduction of anxiety in athletes. Thorough analysis of the contents of an autobiography of the athlete may help the coach ascertain what immediate social pressures may be impinging upon the athlete, and also what prior pressures—family, friends, etc.—the athlete may be concerned about before competition.

Data obtained on youthful sports competitors has also indicated that the youth who is overly anxious at the completion of a contest is not always one who fears the demanding coach, but one whose own feelings of self-esteem may be lower than usual. Thus, the coach should realize that the younger athlete's "psychologic base," feelings of self-worth, if generally high are likely to sustain him when losing (or prior to a difficult contest). On the other hand, if the coach or other person important in the life of the younger athlete has instilled a negative self-image, it is possible that at least temporary feelings of fear will be engendered before and after sports competitions. These temporary feelings may transform themselves into more permanent trait anxiety as the competitive years go by.

Finally, the coach may have to deal with the problem of success phobia in individual athletes and in groups. More than one athlete has withdrawn from winning owing to the unconscious or conscious need to keep away from the pressures of being at the top. I recently counseled a ranking tennis player who, when about to beat a top opponent, "began to shake all over" and eventually lost matches that might have been won.

This same problem has been documented by clinicians dealing with athletes throughout the world, participating in a number of sports. Among the strategies helpful in overcoming this problem are:

1. Inform the athlete that you are aware of the problems encountered by superior athletes in maintaining high performance levels, keeping friends, and otherwise maintaining themselves psychologically.

2. Explain that these problems are part of the price other superior athletes had to pay for their success, and it is a price that *they* must pay for *their* success.

3. Point out that others superior in other sports and in other endeavors will appreciate their excellence, and the price paid to earn it.

4. Suggest to the athlete that he or she, having achieved in a superior manner, will have a lifetime to look back with pride upon accomplishment, an opportunity that may be worth the immediate psychologic strains of winning and of becoming the best.

SUMMARY

This chapter has focused on principles of use to the athlete, derived from the body of the text. For example, there may be certain stresses that are relatively predictable and unavoidable, and thus athletes should accommodate to them as best they can. Examples of these are fickle fans and teammates or opponents who may be jealous of the too successful athlete.

Success phobia in athletics was discussed briefly, with the implication that often the athlete must compromise, and accept social rejection, while attaining superior performance. The blunting effect of teammate rejection was elaborated on.

Ways were also pointed out in which athletes might seek to optimize the social-psychologic conditions under which they must function. For example, the athlete should change coaches, without undue anxiety, if a mentor proves abusive socially or/and incompetent. Prior to contest, the athlete should also seek the association of teammates who may help the athlete to relax, if it is warranted, or to activate himself or herself to optimum levels.

QUESTIONS FOR DISCUSSION

1. What emotional resources may aid an athlete to improve his own performance and the performance of others on a team?
2. What feelings might an athlete have about the fans? How might these feelings either help or hinder performance?
3. What are the possible fan influences upon hostility evidenced during a contest? How might this hostility be reduced or controlled by the athlete?
4. How does a world class athlete in swimming or track and field compete against the entire world, even though those actually present on a given day may be few in number?
5. How might an athlete improve his relationships with his or her coach? What steps might be taken to reduce the interpersonal hostility that sometimes occurs between the two individuals?
6. How might the athlete have to deal with feelings about close personal relationships and friendships when becoming more and more successful in sport?
7. How might a sports team deal with the forming of closer friendships and performance needs during the course of a competitive season?
8. What is likely to take precedence when an athlete interacts with a coach, the athlete's feelings about his technical expertise, or his feelings about the coach as a friend? Is this importance likely to be different in world class competitions?

14

The Coach and Behavioral Scientist

For several decades, countries in Eastern Europe have involved physiologists, psychologists, social psychologists, and biomechanists in the group of people who coach, advise, and otherwise attempt to improve the welfare of athletes and the teams to which they belong. This same close coordination between the human sciences and the coaching fraternity is not usually the case in the United States, and in other countries of the world.

This chapter will outline how such cooperation might take place. The focus is on how the coach might interact with the psychologist or social psychologist when attempting to optimize performance of the team and of the individuals who make it up.

SOCIAL-PSYCHOLOGIC DATA

The coach may permit a qualified behavioral scientist to associate with the team in order to collect objective data on the social dynamics present. Such professionals (psychiatrists, social psychologists, psychologists, etc.) should be selected with care, and their interactions with the team and testing program scrutinized carefully.[1]

The presence of such individuals can lead to controversy, and has

[1]Criteria for the evaluation of a psychological testing program may be found in Chapter 4, Cratty, BJ: *Psychology in Contemporary Sport.* Englewood Cliffs, New Jersey, Prentice-Hall, 1974.

285

done so in the United States. If their integrity is high, their contributions may have a positive effect on the emotional health and performance of the team as a whole. The coach and his staff can also be the beneficiaries of positive "fallout."[2]

The person selected for this important job should adhere to the ethics of the American Psychological Association. The following guidelines may prove helpful:

1. Initial meetings between the coach and team psychologist or social psychologist should result in the clarification of exactly what the goals of both are, and how coach (and coaching staff) and social psychologist should interact. Among the questions that should be discussed are the following.

   What kinds of scales and subjective evaluation techniques will be employed?

   How much time will be devoted to the collection of data?

   How often during the season will various kind of information be obtained? An athlete or a team may be overtested, and harassment of this kind can have negative effects. Thus, agreements should be made with team members and leaders about the duration, number, and content of such sessions throughout the sports season.

2. The duration of time to be spent and the remuneration the behavioral scientist will receive should be decided upon. Unfortunately, brief association with an athlete or a team with the main intent to collect data for a dissertation has been the pattern in the United States. This brief and superficial relationship is seldom helpful to the team, and at times may have harmful effects on the team's performance and on the overall social tone of the group.

3. It should be made clear just how the psychologist or social psychologist will work with other interested individuals surrounding the team, including parents, trainers, physiologists, and coaches. Some of the important questions to be answered *in advance* are:

   Will there be group discussions involving some or all of these people?

   Will data be obtained from them? In what form?

   How will *these* data be used?

4. The way data are to be obtained from the athletes should be decided on. How will the data be written up, summarized, and otherwise made available to the athletes themselves? What data obtained from the athletes will be shown to the staff? Will the athlete be present? What data obtained from the coaching staff may be studied by the athletes?

5. How available will the social psychologist be to coaches, players, and others, including parents? Will his or her attendance be obtained for practices, games, trips, and for how many group and individual counseling sessions? Will the services of the professional behavioral scientist be available at the season's end? at the end of the athlete's career?

---

[2] I am aware of at least one sport psychologist in the United States whose main contribution to a university football team consisted of keeping the head coach calmed down, so that he could make reasonably rational decisions on the day of the game.

Although the coach and social psychologist may arrive at any number of answers to these questions, this writer has certain biases, reflected in the above queries. It is believed that the effective use of a social psychologist or psychologist will occur under the following conditions:

1. The association between the team, coach, and social psychologist should be a prolonged and professional one. It should last at least an entire sports season, and preferably longer.

2. The only way valid data may be obtained via formal questionnaires, autobiographies, and/or discussions and less formal means is if the athletes are assured that their utterances will be kept in complete confidence. Data obtained from athletes should be explained carefully to them, and then with their permission part or all of it could be used to enhance a group discussion composed of athlete, coach, and social psychologist.

3. The social psychologist should avoid excess exposure to the press. His job is to help the team's performance and the emotional health of all concerned, not to enhance his own reputation by seeking publicity.

4. The calling in of a behavioral scientist should be looked on as a form of preventive medicine, and should not always be a reaction to the onset of problems. Rather, the behavioral scientist's role should be looked on as a positive one, meant to enhance performance, rather than only prevent a future problem or reduce a present one.

5. A first meeting with athletes should consist of discussions about their "rights of confidentiality" and how data emanating from them will be used. This first discussion could also consist of information as to how useful the information obtained via various assessment tools could be to their performance success, and to the "health" of the team.

6. The athletes often-limited time and energy should be considered at all times, by both the coach and psychologist, when setting up an evaluation and counseling program. Personal counseling should be optional, not mandatory.

The social psychologist may thus assume many roles. He or she may act as a personal counselor, or as a buffer between coach and athlete in attempts to improve interpersonal communication. He may also serve as an advisor to the coach and coaching staff.

Operations, Meetings, and Evaluations

Following a coming together of the coaches and social psychologist concerning the groundrules, there are more operational decisions to be made, including the number and frequency of meetings and the exact nature of the evaluation tools that may be employed. It would seem that the following types of meetings should be scheduled initially.

1. A meeting with the head coach, and possibly the athletic director, should be first, during which salary, frequency of contacts, and the

possible uses of data obtained might be aired. The general philosophy of the psychologist, as well as that of the athletic director and coach, should be contrasted; if obvious differences abound, this first meeting could be a last meeting. Differences may be irreconcilable.

2. Next, a meeting should be held with the athletes as a group, during which the psychologist's (or social psychologist's) role may be explained. The athlete's rights to privacy should similarly be covered. Questions about the nature of the data to be obtained and the uses to which it may be put should also be answered.

3. Conferences with individual athletes should take place. During these, questions the athlete may not have felt comfortable answering in front of the group may be dealt with. This meeting may be a good time to begin to obtain data from the athlete; writing or taping an autobiography may be helpful. During this meeting, it should be made clear just how available to the athlete the psychologist will be, whether or not the athlete can initiate a meeting with the social psychologist, and how often and under what circumstances such contacts might occur.

4. Another kind of meeting is that during which information and formal data may be obtained. Sociograms indicating teammate choices of friendship, physical expertise of teammates, together with personality tests, attitude surveys, and the like may be used. These meetings should not last too long. Much longer than an hour is not usually desirable. They should not be scheduled at times that interfere with the athletes' rest, recreation, and/or physical training.

Evaluation Tools

The nature of the specific strategies and types of evaluative tools that may be employed by a team psychologist or social psychologist are almost infinite. And as is true with any type of psychologic work-up, the assessment devices depend on the theoretical orientation, background, and expertise of the evaluator, as well as on the demands and constraints of the situation.

Very helpful data can be obtained through an autobiography, written (or taped) by each athlete on the team. Instructions should encourage the athlete to relate the way his early childhood and family background seemed to mold decisions relative to athletics. Understanding early influences is important when the social psychologist attempts to unravel contemporary forces impinging on the athlete. In addition, the athletes should deal with their immediate situation, their feelings about the current sports team and their own part in its success.

The autobiography may at first be unstructured, giving the athlete 2 to 3 hours, or more, to write it. After reading it, the psychologist may wish to ask additional questions, whose answers are added to the document.

Contemporary motives are an important part of the information to be obtained from such an essay. Thus, athletes' feelings about how teammates, family, close friends, and others important to them look upon their athletic competition are important. Impediments to their successful performance within the current team might also be the subject of discussion based on the autobiography.

Discussion about both positive and negative forces with which the athlete might be concerned could revolve around the following questions:

1. What factors help you in or hinder you from performing well?
2. How much thought have you given these variables?
3. What forces on or around the team do you feel helpless to change?
4. What do you feel about the worth, short-term and long-term, of the current social-psychologic evaluation session?

In addition to these semiformal strategies for the collection of personal data, the social psychologist might obtain information on other questions:

1. What are the permanent personality traits of the athletes?
2. What fluctuations seem to occur in their mood states, during practices and before and after games and competitions?
3. What is the nature of group cohesion within the team?
4. What friendship patterns and patterns of mutual respect exist on the team?
5. How do various members feel about the performance capacities of others on the team?
6. How do they feel about their own performance capacities, and their potential or actual contribution to the team's success?
7. To what degree do they value performance success vs. social affiliations within the team? (Fiedler's test relative to "most preferred" and "least preferred" co-workers has been discussed.)

Following the collection of this type of data, decisions must be made about how it is to be employed. Superior athletes may or may not seek the counseling of a behavioral scientist attached to a sports team, but the best performers invariably wish to obtain a description and thorough explanation of the nature of the information contained in personality tests and other measures to which they have been exposed.

Various kinds of sociometric data, charted and summarized, should be presented and interpreted to the coaching staff. Individual athletes should be counseled about possible fluctuations in measures of temporary mood state, and this information may help them be ready for maximum competitive effort.

Several of the measures should be administered to the team members at various times in the sports season. This is particularly important in the case of team sports. However, even in individual sports, measures of temporary mood (i.e., Spielberger's trait and state anxiety test) should be given enough times to permit both psychologist and athlete to view patterns of anxiety and activation that seem to indicate good *vs.* less-than-optimum performance. Measures of mood may also include physiologic indices, including heart rate and blood pressure. And biofeedback training, in an effort to lower high anxiety levels, may be used with good results prior to sports competition.

It is not inappropriate to expose members of the coaching staff to the same measures that have been given to their athletes. Indeed, some sport psychologists in the United States do not give their tests to the athletes on a team unless the coaches agree to take the tests also.

Sociometric data, when obtained at different points in the season, may reveal changes in friendship and preferred teammate patterns as the result of losing and winning efforts. These fluctuations are as important to consider.

Group Therapy, Rap Sessions, Counseling

There are numerous ways in which informal and formally collected data can be employed to improve both the emotional tone and the performance of an athletic team. These strategies range from casual one-to-one encounters between coach and athlete, or between social psychologist and athlete, to carefully planned and regularly scheduled group therapy sessions involving many or most team members.

It is important that the athletes concerned be made to feel that they need not carefully schedule contacts with the coach or (social) psychologist, but that these people are available to them most of the time for informal chats. Furthermore, while attendance at group sessions should be made attractive, whether or not attendance is mandatory is best left to the discretion of the coach and psychologist.

For years, sports teams have engaged in informal strategies that have helped to ventilate feelings and emotions. Coaches have been satirized at the completion of training camp in plays put on by athletes, which may help reduce interpersonal hostilities harbored by the athletes during a rigorous training regime. Rookies (first-year players) on professional sports teams in the United States are "tested" via ridicule both on and off the practice field, in an effort to help them place their egos in proper perspective.

There are, however, more formal ways in which the sport psychologist, or industrial psychologist, may work with groups under the stress of competition. The "psychodrama" is frequently used to enact and illuminate individuals' roles and problems. In this way, hostilities that may have arisen between various team members are first exposed and then reduced. Interpersonal communication is also improved by this means, as is self-understanding. Group therapy taking this and other forms helps athletes assess their own impact on other members of the team, which in turn aids them to understand better how others may be reacting to them. The problems and advantages of acting as a leader or follower may also be illuminated in sessions such as these.

For the most part, free communication will occur if the group members know their utterances will not in some way be used against them. Communication in a judgment-free environment, a situation in which they will not likely be rewarded or punished, is far more likely to be free-flowing and honest. Thus, it is usually highly desirable if initially the coach or a member of his staff is not present during rap sessions in which team members participate. The athletes involved should be convinced that the group leader (usually the psychologist) will honor client-patient confidentiality inherent in this type of professional contact. Coaches may be generally informed of the overall "tone" of such meetings with athletes, but should not be told who said what about and to whom.[3]

At the same time, it may be highly desirable, particularly if the coaching staff is large (four or more), to conduct separate sessions for them. During these meetings, their own feelings about authority, personal differences, and their own roles and team members may be the subject of helpful discussions.

Most important, the head coach should not be reluctant to obtain counseling about his or her behavior(s) and interactions, both with the other coaches and with the team. The head coach should also give the psychologist the authority to work directly and independently with other members of the coaching staff.

Thus, after the selection of a social psychologist or psychologist has been made with confidence, the coach and coaching staff should extend their fullest support. The member of the scientific community selected should attempt to operate in as professional manner as possible, in order to enhance effectiveness with team members and coaches alike.

SUMMARY

This chapter has attempted to indicate guidelines for the selection and utilization of a team (social) psychologist. Included in these guidelines were suggestions about how the behavioral scientist might operate

---

[3]A colleague of mine, after weeks of group sessions with members of a sport team, drew from the members that their apparent lack of ability to win games at the completion of the season was due to deep-seated dislike (even hate) of the coach. They simply did not wish to contribute to his success. It is highly unlikely that these feelings would have "surfaced" if the principles outlined above had not been followed.

ethically and practically both with members of the team and with the coaching staff. Among the operational principles presented were suggestions for both formal and informal evaluation instruments, as well as suggestions concerning the nature of the contacts between psychologist, coach, and team members. Suggestions indicated that the social psychologist should be placed in a position that permits him or her to have prolonged and thorough contact with team members and coaches. Furthermore, it was pointed out that the effectiveness of a social psychologist attached to a team hinges largely on his not being pressured to violate client (athlete) confidentiality.

The chapter concluded with suggestions as to how group therapy and individual counseling sessions may be made positive experiences for all.

QUESTIONS FOR DISCUSSION

1. In what ways might the behavioral scientist provide an impetus for positive change on the athletic team?

2. In what kinds of operations might the behavioral scientist act differently when working with an individual sport in contrast to a team sport?

3. In what ways might the behavior or professional conduct of the team social psychologist prove a detriment to individual and/or team success?

4. What kinds of items for discussion might one have on the agenda for the first meeting of the team with the behavioral scientist?

5. What kinds of issues might be discussed during the final meeting of the year between the behavioral scientist attached to a team and the athletes?

6. What kinds of general issues, nuances of emotional tone, and information might the behavioral scientist discuss with the coach without violating player confidentiality?

7. What kinds of information obtained from athletes should not be discussed with the coach by the behavioral scientist attached to the team?

8. What kinds of evaluation tools might be employed by the behavioral scientist which reflect social-psychologic dimensions within and surrounding the team?

INDEX